The McCall's Book of Christmas

by The Editors of McCall's Needlework & Crafts Publications

Simon and Schuster / The McCall Pattern Company • New York

Published by Simon and Schuster
Rockefeller Center, 630 Fifth Avenue
New York, New York 10020

Photograph on page 145 courtesy of
Kaycrest Gift Wrapping, Papercraft Corporation.

Designed by Beri Greenwald

Manufactured in the United States of America

1   2   3   4   5   6   7   8   9   10

Library of Congress Cataloging in Publication Data

Main entry under title:
The McCall's book of Christmas.
1. Christmas decorations.   2. Christmas cookery.
I. McCall's needlework & crafts.   II. Title: Book of Christmas.
TT900.C4M3   745.59'41   75-17729
ISBN 0-671-22105-1

Contents

Christmas Greetings

The McCall's Book of Christmas is a timeless treasure for everyone who delights in the joyous season. We have gathered the very best of designs and have carefully selected the projects to give people of all ages, all abilities and all interests a collection of unique and beautiful decorations to make for the holidays. We hope this book will become a cherished heirloom, reflecting the tradition and spirit of joy and giving and making the holiday season not only a time of festivity but also a time of thoughtful creativity. There are hundreds of ideas from which to choose, so that you may express the meaning of Christmas year after year in your own special way.

All you need to fill your home with warmth and cheer is here in abundant variety. Ornaments, wreaths, trees, festive tablecloths, charming wall hangings, crèches, cards, stockings, Santas, and more are all boldly illustrated in brilliant color. Whatever technique you choose—knitting, crochet, embroidery, stained glass, papier-mâché, or bread dough sculpture—you will find that each project has its individual set of step-by-step instructions and a list of all equipment and materials required. The crafts range from the very easy cut-and-paste projects to more difficult ones; but none is too complicated for any patient and determined novice to attempt and successfully complete.

To us, "made by hand" means "made with love." We give you our very best to fulfill the joyful spirit of the season.

The Editors of McCall's

ORNAMENTS

Ukrainian Eggs

Drawing wax designs on eggs and dipping them in a series of dye baths is a traditional Russian folk art. Similar to batik, the process is easier than it may seem—the delicate patterns appear on the eggs as if by magic. These old world ornaments are so beautiful you will want to display them long after the trimmings are off the tree.

EQUIPMENT: Newspapers. Paper towels. Bowl for egg contents. Bowls or glasses for dye baths. Very long darning needle (at least 2½"). Rubber bands. Pencil. Fine tjanting needle or a very fine pointed paintbrush. Designs for copying on eggs (see directions below). Plain candle. Aluminum foil.

MATERIALS: Large white eggs. Beeswax. Dyes (aniline): Yellow, orange, red, and black (or desired colors). Vinegar. Fine pearl embroidery floss. Small beads. All-purpose glue.

DIRECTIONS: Note: The eggshell ornament designs were copied from postcards of the traditional Ukrainian egg designs. Designs were drawn freehand with pencil on the eggshell, painted with wax, and placed in a series of dye baths, using the traditional Ukrainian egg colors. You may use your own designs and color combinations. If you wish to reproduce our designs, work from color illustration opposite.

We suggest that you have several extra eggshells on hand for experimenting with designs (also in case of breakage, although eggshells are sturdier than expected if carefully handled).

Cover working area completely with newspapers. To empty eggshell, prick hole in each end of egg with needle; make hole in larger end a little bigger. Holding egg over bowl, blow through hole in smaller end until eggshell is empty. Be sure holes are large enough to accommodate double thickness of embroidery floss and needle for making hangers for ornaments later. Rinse empty eggshells thoroughly. Wipe with paper towels; let dry.

Prepare dyes, mixing with vinegar according to instructions on package. Dyes do not need to be kept hot.

Use rubber bands around the eggshell to halve and quarter it as a guide to spacing and planning design.

Lightly pencil-in design on shell. Fill the tjanting needle with wax; melt wax by holding needle over the candle flame. If using paintbrush, melt wax in can or pan and dip brush in wax. Test the line of wax the tjanting needle makes on your fingernail. If it flows smoothly, start drawing in the lines and areas that are to remain white. (**Note:** Do not remove any wax until all dye baths have been completed.) Place eggshell in the lightest dye bath (yellow or orange) for about 10 to 20 minutes, depending upon how well the dye takes (some eggshells will absorb color faster than others). When thoroughly colored, dry eggshell with paper towel. Using tjanting needle, wax the areas of the design that are to remain yellow or orange. Place egg in next color bath (red) until shell is thoroughly colored (about 10 to 20 minutes). Dry eggshell with paper towel. Using tjanting needle, wax the areas of the design that are to remain red. Place eggshell in darkest color dye bath (black) until color takes (10 to 20 minutes). Dry.

Remove all wax by carefully heating eggshell directly over candle flame or by heating it in the oven (make sure you have aluminum foil under eggshell to catch the melting wax). Wipe wax away with paper towels.

To make hangers for eggshell ornaments, cut a 10" length of floss; fold in half. Thread darning needle with both ends of floss. Insert threaded needle through hole at wider end of eggshell; pull needle out through hole at narrower end of shell, leaving a 2" loop extending at wider end. Insert needle through small bead; remove needle and knot floss ends so bead cannot slip off. Dab glue at holes if necessary to keep hanger from slipping.

Plumed Partridges

*Colorful felt pieces, decoratively stitched with embroidery
floss, are assembled and stuffed to make these five proud birds.*

EQUIPMENT: Scissors. Pencil. Embroidery
needles. Paper for patterns. Straight pins.
Steel crochet hook No. 0. Knitting needle.
Small piece of cardboard.

MATERIALS: Small pieces of felt in the following colors: Off-white, white, aqua, light
and dark orange, lavender, fuchsia, turquoise.
Dacron or cotton fiberfill. Six-strand embroidery floss, one skein each of teal blue, yellow-
green, apple green, lavender, aqua, purple,
orange, tan, off-white, gray, red-orange.

GENERAL DIRECTIONS: Enlarge patterns
by copying on paper ruled in 1″ squares. Cut
all pieces out of felt as indicated in individual
directions. Dash lines indicate running
stitches; fine lines indicate other embroidery.
Mark these lines lightly with pencil on felt.

To embroider and assemble: Use three
strands of floss in needle unless otherwise
directed. See Stitch Details on page 186. Make
blanket stitches along edges of each wing. Pin
a wing to each body piece, placing as illustrated. To secure wing to body, work at least
one row of satin stitch following design over
edge of wing and through body (see illustration). Embroider French knot for each eye
at dot on pattern.

For hanger, use six strands of floss and
crochet a chain 8″ long. Fold in half to make
a loop; pin ends on wrong side of one body
piece at top edge; tack.

Finish embroidery following individual directions.

Place two body pieces together, wrong sides
facing. Blanket stitch edges together around
head and body, up to dash line, leaving tail
end open. Use knitting needle to push stuffing
into head and body. Stitch tail ends together
with running stitch along dash line.

Note: Partridges are numbered 1–5, starting
from top of illustration.

Partridge #1: From turquoise, cut two of body
pattern B. From dark orange, cut two of wing
pattern D. Using purple floss, embroider
blanket stitch around each wing. To attach
wings to body, use purple, orange, and apple
green floss, embroidering one row each of
satin stitch. Using teal blue floss and blanket
stitch, sew pieces together; stuff and complete.

For comb, use ½ yard each of fuchsia,
apple green, and orange floss (six strands).
Wind each around a piece of ½″-wide cardboard. Slip a needle threaded with three
strands of apple green floss under strands at
one edge of cardboard; remove needle; tie
ends tightly. Clip strands at other edge; fluff
with fingers; stitch to top of head.

For tail plumage, wind 3 yards each of
fuchsia, apple green, and orange six-strand
floss around a piece of 1″-wide cardboard.
Use six strands of fuchsia floss in needle and
make in same manner as comb. Stitch in place
between turquoise tails.

Partridge #2: From off-white, cut two of body pattern A. From lavender, cut two of wing pattern G and one of tail pattern F. From fuchsia, cut two of wing pattern G and one of tail pattern F. Mark design on each fuchsia wing piece; do not mark design on head.

To make wings at each side, pin one fuchsia and one lavender wing together, with marked fuchsia wing on top. To attach each set of wings to body use lavender, yellow-green, and teal blue floss to embroider three rows of satin stitch, following design.

For comb, using six strands of embroidery floss, crochet a 3″ chain in each of the following colors: lavender, apple green, teal blue. Fold each chain in half to form a loop. Attach the three loops to top of head on wrong side of one body piece.

With wrong sides facing, place two body pieces together, having fuchsia and lavender tail pieces pinned in place between the two body pieces, matching dash lines (see pattern). Using off-white floss and blanket stitch, sew body pieces together.

Partridge #3: From off-white, cut two of body pattern A and two of wing pattern D. From white, cut two of wing pattern D and one of tail pattern F.

Using aqua floss, embroider blanket stitch all around each white wing piece.

To make wings at each side, pin one off-white and one white piece together, with white embroidered wing on top. Using tan floss and satin stitch, attach wing to body.

Following illustration, embroider each section of head design in satin stitch, alternating aqua and gray.

Use off-white floss to sew body pieces together. Before sewing tail ends together, pin white tail piece between two body tails.

For comb, use aqua embroidery floss. Make and attach as for Partridge #1.

Partridge #4: From orange, cut two of body pattern B. From lavender, cut two of wing pattern C and two of tail pattern E. From fuchsia, cut two of wing pattern C and one of tail pattern E. Mark embroidery lines on each orange body piece and on each lavender wing piece.

To make wings at each side of body, place one lavender and one fuchsia wing together with lavender piece on top. Pin to orange body.

Using teal blue floss, outline lavender wings with blanket stitch, and attach each set of wings to each side of body with a row of satin stitch. Embroider lines on head and wings in running stitch, using apple green, fuchsia, red-orange, and purple floss.

Place one fuchsia tail piece between two lavender tail pieces; pin to wrong side of one body piece, matching tail tips.

Blanket stitch bodies together, then sew tail ends together with orange floss.

Make comb as for Partridge #1, using 1½ yards of orange floss.

Partridge #5: From white, cut two of body pattern A. From off-white, cut two of wing pattern D. From turquoise, cut two of wing pattern D.

Mark design shown on head #5 on both heads. Use yellow-green and aqua floss to embroider three rows of running stitch, following design.

Blanket stitch wings with aqua floss. Using tan floss and satin stitch, sew wings to body.

Blanket stitch bodies together, then sew tail ends together with off-white floss.

For comb, use tan embroidery floss. Make and attach as for Partridge #1.

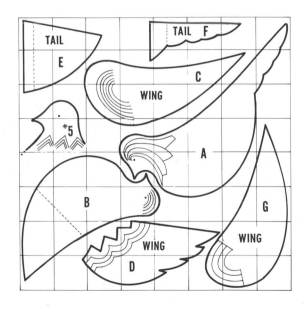

Silk Baubles

Embroidery motifs in shining pearl cotton embellish these lustrous circles of silk.

EQUIPMENT: Tracing paper. Dressmaker's tracing (carbon) paper. Scissors. Pencil. Compass. Embroidery needle. Zigzag sewing machine.

MATERIALS: Silk fabric, 10 pieces, each approximately 5″ x 5″ in shades of pink to red. Dacron fiberfill for stuffing. Sewing thread to contrast with fabric. Pearl cotton in the following colors: medium blue (A); bright red

(B); coral (C); dark yellow-green (D); hot pink (E); orange (F); maroon (G); light yellow-green (H); light pink (I); teal blue (J); turquoise (K); yellow-green (L). Ribbon for hangings: Five pieces narrow gold satin ribbon, each 8″ long.

DIRECTIONS: For each bauble, cut two 4¾″-diameter circles from silk. With contrasting thread, use machine zigzag stitch to make decorative finish around edge of each circle and to keep edges from raveling. Trace designs and transfer to one piece for front of each. Following patterns and the letters below for colors, embroider motifs. Stems are split stitch; tiny petals are lazy daisy stitch; small dots are French knots; blue bow is split stitch; remainder of designs are filled in with satin stitch. See Embroidery Stitch Details on page

186. With wrong sides facing and edges flush, sew front and back circles together with contrasting thread around perimeter, ¼″ in from edges. Leave an opening for stuffing; leave needle in fabric. Stuff lightly; continue stitching to close.

For hanger, double each piece of ribbon to form a loop; fold under raw edges; stitch one looped hanger to the back of each bauble.

ACTUAL-SIZE PATTERNS.

Wound-Thread Ornaments

This wound-thread technique is adapted from a traditional craft of Ecuador to make these fascinating trimmings. Pins are inserted into the basic cardboard shapes; pearl cotton is wound around the pins.

EQUIPMENT: Ruler. Pencil. Scissors. Mat knife. Masking tape. Large-eyed needle or small crochet hook.

MATERIALS: Pearl cotton, size 3, 1 skein for each color desired (see illustration and individual directions). Cardboard, ⅛″ thick. Craft pins, ½″ long. Silver or gold foil paper. All-purpose glue.

GENERAL DIRECTIONS: With mat knife, cut two 2″ squares of cardboard for each ornament (except No. 5; see individual directions). Turn squares so that corners alternate, making an octagon with eight evenly spaced points; glue squares together in this position.

Insert craft pin in each point, leaving 1/16″ extending. Tape beginning end of pearl cotton to center of cardboard (this is front; always work from this side). Glue a piece of foil paper, at least 1½″ square, over taped end (and/or on center back; see individual directions). Technique consists of winding the thread around the cardboard in a certain sequence. The thread is wound either from the points of the octagon toward the spaces between points (joints), or from the joints toward the points. Keep threads taut, placing them close together, but not overlapping. Following the individual sequences and accompanying diagrams, repeat each sequence in color directed for the specified number of rows. Because ornaments are reversible, check the back periodically to make sure you are winding correctly.

To join a new color, tie end of last color and beginning end of the next color together. With pin, tuck knot into wound threads; continue winding. Before starting new color, count threads of last color, making sure count is the same all around.

To finish, weave end of final color under the threads at one corner; knot close to work and trim. Make a loop for hanging from final color as follows: Cut 8″ length; fold in half and pull folded end through threads at a point or between points. Knot cut ends; pull knot under threads to conceal.

No. 1 and No. 8 (Fig. 1): Glue foil to front only. Work from points toward joints. Begin at point A, wind under (to back), skipping two points going clockwise; bring to front at next point (B). Wind over (to front), skipping one point counterclockwise; bring to back at next point (C). Work next repeat, winding to D and E; repeat until you are back at A to complete the first row. Wind each successive row laying thread to the left of previous row, and turning work in counterclockwise direction. For No. 1, work 7 rows yellow-orange; then 4 rows red (reverse side shown in illustration). For No. 8, work 6 rows light green; 3 yellow; 4 medium blue.

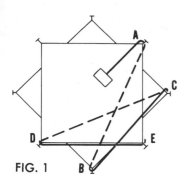

FIG. 1

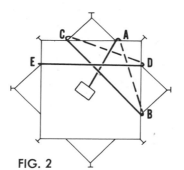

FIG. 2

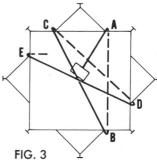

FIG. 3

No. 2 and No. 7 (Fig. 2): Glue foil on both sides. Work from joints toward points. Begin at A, wind under, skipping two points going clockwise; bring to front at next joint (B). Wind over, skipping three points counterclockwise; bring to back at next joint (C). Work next repeat, winding to D and E; repeat until you are back at A to complete the first row. Wind each successive row, laying thread to the right of previous row and turning work in clockwise direction. For No. 2, work 5 rows blue; 2 red; 5 green. For No. 7, work 3 rows light green; 2 red; 2 green; 4 red.

No. 3 and No. 4 (Fig. 3): Glue foil to back only. Work from joints toward points. Begin at A, wind under, skipping three points going clockwise; bring to front at next joint (B). Wind over, skipping four points counterclockwise; bring to back at next joint (C). Work next repeat, winding to D and E; repeat until you are back at A to complete the first row. Wind each successive row, laying thread to the right of previous row and turning work clockwise. For No. 3, work 8 rows light blue; 2 dark blue; 4 red. For No. 4, work 4 rows red; 8 yellow-orange.

No. 5 (Fig. 4): Use winding diagram as actual-size pattern for cutting seven-pointed star from one piece of cardboard; insert pins in points. Glue foil on both sides of cardboard.

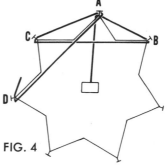

FIG. 4

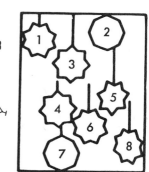

Work from points toward joints. Begin at A, wind under, going clockwise, and bring to front at next point (B). Wind over, skipping one point counterclockwise; bring to back at next point (C). Work next repeat, winding under to A and over to D; repeat until you are back at A for first row. Wind each successive row laying thread to the left of previous row, and turning work clockwise. Work 5 rows russet; 1 light green; 4 light blue; 4 medium blue.

No. 6: Following General Directions, make eight-pointed star. Follow diagram and winding directions for No. 5 exactly (the only difference consists in working one more point). Work 6 rows medium blue; 7 light green.

Felt Mini-Figures

Embroidered tiny felt toys make endearing little package or tree trims.

EQUIPMENT: Tracing paper. Pencil. Ruler. Scissors. Sewing needle and embroidery needle. Straight pins.
MATERIALS: Small pieces of felt. Scraps of fabric. Sewing thread to match felt and fabric. Heavy white thread. Six-strand embroidery floss and fine yarn in contrasting colors. Sequins, bangles, and seed beads. Pipe cleaners. Absorbent cotton for stuffing. See individual directions for additional materials.

Pin two head-bodies together. Insert a small piece of pipe cleaner (bent in half) between arms. Place each inner and outer ear together with bottom ends flush; pinch sides together at bottom and insert into top of head where indicated by X on pattern. Whipstitch head-body together, securing ears in place; leave bottom open.

Cut two strips of chartreuse felt about ¼" wide to fit across one stocking piece; secure in place with chain stitch, using six strands of pink floss. Using same floss, make three double cross-stitches between strips. Tack five pink sequins between strips. Pin stockings together; whipstitch together; leave top open. Stuff Mouse and stocking softly; insert Mouse in stocking and whipstitch in place to top edge of stocking. Bend paws down.

Puppy in Stocking: From tan felt, cut two head-body pieces and two outer ears. Cut two inner ears of pale pink felt. Cut two larger stockings of shocking pink felt.

With three strands of beige floss or one strand of fine yarn, embroider muzzle in buttonhole stitch worked in a circle. Embroider mouth with two strands of pink floss in small chain stitch. Sew on black seed beads for eyes at small dots; sew on black sequin for nose at larger dot. Pin head-body pieces together; insert a small piece of pipe cleaner (bent in half) between arms. Place each inner and outer ear together with bottom edges even; fold sides of outer ears over to center; insert ears in place at X as indicated. Sew Puppy together as for Mouse. With three strands of chartreuse floss, make a chain stitch around neck of Puppy; tack a gold sequin just below to look like a dog tag.

With three strands of chartreuse floss, embroider a chain stitch bow design on one stocking and sew on a bangle as shown. Whipstitch stocking together, leaving top open. Stuff Puppy and stocking; insert Puppy into stocking and tack around top edge of stocking. Bend paws down.

Doll in Stocking: Cut two head-bodies of pink felt; cut two dress pieces of print cotton fabric; cut two larger stockings of red felt. Sew black seed beads at dots for eyes. With single strand of bright pink floss, embroider mouth in chain stitch and nose in satin stitch. Sew head-bodies together as for Mouse with pipe-cleaner piece in arms. For hair, cover back of head with straight stitches of fine red yarn; make loops of yarn around top and sides of head, anchoring each loop with a tiny stitch. Clip some loops.

With right sides facing, sew underarm and shoulder seams of dress, making ⅛" seams.

GENERAL DIRECTIONS: Enlarge patterns by copying on paper ruled in 1" squares; complete the half- and quarter-patterns indicated by long dash lines. Following individual directions, cut pieces, sew together with matching thread and stuff. See page 186 for Stitch Details. When finished, tack loop of thread or floss to top of ornament.

Mouse in Stocking: From gray felt, cut two mouse head-body pieces and two outer ears. Cut two inner ears of pale pink felt. Cut two larger stockings of shocking pink felt. Sew on black sequins for eyes at small dots; sew on black bead for nose at larger dot. For whiskers, use double strand of heavy white thread and pull through face, leaving 1" strands extending at each side of nose; knot close to felt.

Turn dress to right side and put on doll. With three strands of bright pink floss, make chain stitch around sleeves, neck, and down front of dress, securing dress to body at same time. Make shoulder straps down front and back with fancy bias binding tape; stitch to dress. Make stocking and embroider as for Puppy. Stuff and attach Doll in stocking as for Mouse and Puppy; bend arms down.

Larger Mouse: From gray felt, cut two heads, two ears, and tail. From green felt, cut two complete body pieces and one bottom. Cut small stocking of shocking pink felt. Sew black sequins at dots for eyes. For nose, use three strands of black floss and work satin stitch across nose area. With right sides facing, place the two heads together; pinch straight ends of ears together slightly and insert ears between head pieces so that pinched ends of ears and edges of head are even; whipstitch heads together along sides and top, securing ears at same time. Turn to other side.

Whipstitch edges of two body pieces together, leaving bottom open. Whipstitch bottom in place, leaving one half unstitched. Turn to right side. Stuff body fully; sew opening at bottom closed. Place head over top of body, turn bottom edge of head in and sew edge to body.

With fine white yarn, embroider chain stitch line around neck, down front, and a pocket outline at side. Using heavy white thread, pull about four strands through nose area, leaving 1¼" ends for whiskers; knot close to felt. Fold tail in half lengthwise; whipstitch long edges together. Sew straight end to bottom back of body.

With chartreuse floss, make line of chain stitch around top of stocking and work satin stitch on toe and heel areas. Tack two gold sequins on stocking. Fold in half crosswise and whipstitch sides together. Tack stocking to front of one paw.

Raccoon: From gray felt, cut two heads, two ears, and one tail. From shocking pink felt, cut two bodies and one bottom. Cut small stocking of green felt. With three strands of black floss, make close buttonhole stitch to cover middle eye area and work satin stitch for nose. With fine white yarn, buttonhole stitch areas above and below eye area, and whipstitch around edges of ears. With three strands of chartreuse floss, make satin stitch eyes and sew a black seed bead in center of pupil as shown.

With right sides facing, place the head pieces together; insert ears in place between, with ends of ears and edges of head even. Sew heads together along sides and top, leav-

ing bottom open. Turn head to other side. Make body as for Larger Mouse. Place head over top of body; sew head in place as for Larger Mouse.

With fine dark green yarn, make a row of chain stitch around neck and down front of suit; make two rows around waist of suit. Sew four gold sequins to front of suit as shown.

Turn edges of tail under and sew tail to back of body at bottom of suit with point up. Using white and black yarns alternately, make rows of straight stitches across tail to resemble raccoon's stripes. Make small stockings as for Mouse, using shocking pink floss for embroidered details.

Angel: From pale pink felt, cut two complete bodies and two separate arms. Cut two dress pieces of printed fabric adding ¼" for turn-in allowance all around. Cut two wings of white felt. Sew blue seed beads at dots for eyes. Embroider mouth with two strands of shocking pink floss in tiny chain stitches. Sew the edges of the two bodies together, leaving open at bottom. Stuff fully; sew opening

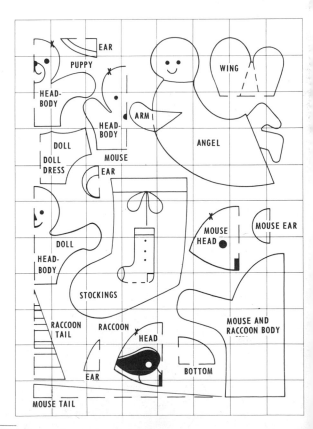

closed. Place the dress pieces on body; turn in edges and sew dress pieces together, securing dress to body at neck and legs. Whipstitch hand part of arms together; stuff this area and tack arm ends in place on body.

Make a tuck in each wing piece where indicated by two rows of short dash lines. Sew bottom edge of each to back of angel. If desired, glue a little crystal glitter on wings. Glue white baby rickrack along edges of dress at bottom, neck, and arm. For hair, use fluffy red yarn and make as for Doll.

Jumping Jacks

Six whimsical "animated" figures will delight all ages as they dangle from the tree or fascinate a child as toys. Brightly painted bodies are made from tongue depressors and ice-cream sticks; legs and arms are attached by brass paper fasteners. Pull the golden cord and the limbs move!

EQUIPMENT: Tracing paper. Hard and soft pencils. Sharp kitchen shears. Drill with ⅛" bit. Awl or ice pick. Knife. Small pointed paintbrush. Ruler. Bowl.

MATERIALS: Wooden tongue depressors and ice-cream sticks. Brass paper fasteners (pronged). Pipe cleaners. Heavy thread. Gold cord. Poster paints. Clear spray varnish. All-purpose glue. Wooden beads 1" diameter for heads, ⅜" for pulls.

GENERAL DIRECTIONS: Soak wooden tongue depressors and ice-cream sticks in a bowl of hot water so they can be cut with kitchen shears without splintering. Use depressors for body pieces and ice-cream sticks or depressors for arms and legs. See Figs. 1-3 for basic assembly of Jumping Jacks. All Figs. are back views.

All bodies (except Columbine) are made of three pieces of depressors. Cut off one end of depressor straight across to length given in individual directions. Overlap the three pieces as shown in Fig. 1 for basic body, and glue together; dash lines show overlapping pieces. Cut arms and legs as directed in individual directions. Drill a ⅛" hole through center top of arms and legs, and through matching place of body (see Fig. 2). With awl, make a tiny hole through arms and legs above drilled hole (see Fig. 2). Cut hands and feet according to individual directions and glue to ends of arms and legs.

For head, fold a 6" pipe cleaner in half. Glue inside 1" diameter wooden bead with folded end extending about ¼" above bead. Glue ends of pipe cleaner to center back of body, leaving a short section between head and body for neck. Let dry.

Assemble figure (see Fig. 3). Fasten arms and legs to body with pronged paper fasteners, inserting them from front to back and spreading prongs out on back; fasten limbs rather loosely to allow them to move freely. Tie heavy thread through small holes in arms, allowing some slack so they can move easily (see Fig. 3). Do the same with legs. Tie gold cord around center of arm thread, bring down back to leg thread and tie to center; let about 6" of cord hang down for pull. Slip a small bead on gold cord and knot end of cord.

Trace faces given at right; go over back of tracing with a soft pencil. Holding tracing around bead head, right side up, go over lines again with a sharp hard pencil to transfer lines to bead. Paint features as shown in photograph; continue painting hair or hats around top, sides and back of head. Paint bodies, arms, and legs as shown, or as de-

ANGEL

COLUMBINE

DRUM MAJOR

HARLEQUIN

SANTA

PEASANT

sired. Spray completely with a light coat of varnish.

To hang Jumping Jacks, tie 4" piece of gold cord through pipe cleaner at top of head, knotting ends together.

Harlequin: Cut three body pieces 3" long. Use 2½" pieces of depressors for arms, cutting off ends diagonally. Cut 3" pieces of depressors for legs. For hands, cut 1½" pieces of ice-cream sticks and glue to back of arms with round ends out. For feet, cut off 1½" pieces of ice-cream sticks diagonally and glue horizontally across front of legs.

Finish following General Directions.

Peasant: Cut two body pieces 3" long (outside pieces) and piece for center 3¼" long. Glue together with straight ends at top and center piece extending at top ¼". For arms, cut depressors 2" long and attach to body with round end out. Glue on 1¼" pieces of ice-cream sticks for hands, angling them upward with round ends out.

For legs, cut 3″ pieces of ice-cream sticks. Attach to body with straight cut edge down. Cut off ⅜″ round ends of depressor for feet; glue to front of legs with round end up. Finish following General Directions.

Santa: Cut three body pieces 3″ long. Glue together as in Fig. 1 with rounded ends at bottom. With knife, cut off outer top corners to make round shoulders.

For arms, cut two depressors 2¼″ long. Attach to body with round ends out. Glue 1″ pieces of ice-cream stick to back of arms for hands as in Fig. 2.

For legs, cut depressors 3″ long. Attach to body with straight cut end down. Cut off ¾″ round ends of depressor for feet; glue to front of legs with round end up. Finish following General Directions.

Drum Major: Cut 3″ body pieces from depressors. Glue together straight, as shown in Fig. 4. For arms, cut 2½″ pieces of depressors; attach to body with straight cut end out. Cut 1¼″ pieces of ice-cream stick and glue to back of arms as shown; glue a toothpick to one hand for baton.

For legs, cut 3″ pieces of depressors; attach to body with straight cut end down. Cut and glue on feet as for Harlequin. Finish following General Directions.

Angel: For body, cut three pieces 5″ long; glue together as in Fig. 1 with round ends at bottom. For tops of wings, cut two pieces of depressor 1″ long and glue to top corners

of body as shown in Fig. 5. For wing tips, cut two pieces of depressor 3″ long; taper cut ends to points; attach to wing tops as shown in Fig. 6. Tie thread as shown in Fig. 6.

For feet, cut two pieces of ice-cream stick and glue to back of center body piece with round ends down.

For hands, cut two pieces of ice-cream stick ¾″ long; shave off one side, making a straight edge from cut end to round end. Glue cut end of each to front at either side of center body piece 1″ down from top; glue round tips together, forming a point. Tie gold cord pull to wing thread. Finish following General Directions.

Columbine: For skirt, cut five pieces of depressors (see Fig. 7): center piece 3″ long; next two side pieces 3″ long with ends cut off diagonally; outside pieces 2⅛″ long. Glue together as shown in Fig. 7. For legs, cut ice-cream sticks 3″ long; cut off round end diagonally as shown in Fig. 7. Cut 1″ pieces of ice-cream stick for feet with ends cut diagonally, and glue to front of legs as shown.

For bodice, cut two pieces of depressor 2″ long. Overlap cut ends diagonally and cut a mitered joint as shown in Fig. 8. For arms, cut ice-cream sticks 2¼″ long. Cut and shape hands as for Angel; glue to back of arms (see Fig. 8). Glue bodice over top of skirt as indicated by dash lines in Fig. 8. Finish following General Directions.

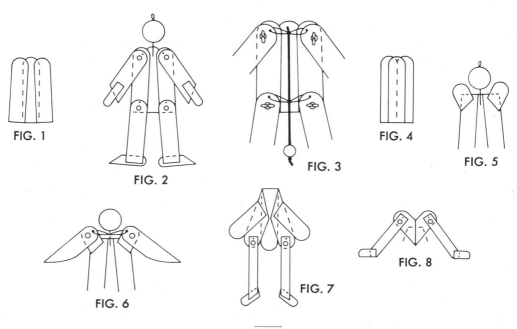

FIG. 1

FIG. 2

FIG. 3

FIG. 4

FIG. 5

FIG. 6

FIG. 7

FIG. 8

Needlepoint Disks

Worked on 10-mesh-to-the-inch canvas with tapestry yarn, the glowing candle and five little faces emerge in no time to add to your Christmas ornament collection. Santa's beard, the clown's hair and cat's whiskers create a third dimension. A cardboard ring and backing form the foundation for each disk, which measures 3" in diameter when completed.

EQUIPMENT: Masking tape. Pencil. Tapestry needle. Scissors. Small paintbrush.

For blocking: Soft wooden surface. Brown wrapping paper. Compass. Thumbtacks.

MATERIALS: Needlepoint canvas, 10-mesh-to-the-inch, 5" square for each disk. Small amounts of tapestry yarn in the colors listed in Color Key. Cardboard rings from narrow masking or other tape, about 3⅛" diameter,

½" to ¾" thick. Acrylic or poster paints (see colors in individual directions). All-purpose glue. Thin cardboard. Small screw eyes. Scraps of pink and brown felt. Small amounts of decorative braid (optional).

GENERAL DIRECTIONS: Bind the edges of the square of needlepoint canvas to keep from raveling. Mark outline of cardboard ring in center of canvas square with pencil.

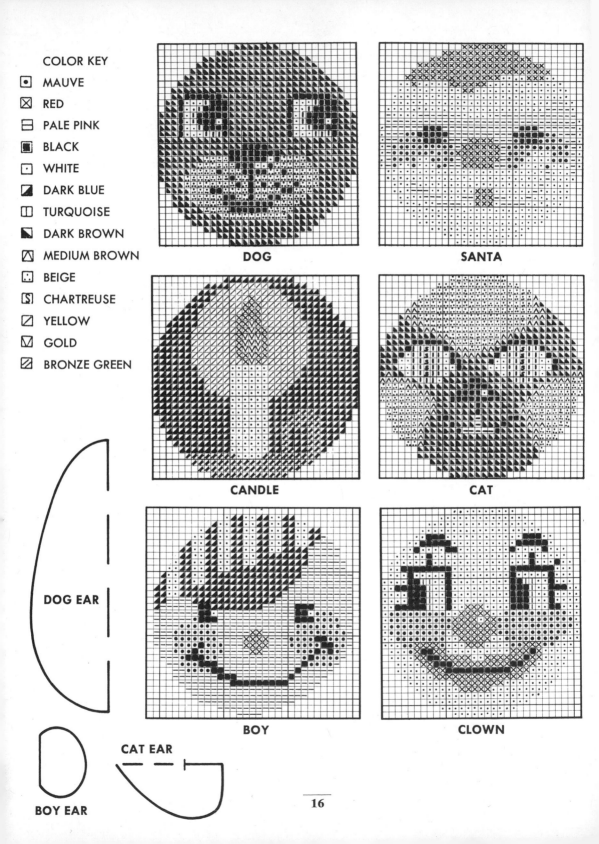

COLOR KEY

- ⊡ MAUVE
- ⊠ RED
- ⊟ PALE PINK
- ⊡ BLACK
- ⊡ WHITE
- ◪ DARK BLUE
- ⊞ TURQUOISE
- ◼ DARK BROWN
- ◩ MEDIUM BROWN
- ⊡ BEIGE
- ⧆ CHARTREUSE
- ◪ YELLOW
- ◩ GOLD
- ◪ BRONZE GREEN

DOG

SANTA

CANDLE

CAT

DOG EAR

BOY

CLOWN

CAT EAR

BOY EAR

16

Using continental stitch, work needlepoint following Color Key and charts opposite.

To work continental stitch, start at upper right corner. Work from right to left. To begin, hold 1″ of yarn at back of canvas; work over end as you do needlepoint. All other strands may be started and finished by running end under stitches on wrong side of work. Work back and forth, turning work upside down to return; aways work from right to left. Details 1 and 2 show position of needle and stitches for the two rows.

Paint rings the color given in individual directions; let dry.

To block, cover wooden surface with brown paper. Using compass, mark on paper the exact size of worked area, being sure the circle is perfect. Place needlepoint right side down over guide. Stretch canvas over guide so needlepoint area matches marked circle; fasten with thumbtacks about ½″ apart along edge of canvas. Wet thoroughly with cold water; let dry.

After piece is blocked, refer to individual directions for embroidering loops and other details.

Cut around finished needlepoint circle, leaving a ¾″ margin of unworked canvas. Bend margin down so it will fit inside cardboard ring. Put a thin layer of glue on inside of cardboard ring and insert canvas margin so that the edge of finished canvas is flush with top edge of cardboard ring. Be sure that canvas margin is securely glued to inside of ring. If any unstitched area of canvas shows, fill in with stitches, using background yarn.

Cut a circle of thin cardboard the same diameter as cardboard ring. Glue to back of disk. Insert and glue screw eye into center of ring at the top of disk.

DETAIL 1   **DETAIL 2**

Candle: Paint ring blue. Glue fancy blue, red, and gold braid around ring.

Santa: Paint bottom and sides of ring white; paint top red to continue needlepoint hat. With white yarn and needle, make loops of various lengths for Santa's beard, moustache ends, and eyebrows by pulling yarn through needlepoint where illustrated.

Clown: Paint ring white. With golden-orange yarn and needle, make long loops for hair at top and sides of head by pulling yarn through needlepoint.

Cat: Paint ring tan or beige. To make whiskers, cut six 3¼″ lengths of beige yarn. With needle, pull yarn through needlepoint under nose area, leaving ends extending as shown. For ears, complete half-pattern and cut two ears of brown felt; cut small slit at bottom (up to crossline); overlap edges of slit and glue each ear to ring as shown. If desired, glue fancy sequined gold braid around bottom to form collar.

Little Boy: Paint bottom and sides of ring pink; paint top of ring where hat is in same colors as hat (blue and white) to continue hat stripes. Cut two ears of pink felt and glue one to each side of head ring.

Dog: Paint ring tan or beige. Complete half-pattern for ear and cut two ears of brown felt; glue one to each side of head ring.

Pleated Paper Ornaments

Delightfully original figures are made from folded paper and styrofoam, embellished with golden and jeweled details.

EQUIPMENT: Scissors. Ruler. Pencil. Tracing paper.
MATERIALS: Sheets of white typing paper. Styrofoam: For figures, five balls 1¼″ diameter; for birds, two balls 1″ diameter and two ovals 2″ long. Gold Christmas beads ¼″ diameter. Fine gold cord. Narrow, flat gold braid. Scallop-edge gold braid ¼″ wide. White pipe cleaners. Tiny glue-on artificial jewels, blue and green for eyes. Red seed beads for mouths. Plain wooden toothpicks. Straight pins. Gold flower bangles and a sequin. All-purpose glue. Lightweight cardboard ¼″ x 6″.

GENERAL DIRECTIONS: All figures are made with styrofoam balls and ovals and pleated white paper. Cut paper to sizes indicated; fold in accordion pleats ¼" wide.

Birds: Glue a 1" styrofoam ball for head to top of the larger end of styrofoam oval: for Goose, use a 1" piece of toothpick inserted into both; for Swan, attach head to bottom front with a 4" piece of pipe cleaner; bend neck upward and curve gracefully backward and forward. Insert and glue two ½" pieces of toothpick into front of head for beak. Cut two pieces of white paper using actual-size wing pattern opposite. Fold in accordion pleats, starting at wide end, as indicated by short dash lines on pattern; continue folding to short end. Holding pleats on straight edge together, force a dab of glue into pleats and press firmly together until set. Clip glued end into V-shape, as shown in Fig. 1. Pin and glue long sides of wings horizontally to sides of body. For tails, cut a piece of white paper 2" x 5"; accordion pleat crosswise. Clip one end diagonally as shown in Fig. 1; clip opposite end in V. Glue V-shaped end to body as indicated in individual directions; make a slit in narrow end of styrofoam body, pin and glue tail into slit. Glue on jewels for eyes. Tie flat braid around neck. Cut a 6" piece of gold cord; knot ends together. Glue and pin knotted end to top of back for hanging.

Ladies' Skirts and Bodies: Cut white paper 4" x 10"; pleat crosswise. Bend pleated strip into a tube. At one end, for top, apply a line of glue touching the edges of each pleat. Insert a 2" piece of pipe cleaner inside glued end with ¼" extending above, for neck. Press pleats around pipe cleaner, holding until glue sets. Insert and glue neck into a 1¼" styrofoam ball for head. Fan out pleats at bottom for skirt. Glue jewels on head for eyes, a red seed bead for mouth, and insert two pins for eyebrows. Tie flat braid around neck in a bow. For hanging loop, knot ends of a 6" piece of gold cord together; pin and glue to top or top back of head to hang ornaments.

Men's Legs and Bodies: For legs, cut a piece of white paper 4" x 10"; pleat lengthwise. Fold in half across pleats and wrap a piece of pipe cleaner around center tightly; twist ends of pipe cleaner together at top for neck. Cut a piece of white paper 2¼" x 10" for body; pleat crosswise. Form into a tube and glue as for Ladies' skirt; glue around pipe cleaner neck, with legs extending below. Glue 1¼" styrofoam ball head onto neck. Glue on features, and attach hanging loop as for Ladies.

Arms: Cut two pieces of white paper same size as bird wings; pleat the same as wings. Glue arms to sides of body following individual directions.

Finish each according to individual directions below.

Golden Ring: Cut a strip of lightweight cardboard ¼" x 6". Glue gold braid on both sides. Bend into a circle and glue ends together. Cut a 1" x 5" piece of white paper; pleat crosswise. Bend pleats across middle; glue at middle. Glue one edge to ring over joining, so that ends fan upward; glue gold bead to center of pleats and three gold beads on ring at each side of paper. Thread a 6" piece of gold cord through center bead and tie into a loop.

Goose: Make bird following General Directions. Attach tail at back, straight out. For nest, cut two strips of white paper 1½" x 10". Pleat each crosswise. Glue one end of each as for tails; fan out other end into half-circle; glue half-circles together to form a full circle. Glue Goose to center of circle nest; glue a few gold beads to nest for eggs.

Swan: Make bird following General Directions. Attach tail to back, pointing upward and fanning out. Glue a flower bangle to top of head, inserting edge into center of head. Pin and glue two gold beads under body for feet.

Milking Maid: Make body and arms following General Directions. Attach long edge of arms at sides, pointing downward. Glue a gold bead at end of each arm for hands. For cap, cut a 1" x 10" piece of white paper; pleat crosswise. Glue cap around top and sides of head on back, so it fans out over front of head. For pail, cut a 1" x 3" strip of white paper; glue ends together to form a ring. Glue a circle of paper to one edge for bottom. Glue ends of a 2" piece of gold cord inside pail for handle. Glue handle to arm over one hand; glue side of pail to body.

Leaping Lord: Make body, legs and arms following General Directions. Glue short edge of arms to sides of body at top. Crease folds sharply and curve arms slightly upward. Glue a bead to end of each arm for hands. Fold one leg in half across pleats, inward. Bend ends of legs outward so ends flair for shoes. Glue folded leg against straight leg. For hat, cut a 1" x 10" strip of paper; pleat crosswise. Glue pleats at one end together; fan out other end to form a circle and glue. Glue hat to top of head. Make another arm. Glue long edge to top of hat from center down over one side. Glue a gold bead at center top of hat.

Dancing Lady: Make body and arms following General Directions. Attach long edge of one arm to side of body; attach short edge of other arm at top of body. Glue a gold bead at end of each arm for hands. Glue gold braid around top and sides of head at center. Make another pleated arm; curve and glue long edge around head over braid.

Piper: Make body, legs and arms following General Directions. Attach arms as for Leaping Lord. For collar, cut a 1" x 10" strip of white paper and pleat crosswise. Glue ends of pleats around neck and glue together at back. For hat, cut a 2" x 8" piece of paper; pleat crosswise. Form into a cone as for body; glue hat on head. Roll a triangular-shaped scrap of paper into a long cone for horn; glue. Curve one arm upward; glue horn to head at mouth and to arm near end.

Drummer: Make body, legs and arms following General Directions. Attach arms as for Leaping Lord. Make drum in same manner as Milking Maid's pail, with paper circles at both ends of tube. Glue drum to front of body. Curve arms upward; glue gold beads near ends for hands. Glue toothpick to each hand and to top of drum. For hat, cut a 1" x 10" strip of white paper; pleat crosswise. Glue piece of gold braid around chin and up sides of head for strap. Glue pleats of hat around head; join at back. For cockade, make another arm; cut off end to make shorter. Glue long edge to front of hat with tip pointing up. Glue a gold sequin to bottom of cockade.

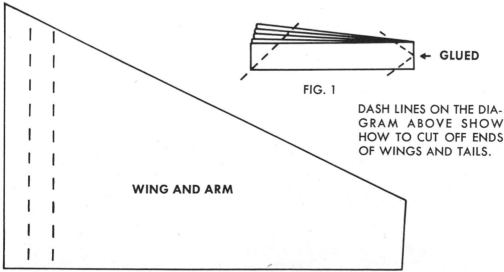

← GLUED

FIG. 1

DASH LINES ON THE DIAGRAM ABOVE SHOW HOW TO CUT OFF ENDS OF WINGS AND TAILS.

WING AND ARM

WREATHS

Della Robbia Wreath

*Della Robbia fruits in luscious colors of felt are lightly stuffed
and glued to a 9"- diameter felt wreath.*

EQUIPMENT: Tracing paper. Pencil. Ruler. Compass. Scissors.

MATERIALS: Felt: 9" x 12" pieces of magenta, dark green, chartreuse; scraps of fuchsia, orange, yellow, gold, purple, lavender, dark olive green, bright green. Piece of dark green gift-tie yarn, 6" long. Absorbent cotton for stuffing. All-purpose glue. Wooden toothpicks.

DIRECTIONS: Trace patterns; complete half and quarter-patterns indicated by dash lines.

For wreath, mark and cut an 8½"-diameter circle of dark green felt and another of magenta felt. Cut a 3½"-diameter circle out of center of each. Spread glue on one surface of each; place small amount of cotton around one circle and press the two glued surfaces together. For bow, cut strip of chartreuse felt 1¾" wide, 11" long; fold ends to center, forming bow loops. Cut another strip 1" x 2"; wrap tightly around center of bow to shape; glue. Cut two more strips, each 1¼" x 3½";

cut off one end of each diagonally for streamers; glue straight ends to back of bow. Glue bow to wreath. Using patterns, cut two pieces for each fruit of appropriate color felt, making two oranges, two pears, two lemons; make one apple of fuchsia with a leaf of dark olive green. For each fruit, glue two pieces of felt together with light cotton stuffing between. For bunch of grapes, cut one base of purple; cut 20 circles in three sizes of lavender to cover base; glue circles on base. Cut 14 holly leaves of bright green; cut 11 holly berries of fuchsia. For fringed leaves, cut twelve of bright green, seven of dark olive green; cut fringe where shown. To form leaves, put a dab of glue at narrower end and wrap around toothpick; glue again at end. When glue is dry, cut off any part of toothpick showing. Arrange pieces on wreath as shown and glue.

To hang, form loop of gift-tie yarn; glue ends to top of wreath at back. Cut a 1" x 2" strip of dark olive green felt and glue over yarn ends at back to cover.

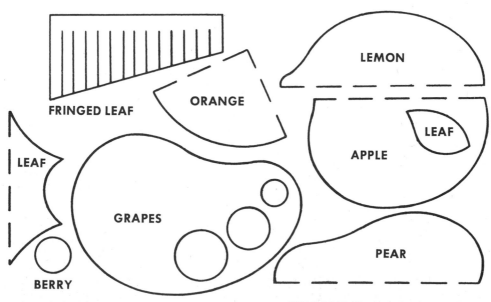

FRUIT FOR DELLA ROBBIA WREATH.

Holly Wreath with Pompon Berries

*Colorful pompon "berries" center this puffed felt holly wreath;
the leaf cutouts are machine appliquéd.*

SIZE: 17″ diameter.

EQUIPMENT: Scissors. Pencil. Paper for patterns. Tracing paper. Dressmaker's tracing (carbon) paper. Sewing needles. Straight pins. Zipper foot. Steam iron.

MATERIALS: Felt: White, two pieces, each 18″ x 18″; kelly green, 26″ x 15″; red, 54″ x 1¼″. Cording, ¼″ thick, 54″ long. Thread to match all felt. Dacron or cotton fiberfill, and small amount of batting. All-purpose glue. Large and small pompons from ball fringe in red and fuchsia, about 100.

DIRECTIONS: Enlarge patterns by copying on paper ruled in 1″ squares. Complete quarter-pattern indicated by long dash lines. Make a separate leaf pattern; trace short dash lines onto leaf pattern.

From white felt, cut two wreath pieces, adding ⅜″ all around scalloped outer edge and inner circle edge. From green, cut sixteen holly leaves. Cut red felt to make a strip 54″ x 1¼″ (may be pieced).

To shape red piping to fit around scalloped edges, fold strip in half lengthwise. Use steam iron to press folded edges while shap-

QUARTER-PATTERN FOR HOLLY WREATH
TO ENLARGE ON 1″ SQUARES.

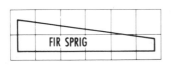

FIR SPRIG

PATTERN FOR
"BALSAM FIR" WREATH

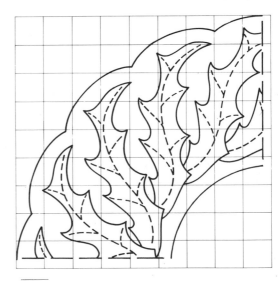

ing strip into a curve (pull and shape felt strip as you press). To make corded piping, open out strip; place cording along lengthwise center; fold strip over, with cut edges flush. Using a zipper foot on machine, stitch along strip close to cording.

Arrange sixteen holly leaves around one white wreath as indicated on pattern. To lightly pad leaves, place a small amount of batting under each one; pin leaves in place. Using matching thread, machine stitch around each leaf close to edge; trim away any excess batting; stitch leaf veins following lines.

With right sides facing and raw edges flush, pin corded piping around scalloped edges of wreath front; baste and clip into seam allowance of cording. With right sides facing and raw edges flush, place back of wreath over front, with cording between; baste. Using zipper foot, stitch all pieces together. Trim seams to ¼"; clip into seam allowance of wreath pieces at curves; turn to right side. Overcast inner circle seams together, leaving about 6" opening; stuff firmly; overcast opening closed.

Glue pompons around front inner circumference of wreath as pictured.

"Balsam Fir" Wreath

Fringed "needles" of felt are wrapped around pipe cleaners and inserted into a styrofoam base to make this ever-green wreath. A red felt bow and pompon berries add the final touches.

EQUIPMENT: Paper for pattern. Pencil. Ruler. Scissors. Needle.

MATERIALS: Felt, three shades of green: apple, kelly, and olive. Pipe cleaners (180), 6" long. All-purpose glue. Miniature Christmas lights. Hairpins. Styrofoam wreath, 12" diameter, ¾" thick, with 1½"-wide rim; small red pompons from ball fringe (24); red felt for bow, 5" x 14"; red sewing thread.

DIRECTIONS: Enlarge pattern for fir sprig by copying on paper ruled in 1" squares. To make fir sprig, cut piece of felt, following pattern. Cut deep, narrow slashes along slanted edge. Glue narrower end to one end of pipe cleaner. Holding pipe cleaner in one hand and felt in the other, twist pipe cleaner, wrapping felt around it as you twist. Glue felt at end. Make 60 sprigs from each shade of green felt. Glue strips of green felt to cover outer and inner edges of rim. Secure miniature light wire to one side of wreath with glued hairpins or small pieces of pipe cleaners. Insert and glue pipe cleaner ends of fir sprigs into styrofoam to cover completely. Glue on red pompons in groups of three as shown.

For bow, cut piece of red felt 2" x 14"; fold in half, each end folded toward center; overlap and glue ends together. Wrap small piece of red felt around center; tack in back. Cut two streamers, 2" x 7"; cut points in one

end of each; taper to ½" at other ends. Tack narrow ends together; tack to back of bow. Glue bow on wreath.

Three-Toned Green Holly Wreath

Felt holly leaves in three tones of green are lightly stuffed and pinned onto a styrofoam base to make this elegant Christmas wreath, highlighted by multicolored Christmas balls.

SIZE: About 18″ diameter.

EQUIPMENT: Scissors. Pencil. Tracing paper. Thin, stiff cardboard.

MATERIALS: Styrofoam wreath, 12″ diameter, ¾″ thick, with 1½″ wide rim. Felt: two strips white, 72″ x 1½″, 72″ x ½″; bright green, ½ yd., 36″ wide; chartreuse, ¼ yd., 36″ wide; blue-green, ⅛ yd., 36″ wide. Thin, all-purpose galvanized wire, 72″ long. Sewing thread to match felt. Miniature Christmas tree balls, approximately 20 25m/m, 15 16m/m in silver, gold, light blue, royal blue

and red. Straight pins. Steel pins, #28, 1¾″ long. Absorbent cotton.

DIRECTIONS: Trace pattern for holly leaf; complete half-pattern indicated by long dash line. Cut pattern out of cardboard. Make several patterns and replace pattern when edges begin to fray.

To Cover Wreath: Trace styrofoam wreath circle on paper. Add ¾″ to inner and outer circle edges. Using paper pattern cut shape from bright-green felt. Clip ¾″ in, along inner and outer curved edges, ½″ apart. Place circle of felt on top of styrofoam; fold clipped tabs over edges of inner and outer sides of wreath; push straight pin through each tab into styrofoam, on both sides, to secure.

For Holly Leaves: From bright-green felt, cut 70 leaves; from chartreuse, cut 40 leaves; from blue-green, cut 30 leaves. To make filled leaves, place two of the same color leaves together; sew together ⅛" in around edge leaving 1" open; leave needle in the fabric. Stuff lightly; continue stitching around to close opening. Insert long steel pin through one point of each filled leaf; insert into wreath at an angle, so pin point does not come out of styrofoam. Completely cover top and sides of wreath as pictured. Sew miniature Christmas balls to leaves, at random, hiding metal Christmas ball hangers under edges of other leaves.

For Bow: Clip both ends of 1½" white felt strip to a "V." With wire between, center narrow strip of white felt on wider strip; stitch along narrow strip, on either side of wire. Tie into a large bow; shape into soft ripples as pictured. Pin bow to top of wreath. Approximately 7" from each streamer end, tack to a leaf at each side, to secure.

Walnut and Pinecone Wreath

Nuts and pinecones are popular ingredients for an everlasting wreath, and here is an elegant version to display proudly through the Christmas season.

EQUIPMENT: Pencil. Ruler. Drill with small bit. Wire snips. Scissors.

MATERIALS: Wire wreath frame, 18" diameter. Wire: Very thin, medium heavy, and heavy covered. Pinecones: Long and narrow for base, about 40; larger round, about 40; small round, about 24. Assorted nuts, about 100. Spray varnish. All-purpose glue.

For Bow: Velvet ribbon, 5 yards each: gold, 2" wide; blue, ⅞" wide.

DIRECTIONS: To attach pinecones to wire wreath frame, wrap a long length of medium wire around each long cone, concealing wire between layers of cone and leaving wire extension to tie around frame. Wrap wire extensions around frame so that each cone radiates from center outward. Continue attaching long cones until wire frame is covered completely.

With medium wire, wrap and tie larger and smaller rounded pinecones in same manner as for long cones, but arrange rounded cones randomly on face of wreath. Conceal wires between base cones and tie on back of frame.

Make about ten groups of six to eight assorted nuts. With drill and small bit, drill a hole through each nut near end. String nuts on fine wire; tie together in a cluster and fasten to wreath as for cones. String smaller clusters of nuts and small pinecones as needed to fill in bare spaces. Spray wreath with two coats of varnish, letting dry between coats.

To hang, fasten covered wire securely to back of frame.

To make bow, see photo, page 26. For bow loops, cut three 30" lengths of each color ribbon. For center bow knot, cut a 5" length of each color. For streamers, cut two 34"

pieces of gold ribbon and two 32" pieces of blue ribbon; cut two 32" pieces of covered wire.

To make bow loops, glue wrong side of each blue ribbon along center on right side of corresponding gold ribbon. Fold ends of ribbon lengths under and overlap 1" at center back. Place the three bow loops together and wrap centers with wire, leaving ends of wire long enough to attach around wreath. To make streamers, center and glue wire along right side of gold ribbons, leaving 1" of ribbon free at each end. Glue blue ribbons, right side up, over wire on gold ribbons. Place the two streamers together and pinch at ends. Attach streamers under bow loops at pinched point by wrapping with wire. To make center knot, glue 5" length of blue ribbon on corresponding gold ribbon as for bow loops. Wrap 5" bow covering around center of bow; glue and wire under bow. Clip V-shape from ends of streamers. Attach bow to wreath. Ripple streamers by bending into soft folds.

Feather Wreath

The subtle shades of real feathers complement the earthy hues of dried wheat and flowers. The materials are attached to a styrofoam base to form a wreath of extraordinary, lasting beauty.

EQUIPMENT: Wire cutters.

MATERIALS: Styrofoam half-round wreath 17" diameter. Feathers: natural dark barred wing feathers, 10" long; pheasant tail feathers, 5"-10" long. Florist's wire. Florist's picks. Dried weeds, such as statice, skyrockets, and wheat.

DIRECTIONS: Break off weed stems, making branches about 6" long. Arrange sprigs of different types in small groups. Attach groups to florist's picks by wrapping a length of wire around both. Insert picks in wreath at an angle. Cover top surface of wreath completely, inserting feathers as you go along (trim quills if necessary). Insert all picks and feathers in same direction.

Dried Wheat and Apple Spray

A styrofoam pyramid forms the base for this lovely arrangement of apples, dried weeds and flowers. Artificial apples can be used or real apples can be added each year.

EQUIPMENT: Wire cutters.
MATERIALS: Styrofoam hexagonal pyramid (12″ high). Dried weeds and flowers, such as wheat, statice, skyrockets, etc. Apples, about 10. Florist's picks, 4″ long. Florist's wire.
DIRECTIONS: Position pyramid with base at top. Break off stems of weeds and flowers so branches measure 16″-18″. Divide into small groups, and attach each group to a pick by wrapping wire around stem and pick. Insert pick into pyramid, arranging as shown or as desired. Insert picks into apples and then into pyramid along center.
Note: Real apples may be used if decoration is to be displayed on outside door, as the cold will preserve them. If hung indoors, use artificial apples (use an ice pick to pierce a hole to receive florist's pick).

Seashell Wreath

The natural forms of seashells create a wreath of exquisite beauty. Large scallop shells are glued in place on styrofoam; smaller shells fill in the curved spaces between. Sprays of dried flowers are added for extra color.

EQUIPMENT: Long knife with serrated edge. Scissors. Masking tape. Straight pins, 1½″ long. Single-edged razor blade. Paintbrush for applying glue.
MATERIALS: Styrofoam half-round wreath, 17″ diameter with center hole 9″ diameter. Lightweight cardboard, 17″ square. Natural raffia, 1 lb. Eight large scalloped baking shells, approximately 4½″ to 5″ (measured straight across widest part). Eight smaller scalloped baking shells, approximately 3″ straight across widest part. Assorted small shells in various shapes and colors (augers, coral, cockleshells, sundial, small scallops, snails, cowries, etc.), about eighty shells. Two small starfish or seahorses, optional. Two bunches of tiny dried flowers, white and russet. All-purpose glue. Household cement. Glue gun.
DIRECTIONS: With serrated knife, slice approximately ½″ off top, rounded side of wreath, making rounded surface flat and slightly slanted toward center. Save scraps of styrofoam for later use.

Wind raffia around ring entirely, beginning and ending on back side and taping ends to hold temporarily. Using paintbrush and glue,

extend over outer edge of ring, with sides of shells almost touching each other. Following manufacturer's instructions, glue securely with glue gun. Weight down heavily, making sure shells are still in proper position after weighting. Let dry thoroughly.

From dried flowers, make small, fan-shaped bunches approximately 3″ long. Hold stems together with masking tape; trim ends. Apply glue to backs of taped stems and secure between large shells, positioning with straight pins.

Using glue gun, secure the smaller scalloped shells, concave side up, on top of flower stems. Base of shell should not extend beyond inner edge of wreath. Weight down, making sure shells are still positioned properly after weighting. Let dry thoroughly.

Make eight groupings of assorted small shells to fill the concave scallop shells (see illustration). With cement, adhere groupings in shells, using bits of styrofoam as needed to prop shells. Cement assorted shells along inside edge of ring; use masking tape to hold shells in place while drying. Let dry. Remove masking tape. Glue starfish or seahorses at random on surface of a large shell.

saturate back of ring and center it on lightweight cardboard; weight down and let dry. With razor blade, trim away excess cardboard just inside outer edges of ring.

On right side, position eight large baking shells around ring, as illustrated. Let shells

Working with Stained Glass

EQUIPMENT: Tracing paper. Carbon paper. Heavy brown paper. Heavy cardboard. Ruler. Ball-point pen or pointed pencil. Felttipped pen. Mat knife. Stencil knife. Glass cutter with tapping ball. Glass pliers, 6″ size. Regular pliers. Adhesive tape. Masking tape. Small, stiff-bristle acid brush. Soldering iron with flat or pyramid tip, 40 watts. Newspaper and plywood board for working surface. Rags. Eyeglasses or plastic goggles. Orange stick for burnishing. Scissors.

MATERIALS: Glass as specified in individual directions. Copper foil tape wth adhesive backing, 36-yd. rolls. Liquid Oleic Acid soldering flux. Whiting powder (powdered chalk). Solid wire solder, 60/40, one-lb. spools. Muriatic acid antique solution. Scraps of glass for practice. Additional materials given with individual projects.

GENERAL DIRECTIONS: Before working on actual glass pieces, practice glass cutting and soldering on scraps. Cover plywood board with newspaper to avoid spreading glass dust. Wear eyeglasses or plastic goggles for protection.

Make patterns and cut pieces out of heavy cardboard. Place cardboard pattern on glass. Mark outline with pen. To make straight cuts, place ruler or straight edge along outline. For curved edges, use pattern edge pressed down on glass, or cut freehand. To score glass with cutter, draw cutter toward you in one continuous, firm motion. Do not go over score line; it dulls cutter and can make an uneven break. If cutter works stiffly, put a drop of any household oil on cutter. Break glass along score as follows: For straight edges, firmly grasp glass at each side of score; bend down and outward, pressing evenly. For curved edges, use ball end of cutter to tap once directly beneath score, ½″ from end; break away glass. Use glass pliers to trim away jagged edges that might remain. On small strips, you may need to use regular pliers, with jaws covered with adhesive tape.

When you have cut all glass shapes needed for one design, arrange pieces over paper pattern to check fit. Wrap foil tape evenly around all edges of each piece. To wrap, place each glass edge in center of strip of copper foil tape, letting equal amounts extend over each side. Overlap foil ends about

¼" where two ends meet; cut. Fold foil edges tightly over glass edges. To flatten or burnish foil to glass, press down with orange stick.

Check fit again. With pieces in place, brush flux over all copper foil surfaces with stiff-bristle brush. Continue brushing frequently during soldering process. *Make sure working area is well ventilated.* **(Note:** If soldering iron has never been used, the copper tip must be tinned as follows: heat iron; brush tip with flux; apply a small amount of solder.)

To solder, hold heated tip of soldering iron close to copper and apply end of solder wire to iron, letting solder flow down tip onto copper. First, spot solder at several points to hold pieces together; then solder pieces together by drawing iron along copper tape, spreading solder. Do not allow soldering iron to remain at any one point for more than an instant. Solder pieces together on front; cool. Solder pieces together on back; cool. Continue soldering until all copper is covered. Repeat soldering process if necessary.

When thoroughly cooled, sprinkle whiting powder on piece, wipe off with cloth to remove excess flux oil. Wash piece until solder is shiny and glass is clean; dry.

Stained-Glass Flowers and Fruit

This glistening window wreath is designed to catch the sun's bright winter light. The glass pinecones are stencilled with copper; some flowers and fruits are slightly overlapped for dimension. Follow General Directions opposite for working with stained glass.

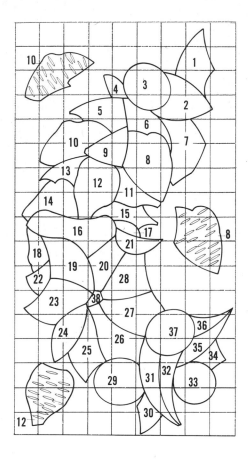

DIRECTIONS: Enlarge pattern by copying on paper ruled in 1″ squares. Trace half-pattern on tracing paper; complete wreath by turning half-pattern upside down and reversing it. Use carbon to transfer wreath pattern to cardboard; cut out pattern pieces.

For each side of wreath, cut out pieces as follows: From dark green antique glass, cut pattern pieces 5, 6, 7, 9, 11, 13, 14, 15; from deep red-orange antique glass, cut pattern pieces 19, 20, 23, 24, 25, 26, 27, 28; from emerald green antique glass, cut pattern pieces 1, 4, 21, 22, 30, 32, 34, 36; from orange antique glass, cut pattern pieces 3, 33; from green-blue opalescent glass, cut pattern pieces 2, 31, 35; from apple green opalescent glass, cut pattern pieces 16, 18; from tortoise (dark amber) cathedral glass, cut pattern pieces 8, 10, 12, 17; from amber semi-opalescent glass, cut pattern pieces 29, 37.

See General Directions for cutting glass.

Cut copper foil sheet into six pieces, each 2″ x 5″. For each side of wreath, place one 2″ x 5″ piece of foil, adhesive side down, on top of tortoise (dark amber) pieces 8, 10, 12. Trace pattern for pinecone design onto tracing paper. Place pattern on foil; trace design lines with ball-point pen to imprint on foil-covered piece. Remove pattern. Use stencil knife to carefully cut out small oval areas. Leaving a ¼″ border beyond glass edges, trim foil around each piece; fold this ¼″ around sides; burnish foil to glass.

See General Directions for preparing, fitting, and soldering glass.

For each red-orange poinsettia center (#38), wrap a narrow strip of foil around four small amber nuggets; solder nuggets over center ends of poinsettia leaves and to each other. To give a three-dimensional effect, build up and fill in spaces between nuggets with additional solder.

Using a cotton swab, apply muriatic acid solution to solder and stenciled foil sheet; rub with cloth until solder and foil sheet become a dull, mottled silver. Let dry; wash with soapy water; rinse; dry again.

For hanging wreath, shape two pieces of stiff wire into small U-shaped loops. Solder ends of loops to top back of wreath at each side, about 2″ in from inside edges. Attach each end of picture wire to one loop at each side of wreath.

(**Note:** Refer to Equipment, Materials, and General Directions for Stained Glass on page 28.)

ADDITIONAL MATERIALS: Antique glass: dark green, two sheets, each 8″ x 10″; deep red-orange, two sheets, each 8″ x 10″; emerald green, about 12 small pieces; orange, about four small pieces. Opalescent glass: green-blue, about six small pieces; apple green, about four small pieces. Cathedral glass: tortoise (dark amber) 1 sheet 8″ x 1″. Semi-opalescent: amber, about four small pieces. Eight small amber nuggets. Adhesive backed copper foil sheet 5″ x 12″. Muriatic acid antique solution. Two pieces of stiff wire for hanging loops, each 1½″ long. Picture wire 22″ long.

Stained-Glass Dove and Holly Wreath

Glowing cathedral stained glass, cut into easy-to-work-with shapes, are soldered into place to create this stunning snow-white dove in a holly wreath.

(**Note:** Refer to Equipment, Materials, and General Directions for Stained Glass on page 28.)

ADDITIONAL MATERIALS: Cathedral stained glass: small amounts of white, green, and red; scrap of yellow for beak. One blue glass nugget for eye. Stiff wire for hanging.

DIRECTIONS: Enlarge pattern by copying on paper ruled in ½" squares. Cut each piece out of cardboard (except eye).

Cut pieces out of glass. To check fit, arrange pieces together. Then wrap copper foil tape evenly around edges of each piece, including nugget for eye. Place pieces together again for complete design, with eye in place on one side of head. Brush with flux and solder pieces together following General Directions. Solder wire loop to center top for hanging.

When finished, clean well with soap and hot water; wipe dry.

Calico Wreath

A cheerful calico fabric is used to create a tufted, puffy wreath that will welcome smiles when friends come calling. The print motifs are cut and sewn into the wreath shape; front and backing are sewn to boxing strips and stuffed before tufting. (Shown on page 34.)

EQUIPMENT: Tracing paper. Lightweight cardboard. Ruler. Scissors. Single-edged razor blade. Pencil. Thumbtack. String. Needle. Compass (optional). Straight pins. Narrow masking tape.

MATERIALS: Fabric: Green cotton print, 45" wide, preferably with 4" to 4½" motif, 1 yd. White vinyl, 6" x 48" (or use a stiff fabric as a substitute). Polyester fiberfill. Sewing thread. Cafe curtain ring.

DIRECTIONS: Wreath has 17" outer diameter and 8½" inner diameter. To make pattern, use a large compass, or mark on cardboard as follows: Tie a knot in end of a length of string; measure 8½" from knot and tie string beyond this point around a pencil; push thumbtack through knot at end, into center of cardboard. Mark off circle on cardboard by pivoting pencil around. Do same for inner wreath diameter (4¼" from knot) or use compass. Using razor blade, cut out on pencil lines.

Divide cardboard wreath into eight equal parts; do not cut apart. Trace one section to make cardboard pattern for cutting fabric. Cut out eight fabric sections, centering a motif on each piece and allowing ½" extra all around for seams. If motifs run into one another, try to match as we have done. For wreath back, cut out one entire ring of fabric with ½" seam allowance on both edges. Cut out two strips of fabric for boxing: one 3" x 60" for outer edge, and one 2" x 27" for inner edge, piecing where necessary.

With right sides facing, pin, then sew motif sections together into wreath shape, making ½" seams. With right sides together, sew 3"-wide boxing strip around outside of pieced wreath shape, making ½" seams; seam ends of strip together; trim excess stripping. Do same with strip for center hole. With right sides together, sew wreath back to other edge of outer boxing strip. Slash into seam allowances all around for smooth curves. Turn to right side. Turn in ½" around remaining edges of inner boxing and wreath back and slip-stitch together leaving 6" opening for stuffing.

Pinch outer seam edges of wreath between fingers; topstitch all around, 1/16" in from edge. Stuff fully; slip-stitch opening closed.

For tufting, thread needle with doubled sewing thread and make 3 or 4 stitches through entire thickness of wreath 1½" from outer edge between each section on seam line; knot on back.

To make bow, cut vinyl 45" long, 6" wide. Gather center of strip with fingers; fold ends back to center, leaving approximately 6" of fold on each side for bow loops. Overlap and gather ends at center; tape around center to hold. Cut piece for center of bow 3" x 4". Fold shorter ends under to make strip approximately 1¼" x 4". Wrap around center of bow to back; fasten with tape; trim excess. Pin bow to wreath. Trim ends of bow evenly and cut out a triangle in both ends. Sew cafe curtain ring to top back of wreath for hanging.

TREES

Calico Tree

To match the calico wreath, here is a fabric tree complete with its calico star. The tree is sewn in tubular sections, trimmed with bright yarn pompons.

SIZE: 33" high (with base).

EQUIPMENT: Pencil. Yardstick. Scissors. Lightweight cardboard, 34" x 20". Needle. Straight pins, 1¾" long. Narrow stick.

MATERIALS: Green cotton print fabric with 4"-5" wide motifs, 3 yds, 45" wide. Interfacing, 25" wide, 6 yds. Fusible web. Polyester fiberfill, approximately 2 lbs. Sewing thread. Plastic flowerpot, 7" diameter. Red acrylic yarn for pompons. Red moss fringe (optional) 12". All-purpose glue.

DIRECTIONS: To make pattern, rule a 33½" line vertically down center of cardboard. Mark top A and bottom C. From A measure down 29"; center a 19" horizontal line across AC line. Letter each end of horizontal line B. Connect A to B and B to C for both sides. Round off point at C. Using pattern and allowing ¾" extra all around for seam allowance, cut out six pieces from fabric. If there is a motif pattern, center it on each piece, using the vertical line as a guide. Using same pattern and seam allowance, cut out six pieces of interfacing. Place interfacing on wrong side of each fabric piece; baste close to edge all around. Sew all six pieces together; start by laying two sections' right sides together and stitching from A to B using given seam allowances. Sew another section to opposite side of one sewn section, again from A to B. Do this for all six sections until you have one continuous circular shape.

Turn bottom edge under ¾" and topstitch ½" from edge all around.

With right sides facing out, fold each section out down the center, matching each section's seam lines; stitch sides of section together from A to B approximately ⅜" from seam line. Do this with all six sections.

With narrow stick, pack each section fully with fiberfill, smoothing each cone shape as you stuff. Bottom of each section is left open so stuffing may be removed for storage.

Ornament for top of tree consists of two motifs cut from fabric and fused back to back with fusible web. Trim edges of ornament with moss fringe. Insert straight pin into bottom of ornament. Concealing head of pin, insert into top of tree.

To cover base, lay out fabric wrong side up. Place flowerpot on its side on fabric; roll pot across fabric until it is completely covered. Overlap at back; trim and fold back ends under; pin temporarily. On inside top and bottom, trace along pot edges onto wrong side of fabric; unpin and cut out, leaving 1" excess on both top and bottom for turning in. Cut out and back this fabric with interfacing, fusing with webbing. Glue to pot.

To make pompon ornaments, see How To Make Pompons, on page 184, and use a 2" diameter for making pompon form. Make as many as desired. Conceal head of pin in pompon and insert into tree.

Star Pillow Tree

Five patchwork plaid pillows, each a star, stack up to make this whimsical tree. When the festivities are over, each star becomes a comfy throw pillow.

EQUIPMENT: Pencil. Paper for patterns. Thin, stiff cardboard. Ruler. Scissors. Straight pins. Wooden dowel about 12" long. Sewing and darning needles.

MATERIALS: Cotton tartan plaids in predominantly reds and greens, 45" wide (yardage varies according to allowance for matching of plaids; that is, larger plaids require

more fabric than the smaller ones). Our tree used one yd. of plaid A (see directions below), ¾ yd. of plaid B, ⅞ yd. of plaid C, and ½ yd. of plaid D. Polyester filling, about 3¼ lbs. Four-hole, smoky pearl buttons: ¾" diameter, two; 1" diameter, eight. Small skein pearl cotton, red.

DIRECTIONS: Enlarge patterns by copying on paper ruled in 1" squares. Complete half-patterns indicated by dash lines. Make a separate pattern for each of five diamonds (1-5) on cardboard, adding ¼" seam allowances on all sides. Make a separate side pattern for each length on cardboard, adding ¼" seam allowances along curved sides and ½" seam allowances at each end.

Each star is a plaid combination: one plaid for sides, two plaids for patchwork stars; combinations in each star pillow vary. Designate each of your four plaids with a letter from A to D, ranging from largest plaid to smallest.

Tree shown uses a variety of plaid combinations. **Bottom Pillow:** Plaid A for sides; plaids B and C for patchwork star. **Second Pillow:** Plaid C for sides; plaids A and D for patchwork star. **Third Pillow:** Plaid B for sides; plaids D and C for patchwork star. **Fourth Pillow:** Plaid A for sides; plaids B and C for patchwork star. **Fifth Pillow:** Plaid D for sides; plaids C and B for patchwork star.

For largest pillow, cut six side pieces with the center (half pattern dash line) along lengthwise grain of fabric; place pattern so that plaids of each side piece match. From each of two plaids for patchwork star, cut six pieces to make top and bottom of pillow. Use diamond pattern #1, with long points along lengthwise grain of fabric; match designs of the same plaids for each piece. With right sides together, stitch diamond of plaid B to diamond of plaid C along one short side

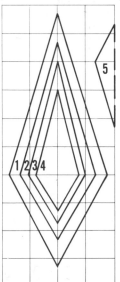

DIAMOND PATTERNS FOR EACH PATCHWORK STAR.

5

1 2 3 4

12" 9½" 8" 6" 4½"

SIDE PATTERNS FOR EACH PILLOW TO ENLARGE ON 1" SQUARES.

with ¼" seam. Alternating plaids, join six diamonds for top and six for bottom of pillow. With right sides together, join side pieces to one patchwork star, making ¼" seams. Stitch curved edge of each side piece along sides of star points, matching point of side and point of star. Clip into seam allowance of side pieces at point; trim points off to ¼". In same manner, stitch opposite curved edges of side pieces to second star. Seam ends of side pieces together with ½" seams, leaving one pair open for stuffing.

Repeat in same manner for the other four star pillows using smaller diamond patterns (numbers 2-5) and shorter side patterns successively. When pillows are finished, turn right side out. Stuff fully, using dowel to get stuffing into points.

Before closing opening of each star pillow, tuft the pillow using two buttons for each. Using long length of pearl cotton threaded through darning needle, make knot about 5" from the end. Pull needle through center of star on one side, out through center of star on the other; you will need to use your hand inside the pillow to guide the needle through. Make stitch across one button through diagonally opposite holes. Then bring needle back through pillow and out on first side next to knotted end. Make diagonal stitch across other button and bring needle back through pillow to second side, pulling firmly at the pearl cotton. Make second stitch through remaining holes of button, then carry needle back to first side and through one open hole of button; pull cotton to tuft pillow. Pull 5" end through remaining open hole; knot ends together firmly; trim. Tuft all five stars, then slip-stitch each opening closed.

Stack star pillows in graduating sizes as shown to form tree.

Star-Topped Felt Tree

This charming pear tree of felt is filled with colorful partridges. The central styrofoam cone is covered with green felt; felt loops are glued down to form the branches. A bright felt star adds the final touch.

EQUIPMENT: Pencil. Ruler. Scissors. Tracing paper for patterns. Lightweight cardboard. Straight pins.
MATERIALS: Styrofoam cone, 6" x 24". Felt: green, 72" wide, 1 yd.; small pieces of felt in assorted bright colors, including black, white, orange, and yellow. Pipe cleaner. All-purpose glue.
DIRECTIONS: To cover cone, align length of cone with straight edge of felt; pin to secure. Roll cone until felt covers; pin at center back; leaving ½" overlap, trim away excess felt. Glue felt to cone. Bottom may be covered also, but it is not necessary. Cut approximately 120 strips of green felt, 6" x ¾" each. Form into loops by following looping diagram on page 38, gluing ends together. (**Note:** The number of loops needed depends on how closely you distribute them on the cone.)

Cover cone entirely with loops by working in circular rows from bottom up, gluing as you go along. Overlap loops of each row over ends of previous row.

Birds, pears, and eggs are made from actual-size patterns on page 38. Dash lines indicate overlapped edges. Trace patterns, making a separate cardboard pattern for each part. Using coordinating colors for each bird and wing, cut pieces from felt. Make tails for some birds by cutting one or two narrow strips (approximately ⅛" x 1½") of felt; loop and glue on back of tail area. For eyes, cut bits of black felt; glue on where indicated on patterns. Glue stems of pears to front of pear as indicated.

Each nest is made of six 3½" x ⅛" strips of felt. Bring ends of each together, forming six loops. Crisscross loops on top of each other; glue together at center. Glue egg on; hold until set.

To decorate tree with birds, nests, and pears, glue and hold each in place until set. Refer to illustration for placement. You will need approximately 60 birds, 9 nests and 12 pears.

Make 4" and 2½" star patterns as instructed on page 184. Make cardboard patterns for

each. Cut three of each, making smaller star orange and larger star bright yellow. Center and glue smaller stars onto larger stars. This is a three-sided star; glue half of first star to back of first half of second; glue remaining half of second star to back of first half of third; glue remaining half of third star to back of remaining half of first. Insert and glue pipe cleaner through bottom of star and insert opposite end into top of cone. Cut small strip of green felt 1″ wide; wrap around top of cone, covering top loops and pipe cleaner. Overlap in back; trim; glue.

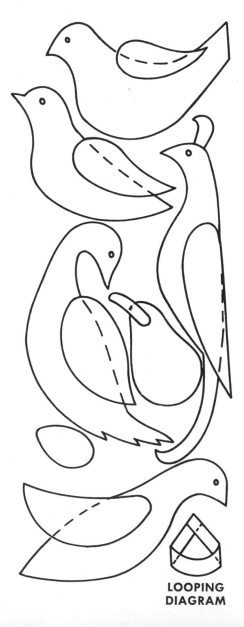

LOOPING DIAGRAM

Fringed Tissue Tree with Fruits and Vegetables

A wooden dowel and coat hangers form the framework for the fringed tissue tree. Tree's fruit and vegetable ornaments make wonderful pot holders, too.

TREE

EQUIPMENT: Handsaw. Drill with ⅛″ bit. Wire cutters. Ruler. Hammer.

MATERIALS: Wooden dowel ½″ diameter, 21″ long. Three wire coat hangers. Bright green tissue paper, two sheets. Scrap of bright pink tissue paper. Clay flowerpot about 5″

diameter at top, 3½″ diameter at bottom. Styrofoam to fill pot. Green florist's clay. All-purpose glue. Brass cafe curtain rings (12 pinch type).

DIRECTIONS: For base: Fill pot with styrofoam and cover with clay. Cover outside of pot with green and pink tissue paper as illustrated; glue.

For tree limbs: Cut from bottom and sides of coat hanger, three pieces: one each 20″, 14″, and 8″; straighten bends in wire. Drill a hole through dowel 8¼″ from one end, another hole through dowel 6″ above first hole, and a third hole through dowel 5″ above last hole. Insert 20″ wire through first hole, 14″ wire through second hole, 8″ wire through third hole, leaving equal lengths of wire at each side of dowel. Glue wire at holes to secure.

For fringe: Cut strips across green tissue paper 1¼″ wide. Fold strips in half lengthwise. Cut fringe on folded edge of the strips ⅜″ deep and about ⅛″ apart. Wrap strips slightly on the diagonal, around wire limbs, starting at ends with fringe out, and working into dowel; glue ends of strips to wire. Starting at bottom of dowel with fringe down, wrap strips around in same manner, working up to top.

To Assemble: Poke hole into styrofoam in pot with sharp instrument. Insert dowel end into clay pot.

Attach a curtain ring to tab of each felt Fruit and Vegetable Ornament. Slip rings over tree limbs as illustrated. Tack on top ornament.

FRUIT AND VEGETABLE ORNAMENTS

EQUIPMENT: Scissors. Paper for patterns. Pencil. Ruler. Embroidery and sewing needles. Hole punch.

MATERIALS: Felt for each ornament, an 8″ square of main color. Matching sewing thread. Scraps of felt and medium-weight yarns. (See illustration for specific colors.) Absorbent cotton for stuffing. All-purpose glue.

DIRECTIONS: Enlarge patterns by copying on paper ruled in 1″ squares. Refer to illustration for colors. Cut two main pieces of felt for each. Cut front designs of another color felt; glue to front of one main piece. Embroider with yarn as indicated on pattern and below (see Stitch Details on page 186). Make seeds on apple, watermelon, and pear in lazy daisy stitch. Make lines on strawberry and beet in running stitch. Make closed buttonhole stitch on plum center. On orange, embroider straight stitches radiating out from center. Make dots on lemon in French knots. Make crosses on grapes in cross-stitch.

Whip two main pieces together, leaving a 1″ opening. Through this opening, insert enough cotton to stuff lightly; whip closed. Punch hole in top end of each ornament.

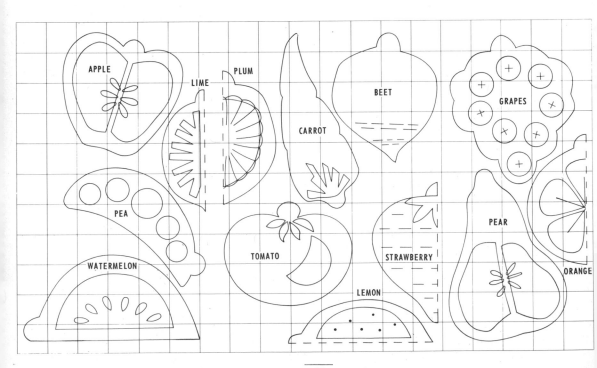

Beaded Tree

*Beads and baubles glitter and glow on this tiny treasure tree.
The wire framework is set in a plaster-filled flowerpot base;
the lavish decorations are wired into place on the
beaded boughs.*

SIZE: 10″ tall.

EQUIPMENT: Wire cutters. Jeweler's pliers. Ruler. Scissors.

MATERIALS: Beads: 6mm transparent emerald green (faceted), about 600; larger green, about 15; multicolored E beads (like seed beads, but larger), about 150; 15mm rhinestone star, one; plastic snowflakes, about five. Assorted beads as desired to fill in (pearls, crystal, seed, pearl drop, rhinestone). Wire: Green covered stem, 16 gauge, one piece 10″ long; silver colored, 32 gauge, one spool; green colored, 26 gauge, one spool. Small plastic flowerpot, 2½″ high, 2″ in diameter. Spackle or plaster to fill pot. Decorative foil to cover pot. One piece each of lightweight cardboard and felt, approximately 2″ x 2″. Glue.

DIRECTIONS: Using bottom of flowerpot as a pattern, cut a circle from cardboard and felt; glue cardboard to base of pot; glue felt over it.

Prepare spackle or plaster according to package directions; pour mixture into flowerpot. Before spackle hardens, insert the 10″ piece of stem wire into center of pot. Place large pale green beads around stem wire on top of plaster; allow to harden.

From green colored wire, cut approximately 15 pieces of each of the following lengths: 1½″, 2″, 2½″, 3″, 3½″.

To form bottom branches, start at base of tree. Twist ends of the 15 longest pieces of green-colored wire around stem wire, spacing around stem. String emerald green beads onto each wire; leave about ¼″ of wire at end; twist into a loop to prevent beads from falling off. Use the 15 next longest pieces of green wire for next row of branches. Use graduated shorter lengths as you work around stem to the top, to give tree shape. Bead each wire after it has been attached to tree; twist each end into a loop.

For decorations, cut pieces of silver-colored wire about 2″ long. String multicolored beads as desired, leaving short ends of wire; twist into a circle; twist ends to branches at random on tree. String other beads separately

onto small pieces of wire and attach to tree, arranging as desired. Attach rhinestone star to top of tree, using small piece of wire. Cover flowerpot with decorative foil; glue.

Ruffled Tree

Soft ruffle trim is glued in place in a spiraling climb to the top of this glorious, easy-to-make tree. Base is a styrofoam cone; pompons and green felt leaves add color to the delicate tiers.

SIZE: About 15" tall.

EQUIPMENT: Tracing paper. Pencil. Scissors.

MATERIALS: Styrofoam cone, 6" in diameter at base, 12" tall. Styrofoam disk ¾" thick, 3¼" diameter. White and gold ruffle trim, 1½" wide, 3 yards. Double-fold bias tape, green, 1 package. Red ball fringe, 1 yard. Gold metallic cord, 1 yard. Olive green felt, 9" x 12". All-purpose glue. Straight pins. Scrap of wire.

DIRECTIONS: Glue styrofoam disk to center bottom of cone. Cut off about ½" from tip of cone. Starting at bottom of cone, glue ruffle trim around in close rows, spiraling up to top. For tree decorations, cut about 34 pieces of bias tape, each 1½" long. Fold one piece in half crosswise at a slant. Pin and glue to cone at center of one row of ruffle. Cut a pompon from red ball fringe. Pin and glue to cone on top of folded bias tape. Make 33 more decorations and attach around cone in every other row of ruffles, making about four in rows around lower portion, and three around as you move up to top.

Trace actual-size half-pattern for leaf; complete pattern. Cut 13 leaves from green felt. Make a tuck in each at center of straight end and glue to base of cone around disk, with points of leaves extending beyond ruffle.

For looped star, cut a 10" piece of gold cord and bend it into nine ½" loops; bring ends together and secure with wire. Bend remaining 26" piece into about 24 loops. Arrange around loops of smaller piece and wire all ends together. Glue and pin to top of tree.

LEAF

Teardrop Tree

Small silver beads highlight each graceful teardrop cut from a double-faced fabric you make yourself. Tree gets its shape from a cardboard cone, and it stands on a cardboard tube base.

FINISHED SIZE: 17″ high.

EQUIPMENT: Paper for pattern. Dressmaker's tracing (carbon) paper. Sharp scissors. Pinking shears. Sewing needles. Staple gun. Iron. Straight pins.

MATERIALS: Fabric: Red chintz, 36″ wide, ½ yd; shiny green satin, rayon, or silk fabric, 15″ x 16″. One piece fusible web, 14″ x 15″. Small silver beads, 56. Styrofoam cylinder for stand, 10″ high, 3½″ diameter. Two pieces of lightweight cardboard, one 10″ x 11½″, one 15″ x 20″. Masking tape. Glue. Spray adhesive. Green and red sewing thread.

DIRECTIONS: Enlarge pattern by copying on paper ruled in 1″ squares; complete half-pattern indicated by long dash line. Using pattern, cut one cardboard shape, adding ½″ to each straight side of pattern. Overlap straight edges ½″ to form a cone. Use masking tape to hold together.

Using pattern, cut one green and two red fabric shapes, adding ½″ to each straight edge and 1″ to bottom. Transfer design for teardrop cutouts to right side of one red shape. Spray adhesive all over cone. Wrap other red piece around cardboard cone, leaving 1″ extending at bottom. Trim point; glue down. Trim bottom edge of fabric with pinking shears; turn excess fabric to inside of cone; staple to cardboard along edges of fabric.

Using pattern, cut fusing web without seam or hem allowance; place between red and green fabric shapes, wrong sides facing. Following manufacturer's directions, fuse fabrics together with iron.

For teardrop cutouts, use sharp scissors to cut along curved lines of design on red side. Fold each cutout in half lengthwise, with green sides facing, exposing red fabric beneath. Pinch edges and sew together with a silver bead to approximate center of cut edges.

Press seam allowance of one straight edge under, with green side out. Pin raw, straight edge over glued seam of red fabric-covered cone, leaving 1″ extending at bottom; match cut-out designs at seam; lap folded edge over raw edge; pin to hold. Fold point at top into

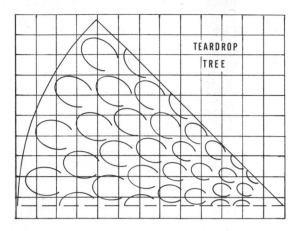

TEARDROP
TREE

seam; slip-stitch along folded seam edge. Trim bottom edge of fabric with pinking shears; turn excess fabric to inside of cone; glue to red stapled fabric.

Base of tree: Wrap 10″ x 12″ lightweight cardboard tightly around styrofoam cylinder; hold together with masking tape.

From red fabric, cut a bias strip 6½″ x 12″. Press under ¼″ to wrong side along one shorter end of fabric. Glue unfolded short end of fabric to cardboard-covered cylinder, leaving ½″ extending at bottom. Wrap fabric tightly around cylinder; glue short folded end over glued edge. Turn under excess fabric at bottom of cylinder; glue to cardboard.

Place tree on stand.

Poinsettia Tree

Bigger-than-life poinsettias are created from crepe paper and bloom on a lattice-strip trellis. Show off the Christmas flower in all its glory—use ten, as shown here, for a tree 41″ high, or make your tree blossom from floor to ceiling. Each blossom is 16″ in diameter.

SIZE: 41″ high.

EQUIPMENT: Staple gun. Screwdriver. Paintbrush. Wire cutter.

MATERIALS: Lattice stripping, ½″ x 1″, four pieces in the following lengths: 18″, 30″, 41″, 42″. Two-plied crepe paper: Five folds flame red; one fold moss-leaf green. Crepe paper: One fold flame red; one fold yellow. Three ¼″ screws and nuts. Moss green water-based tempera or acrylic paint. One spool No. 2 green wire. Seven bundles No. 9 wire (1 dozen pieces in a bundle). One spool green floral tape. All-purpose glue.

DIRECTIONS: Enlarge patterns by copying on paper ruled in 1″ squares.

Flowers: From flame red two-plied crepe paper, cut 80 petals using pattern A; cut 60 petals using pattern B; cut 30 small center petals using pattern C. From moss-leaf green crepe paper, cut 30 leaves using pattern D. From No. 9 wire, cut 80 pieces 11″ long and 60 pieces 9″ long. From No. 2 green wire, cut 30 pieces, each 12″ long.

Cut 1″ strips across the entire lengthwise fold of flame red crepe paper to cover all the 9″ and 11″ wires. Put a small amount of glue at top of wire; wind the strip around the wire two or three times, wrapping securely; twirl the wire with one hand as you guide the strip diagonally downward, stretching the crepe slightly as you wrap; secure the bottom end with more glue.

To wire the petals and leaves, glue the red-covered wire down the back center spine of each petal; do the same with the green wire for each leaf. Use 9″ wire for petal A, 11″ wire for petal B, 12″ green wire for leaves. Use glue sparingly so it will not stain front side. Allow petals and leaves to dry thoroughly overnight.

Flower Centers: Cut a 3″ strip across the grain of the yellow and remaining green crepe paper. Fringe this strip by cutting 2″ deep slashes with the grain, making cuts as close as possible. Cut the fringe into 4″ lengths. Twist the pointed ends of each of the red center petals. For each of the ten flower centers, lay one yellow fringe piece over one green fringe piece. Place three red center petals on top of yellow fringe; with green fringe on outside, roll up tightly to form centers. Wind a small piece of spool wire around base to hold.

To Assemble: For each flower, hold center at base. With smooth sides up and bottoms flush, arrange six medium petals (B) around center; wind a small piece of spool wire around to hold. Arrange eight large petals (A), bottom edges flush, around tied petals and flower center. Wind two 10″ pieces of spool wire around bottom of petals and center, leaving a 4″ end of each piece for stem. Wrap base of flower and the two 4″ ends of spool wire with green floral tape.

Place three leaves, smooth side up, on taped stem at base of flower; secure to stem with green floral tape.

Assemble frame according to diagram, using screws and nuts where indicated by X's. Paint frame moss green; allow to dry thoroughly.

Twist stems of flowers around slats of front of frame following illustration. Staple the stems to the frame to secure. Adjust flowers by bending wire petals and leaves into desired position.

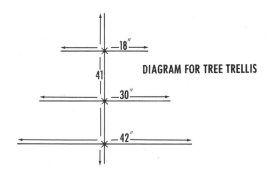

DIAGRAM FOR TREE TRELLIS

PATTERNS FOR POINSETTIA PETALS AND LEAF

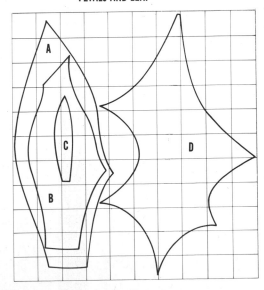

TABLECLOTHS

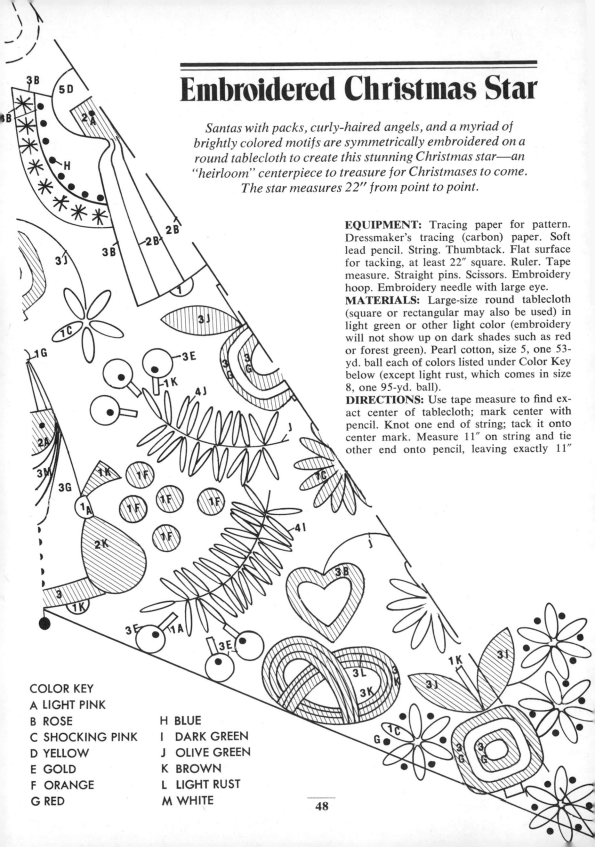

Embroidered Christmas Star

Santas with packs, curly-haired angels, and a myriad of brightly colored motifs are symmetrically embroidered on a round tablecloth to create this stunning Christmas star—an "heirloom" centerpiece to treasure for Christmases to come. The star measures 22" from point to point.

EQUIPMENT: Tracing paper for pattern. Dressmaker's tracing (carbon) paper. Soft lead pencil. String. Thumbtack. Flat surface for tacking, at least 22" square. Ruler. Tape measure. Straight pins. Scissors. Embroidery hoop. Embroidery needle with large eye.

MATERIALS: Large-size round tablecloth (square or rectangular may also be used) in light green or other light color (embroidery will not show up on dark shades such as red or forest green). Pearl cotton, size 5, one 53-yd. ball each of colors listed under Color Key below (except light rust, which comes in size 8, one 95-yd. ball).

DIRECTIONS: Use tape measure to find exact center of tablecloth; mark center with pencil. Knot one end of string; tack it onto center mark. Measure 11" on string and tie other end onto pencil, leaving exactly 11"

COLOR KEY

A LIGHT PINK

B ROSE

C SHOCKING PINK   H BLUE

D YELLOW   I DARK GREEN

E GOLD   J OLIVE GREEN

F ORANGE   K BROWN

G RED   L LIGHT RUST

         M WHITE

48

in between. Holding pencil vertically, swing around center point, making small marks to outline a 22"-diameter circle on tablecloth.

The pattern, which is separated on two pages, is one-sixth of complete star design when joined. Trace section on this page; join this section to pattern on opposite page by matching large dots and all lines of designs; trace pattern and continue star lines at top to meet and form a point. Place tracing carbon on circular area of cloth. Place traced design over carbon on circular area, keeping center point of design on center point of cloth. Using soft lead pencil, trace over the design motifs to transfer pattern to cloth; do not trace star outline. When this section is transferred, turn pattern over and match long dash line to edge of transferred design on cloth; trace pattern again. At points of star the design is not symmetrical (flower motifs extend beyond dash lines) and each point of pattern is the complete design; trace the point only once, then repeat other motifs within star area (see color illustration on pages 46 and 47). Continue turning and tracing design around center until it is traced six times and star design is complete. The center bow motif is indicated by dash line on pattern. Trace the separate bow half-pattern; complete the bow motif and transfer to center of star as shown on page 46, keeping center circle of bow at center of cloth.

STITCH KEY
1. SATIN STITCH   4. LAZY DAISY
2. CHAIN STITCH   5. FRENCH KNOT
3. OUTLINE STITCH   6. BACKSTITCH
        (NOTE: THERE IS NO STITCH KEY
        NUMBER FOR STAR FILLING STITCH.)

Throughout embroidery, use a single strand of pearl cotton about 24" long in the needle, except for the light rust which must be used doubled. To begin and end color areas, knot strand on back; do not carry thread too far across any area on back when working with any one color. Place design area of cloth in embroidery hoop, being careful not to distort fabric; move hoop to new areas as necessary.

Follow Stitch and Color Keys on pages 48 and 49 and Embroidery Stitch Details on page 186 to work design. All stems are outline stitch; only the color is marked on the pattern. The star designs on the angels' wings are not marked as to stitch; use star filling stitch. All solid dots are French knots; for angels' hair, fill entire area with French knots. In shaded areas that call for outline stitch, work rows to fill the shaded area; for pretzel, work two rows of outline stitch in each shaded area; for each heart, work two or three rows; for apples and oranges, work three rows in shaded areas. On lines that are marked for outline stitch or chain stitch, work one row. For leaves, work outline stitch in each half of leaf, following the outline. For the faces, work outline stitch rows across area close together. Work Santa and angel eyes in blue French knots; dots in candle flames are gold French knots.

When embroidery is complete, steam-press with pressing cloth.

Patchwork Star

Hundreds of tiny hexagon patches join together in a subtle blend of bright colors to form this spectacular star tablecloth. Each of the six star points is made separately, then joined for a 78" diameter star.

RIGHT: DIAGRAM FOR ONE-SIXTH OF PATCHWORK STAR.
BELOW: ACTUAL-SIZE HEXAGON PATTERN.

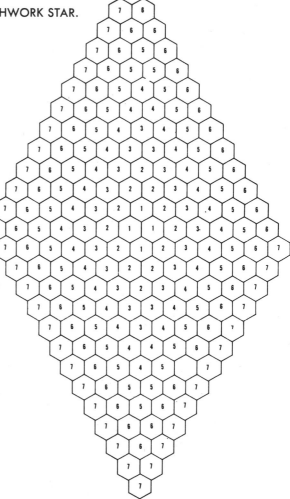

HEXAGON PATCH

SIZE: 78″ diameter.

EQUIPMENT: Tracing paper for pattern. Pencil. Thin, stiff cardboard. Scissors. Tape measure. Straight pins.

MATERIALS: Closely woven fabrics of the same weight and in coordinating colors, 45″ wide; six solid colors and one patterned for the pieced star (numbers refer to the piecing diagram): **(1)** Maroon, ¼ yd.; **(2)** Burgundy, ⅓ yd.; **(3)** Red calico, ½ yd.; **(4)** Dark red, ⅔ yd.; **(5)** Bright red, ⅞ yd.; **(6)** Orange, 1 yd.; **(7)** Gold, ⅞ yd. Matching sewing thread. Polyester-cotton lining fabric in coordinating color, 45″ wide, 2⅓ yds.

DIRECTIONS: Trace hexagon pattern; cut several hexagons from cardboard so you will be able to discard frayed patterns as necessary. Mark arrow onto patterns to be sure pattern lies on the straight grain of the fabric.

Press all fabrics and place them wrong side up. Using pencil, trace around pattern. Allow ½″ between each hexagon for the ¼″ seam allowance on each piece. Yardage was calculated allowing 20 hexagons across the width. Mark and cut the following hexagon pieces adding ¼″ seam allowance all around each: 24 maroon (1); 72 burgundy (2); 120 calico (3); 168 dark red (4); 216 bright red (5); 264 orange (6); 229 gold (7).

Following the diagram for one-sixth of the star, assemble pieces together from the center out. Start with the four maroon pieces (1) at center; add pieces around and out, following the color numbers. With right sides together, stitch hexagons together by machine or hand sew with tiny running stitches along marked outlines. Complete each sixth of star. Press seam allowances together to one side.

Join the six parts together with gold strip of hexagons between each two sixths, and the extra gold hexagon in the center. Turn under and baste outer raw edges of gold hexagons. Cut lining fabric in half; seam two halves together lengthwise. Place star patchwork on lining fabric. Smooth out and baste the two pieces together across complete star in six directions through each point. Cut away excess lining to ¼″ from outer edges of hexagons. Clip into ¼″ seam allowance of lining at each corner of hexagons and turn lining under ¼″ all around. Slip-stitch patchwork and lining together all around edges. Tack patchwork and lining together at center of star and middle of each star point.

Place patchwork star on table over a circular tablecloth.

Macrame and Felt Disk Tablecloth

Felt disks are knotted right into this special table-topper. The macrame fishnet is quick and simple to make—square knots with just a few alternate half hitches to set off the center circle. The finished cloth is 48″ in diameter.

SIZE: Approximately 48″ diameter, without fringe.

EQUIPMENT: Paper for pattern. Pencil. Ruler or tape measure. Compass. Scissors. Straight pins. Large working surface such as a carpeted floor. Hole punch. Rubber bands.

MATERIALS: Braided nylon cord, ¼″ diameter, three (100-yd.) tubes in dark green. Felt in bright colors as shown or as desired. All-purpose glue.

DIRECTIONS: To work macrame, read Macrame Instructions and refer to figures on page 54. Tie all knots as tightly as possible. Because of the nature of nylon cord, if knots are not tied tightly enough, they will loosen. If necessary, secure by dabbing each knot with glue. This may be done on the right side after each knot is tied, or on the wrong side after work is completed. While knotting, allow enough "play" between knots so work remains flat.

Prepare 36 felt circles as follows: For each circle base, use compass to mark two 5¼″ circles on same color felt; cut out. Run a line of glue all around one circle, ⅛″ from edge; glue to other circle. Complete actual-size half-pattern for petal as indicated by dash line. Cut five petals from a contrasting color felt. Arrange petals on right side of double circle base, radiating from center, with petal tips about ¼″ from circle edge. Glue petals in place. From a third color felt, cut a 1″-diameter circle; glue to circle base center, over petals. Punch ten holes in each circle base ¼″ from edges. To space evenly, punch a hole near each petal tip and then one between each two.

Cut ten 10′-long cords; fold each in half and attach to one felt circle (for center of cloth) by poking loop formed by fold through hole in felt. Insert ends in loop and pull taut to form knot (see Mounting Strands, Fig. 1). Divide strands into ten alternate pairs, by using one strand from each adjacent hole. Tie a simple square knot with each pair (Figs. 2A and 2B), making a row all around.

Add a row of five felt circles all around, attaching as follows: Regroup strands into alternate pairs. Tie a simple square knot with any pair; using these two strands, tie a reversed double half hitch (Fig. 3) with each in two adjacent holes in new felt circle. Skip two strands; repeat all around until all circles are attached. With each pair of skipped strands, tie four alternate half hitches (Fig. 4).

Form a group of four strands between circles, using alternate half hitch strands as two center strands and one strand at each side as side strands. Tie a square knot (Figs. 5A, B, C and D) with each group. Cut ten 9′-long cords. Fold each in half and mount one in next hole on each side of each circle. You now have eight strands between circles. Divide into groups of four and tie three alternate rows of square knots (Fig. 6) between circles.

Cut twenty 8′-long cords. Fold each in half and mount one in next hole on each side of each circle. You now have twelve strands between circles. Tie three alternate rows of square knots between circles. Fold each of the remaining cut cords in half and mount them on the cords last attached to circles, between mounting knot and square knot. You now have 16 strands between circles.

There are four holes remaining in each circle; cut twenty 6′-long cords; fold each in half and mount on circles. Use eight new strands, plus one on each side (ten strands). Divide into pairs and tie a simple square

knot with each pair. Tie an alternate row of four square knots with the center sixteen strands between circles.

Cut twenty 6′-long cords; fold in half and mount four, evenly spaced, on the loops formed by the simple square knot cords below each circle. Using new cords as two center strands and adjacent strands as outside strands, form four groups of four strands; tie two square knots with each group. Tie an alternate row of square knots all around.

Attach a row of ten felt circles as follows: In same manner as above, attach one below each previous circle, using the two center strands of the square knot at center of circle (Method A). Then attach the remaining five circles between the five new ones, using two outside strands of the center square knot between previous circles. This second group of five circles will have two free strands at top center; trim them, leaving about a 3″ end. Push ends to underside of circle, to be glued later. Do this also with the two strands attached to the circle, and the next two strands at left and right (total of eight strands) (Method B). Save all cut ends to be used later.

With the remaining cords between circles, tie two alternate rows of square knots. Using strand closet to circle, tie a reversed double half hitch in next hole at each side of each circle. Tie three alternate rows of square knots between circles.

Cut twenty 4′ cords. Fold each in half and mount one in next hole on each side of each circle. Using all strands between circles, tie an alternate row of four square knots. Fold the 40 saved ends in half; mount in remaining holes of felt circles. Divide these new strands into three alternate pairs using one strand from each adjacent hole. Tie a simple square knot with each pair. Tie an alternate row of five square knots with the twenty center strands between circles.

Cut twenty 40″ strands; fold in half and mount on the loops formed by the simple square knots, one on the loop to the left of the right knot, and one on the loop to the right of the left knot.

Using 16 center strands between circles, tie an alternate row of four square knots. Divide the twelve strands below each circle into groups of four; tie two square knots with each group. Tie two alternate rows of square knots all around. Divide the twelve center strands between circles into alternate groups of four; tie a square knot with each.

Attach a row of twenty felt circles as follows: Attach ten using Method A as in previous row. Attach second group of ten circles

PETAL

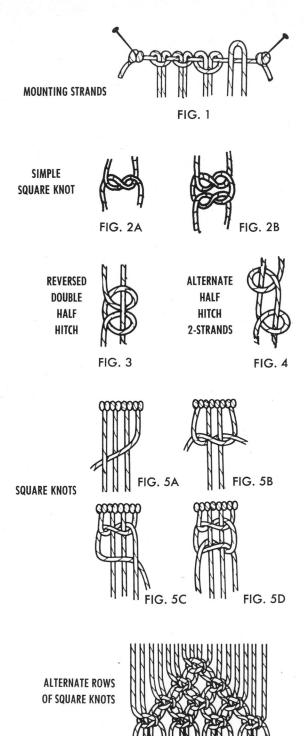

MOUNTING STRANDS

FIG. 1

SIMPLE SQUARE KNOT

FIG. 2A

FIG. 2B

REVERSED DOUBLE HALF HITCH

FIG. 3

ALTERNATE HALF HITCH 2-STRANDS

FIG. 4

SQUARE KNOTS

FIG. 5A

FIG. 5B

FIG. 5C

FIG. 5D

ALTERNATE ROWS OF SQUARE KNOTS

FIG. 6

using Method B, but use the inside strand of knot at each side of center knot to tie the reversed double half hitches. (You will have twelve free strands this time; save ends again.)

There are eight strands between circles; divide into two groups of four and tie a square knot with each group. Tie a square knot with four center strands between circles. *Using strand closest to circle, tie a reversed double half hitch in next hole at each side of each circle. Tie an alternate row of two, then one square knot between circles. Repeat from * once. Tie an alternate row of two square knots. Using strand closest to circle, tie a reversed double half hitch in next hole at each side of each circle. Tie a square knot with four center strands between circles. Form a group of eight strands; use one strand to tie a reversed double half hitch around remaining strands.

From the remaining cord and the trimmed-off ends, cut forty cords, about 20″ long. Fold each in half, and mount on two remaining holes in circles. Tie a square knot with each of the groups of four thus formed. Use one strand of group to tie a reversed double half hitch around the other three. Trim fringe ends evenly around.

Finishing: Turn work to wrong side. For each of the circles where strands were cut, cut a piece of matching felt about 2″ x 3″. Glue the cut ends of cord to felt circle, and then the rectangle on top to cover ends.

MACRAME INSTRUCTIONS

Macrame is worked by making various knots. The knots may be held in place while working by inserting straight pins through them and into the working surface. To make working with long strands of cord easier, wind the ends into a bobbin; fasten each bobbin with a rubber band. As work progresses, unfasten rubber band and allow more cord.

MOUNTING STRANDS: Fold each strand in half; hold doubled strand in front of mounting cord, fold over to back and pull ends through loop, tightening knot.

SQUARE KNOT: Made with four strands. Keeping the two center strands straight, tie knot with the two outer strands as shown in Figs. A, B, C, and D. Always hold center strands taut, and tighten knot by pulling the two outer strands up into place. A simple square knot may also be made with two strands, eliminating the center strands.

ALTERNATE ROWS OF SQUARE KNOTS: Make first row of knots using four strands for each. For second row, redivide strands into groups of four, using two strands from two adjacent knots of first row. Tie row of square knots, spacing row evenly below previous row. Regroup strands in similar manner for next alternate row.

REVERSED DOUBLE HALF HITCH: Follow Fig. 3, using punched hole instead of vertical cord in diagram.

ALTERNATE HALF HITCHES: Work as in Fig. 4, reversing the cords which work the knots, as shown.

Felt Star Table Skirt

A brilliant gold star radiates from the center of a round felt table skirt. The diamond motifs, machine-sewn with zigzag stitches, are repeated until the star is complete. A solid purple background completes the 88″ diameter circle.

SIZE: 88″ diameter.

EQUIPMENT: Ruler. Paper for pattern. Pencil. Thin, stiff cardboard. Sewing machine with zigzag attachment. Iron. Brown wrapping paper 46″ square (pieced, if necessary). String.

MATERIALS: Felt, 72″ wide, in eight bright colors, such as: light gold (color A), ¼ yard; gold (color B), ½ yard; orange (color C), ½ yard; tangerine (color D), ⅔ yard; pink (color E), ½ yard; hot pink (color F), ½ yard; red (color G), ¼ yard; purple (color H), 2 yards. Black sewing thread. Fusible web, ⅝″ strips.

DIRECTIONS: Enlarge pattern for diamond by copying on 1″ squares; complete quarter pattern indicated by dash lines. Cut a few cardboard diamonds; discard each as it frays. For each diamond, place cardboard pattern on wrong side of felt; trace around outline carefully with pencil. Cut eight diamonds from color A; 16 of color B; 24 of C; 32 of color D; 24 of color E; 16 of F; 8 of G.

Star consists of eight points; each point consists of four strips, each made of four dia-

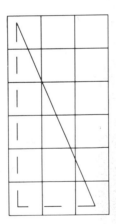

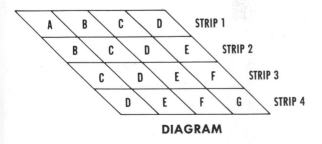

DIAGRAM

monds. Diagram shows color arrangement and how finished strips are placed to form each point of star. Following diagram, make eight each of strips 1, 2, 3, and 4. Join diamonds as follows: Place diamonds to be joined together with edges butting (there are no seam allowances). Set machine for zigzag stitch with stitch width at its widest and stitch length set at 12 stitches to the inch. Stitch along the entire length of butted edges, so stitching is centered over joined edges; make sure edges match exactly.

To make points of star, join the finished strips in same manner as for individual diamonds, following diagram for placement. Make eight points. Then stitch the points together, with color A at center, to form the large center star, as follows: From color A, cut a circle with about a 4″ diameter; this will be used to reinforce skirt at center where points meet. Baste circle to wrong side of one point, with tip of color A diamond at center of circle. Place point to be joined next to first point, and baste circle to wrong side of second point. Stitch points together, as above, stitching through points and circle. Stitch remaining points together, following same procedure.

To make pattern for color H inserts, fold felt star in half between sections, then in quarters consisting of two points. Place quarter star on 46″ square of brown paper, with the center of the star at one corner of the paper. Trace the space between two points onto the paper, marking the tips of the points carefully. Remove felt star from paper. Make a compass by tying one end of string to pencil, near pencil point. Place pencil point at tip of one point of felt star, and bring remainder of string to center of star; make a knot on string at this point (this should be 44″ from pencil point). Place knot at corner of brown paper, and pin in place securely. Hold pencil at other end of string; stretch string taut, and, with pencil perpendicular to paper, mark an arc between marked star points. To mark hem allowance, knot string 1″ beyond first knot, and mark a second arc 1″ outside first, as before.

Using brown paper pattern, cut eight pieces from color H. Stitch in place, between the points, butting edges as above. To make hem, press 1″ to wrong side all around. Insert ⅝″ strip of fusible web in hem, close to cut edge. Press again, following instructions on package, bonding hem to back.

WALL HANGINGS

New England Christmas Scene

The festive spirit of an old-fashioned Christmas is captured in this snowy scene, delightfully reminiscent of an American primitive painting. Following the pattern, it's easy to cut the colorful felt pieces, and glue them into place on a felt background.

SIZE: 28¼" x 16¾" (without mounting).

EQUIPMENT: Ruler. Pencil. Paper for patterns. Tracing paper. Scissors. Mat knife.

MATERIALS: Felt: 28¼" x 16¾", white; 9" x 12" pieces: 1 gray for houses and church; 1 dark green and 1 light green for evergreens; 1 black for bare trees; 1 red for house and sleigh. Small pieces and scraps for remainder of scene. Red yarn, 15". All-purpose glue. Double illustration board for mounting, size depending on margin you allow around scene. Red felt: Size of mounting board. Single and double-faced masking tape.

DIRECTIONS: Enlarge patterns for scene by copying on paper ruled in ½" squares. If possible, we suggest that you have pattern on chart enlarged to 28" x 17" by photostat process (such service is available in most cities). Smallest figures (children, package,

small sled with trees, not including horse and sleigh grouping) are given separately in actual size. Trace these patterns. Short dash lines indicate overlapped pieces.

For each pattern piece, choose colors as desired or refer to illustration for selection. Cut as directed below.

Cut houses and church, then cut out windows and doorways. Cut window curtains slightly larger than pattern; glue to back of window area. The color inside all windows indicates lighting; cut slightly larger than area allotted on pattern, as for curtains; glue to back. Yellow lighting in church windows is applied the same, but may be cut in one continuous piece. Cut and glue lighting in dormer windows on roof of red house. Cut out remaining roof tops; glue down. Cut door decorations, chimneys, shutters, stoops, and

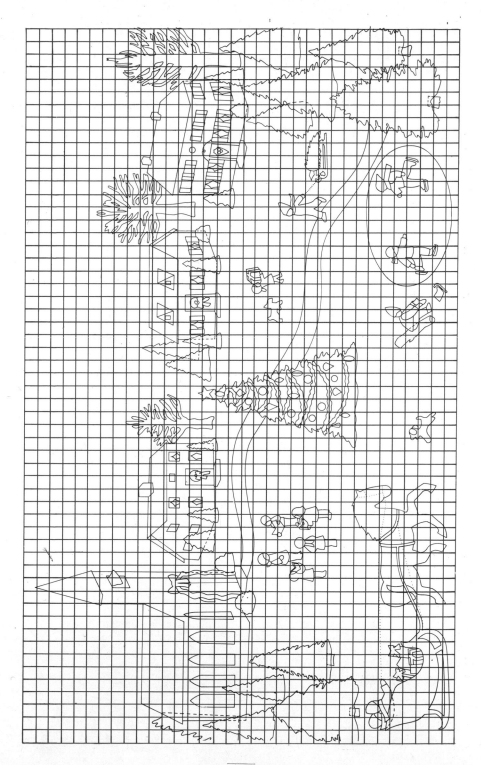

shrubs; glue in place. Glue down path, then black trees and evergreens, overlapping trunks where indicated in pattern.

Extend bottom edges of children and packages in sleigh groupings; overlap these extended edges with sleigh. Glue horse and sleigh to scene. Following dotted lines on pattern, add sled string and reins on horse with yarn. Using actual-size patterns, cut out children; glue in place.

Decide margin desired around scene. Cut illustration board with mat knife to this measurement. Cover entirely with felt; tape felt on wrong surface. With double-faced tape, secure picture to center of covered board.

Felt Tree Wall Hanging

Simple felt cutouts are glued on a red burlap base to make this lovely wall hanging.

SIZE: 24″ x 30″.

EQUIPMENT: Scissors. Paper for patterns. Tracing paper. Pencil. Ruler. Sewing needle.

MATERIALS: Heavy cardboard 24″ x 30″. Red burlap, 36″ wide, 1 yard. Scraps of bright felt: Light yellow-green; medium, emerald, and dark green; mustard; gold; bright yellow; deep turquoise and royal blue; purple; light and deep pink; white. All-purpose glue. Picture hanging wire.

DIRECTIONS: Enlarge patterns by copying on paper ruled in 1″ squares; complete half-patterns indicated by dash lines. Short dash line indicates where piece is overlapped. On cardboard, draw tree shape as triangle with 25″ base, 26½″ high with trunk 6¾″ x 4½″; cut out tree. Make two holes on each side of tree. Secure double length of wire from hole to hole to make hanger.

Cut burlap same shape as cardboard, adding 2″ all around for turning under. Cover front surface of cardboard with burlap; pull to back and glue securely on back only; let dry.

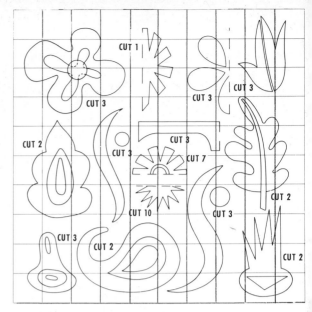

Cut pieces of felt as indicated. Arrange pieces of felt on burlap as shown; glue securely; let dry for several hours.

Bethlehem Glued-Fabric Panel

Scraps of colorful sateen are bonded to a lining fabric and then to the background panel to re-create a starlit view of ancient Bethlehem as Mary and Joseph arrive. Actual dimensions measure 44″ by 72″, but the patterns can be adapted to any size and executed in a variety of materials—from felt to paper.

SIZE: 44″ x 72″

EQUIPMENT: Brown wrapping paper for pattern, at least 44″ x 72″. Pencil. Ruler. Dressmaker's carbon (tracing) paper in white. Dressmaker's tracing wheel. Masking tape. Straight pins. Iron.

MATERIALS: Fiberboard or plywood, 44″ x 72″ x ¼″ thick. Closely woven fabric, such as sateen or cotton broadcloth (in colors shown or as desired): Small amounts for buildings, trees, and figures, plus one piece measuring at least 45″ x 73″ for background. Thin lining fabric. Fusible web.

DIRECTIONS: Enlarge pattern given on page 62 by copying on paper ruled in 2″ squares. Enlarge figures by copying on 1″ squares. Dash lines indicate edges where pieces overlap; draw these on paper also.

Cover board with large fabric piece: fold at least ½″ margins to back; tape in place. Tape or pin enlarged pattern in centered position on top of covered board, with sheets of carbon paper in between. With tracing wheel, mark positions of buildings and trees on fabric (omit details of buildings). Use same pattern to transfer the outlines of individual trees and buildings to the fabric pieces from which they will be cut (transfer the positions of the smaller details to the larger pieces also). Transfer the figures to fabric with carbon paper.

To insure neat edges, proceed with each piece as follows: Cut the shapes out roughly outside of marked outline. Following manufacturer's directions for fusible web, fuse a layer of lining fabric to wrong side of fabric

cutouts. Cut shape out carefully along marked lines. When buildings are completely assembled, fuse the details to the buildings. Cut another piece of fusible web in exact shape of fabric, and fuse each piece in place on background. Fuse figures on last.

Note: Colored papers may be used instead of fabric to make this hanging. Use regular carbon paper instead of dressmaker's carbon, and rubber cement to glue paper directly to background.

Bethlehem in Appliqué

Tiny bells ring out through the streets of this colorful panel. Fabrics in Mediterranean colors are appliquéd on a cotton background, then embellished with embroidery, beads, bells and macrame fringe. The finished piece is quilted and hung by loops from a flat wooden stick.

SIZE: Hanging, 18″ x 32″, with fringe.
EQUIPMENT: Scissors. Pencil. Paper for patterns. Tape measure. Dressmaker's tracing (carbon) paper. Sewing, embroidery, and extra-large-eyed needles. Two thumbtacks. Optional: Sewing machine.
MATERIALS: Cotton fabric: Off-white for background, 16½″ x 26″; backing in desired color, 16¾″ x 26″; small amounts of eight or nine colors for border pieces and buildings; small pieces of orange and peach for sun; scraps of pale pink organdy for sun and windows. Sewing threads to match. Dacron quilt batting, 17″ x 26″. For embroidery: Yarns in about five coordinated colors and various weights; pearl cotton and six-strand embroidery floss in olive green and varied colors. Gold lamé thread, one spool. For Fringe: Small amounts of rug yarn in four colors coordinating with border fabrics (about 23 yds.). Small brass-colored bells, six. Flat wooden stick, ¼″ thick, 1″ x 18″. Optional: Gold beads.
DIRECTIONS: Enlarge complete pattern by copying on paper ruled in 1″ squares. Fine lines are embroidery lines. Make a separate pattern for each area outlined with heavy lines. Lay vertical lines of each pattern piece along lengthwise grain of fabrics. Following photograph and complete pattern, cut each shape from various colors of fabric, adding ¼″ all around for seam allowance. For sun, cut the small circle from orange; cut medium circle from peach color; cut large circle of organdy.

Using tracing carbon, copy complete pattern onto right side of off-white fabric. Turn edges of all shapes under ¼″; baste in place. Place a layer of batting between wrong sides of off-white appliquéd fabric and backing. Baste all layers together around edges. Keeping as close to edges as possible, machine-stitch pieces in place, going through all layers and around all shapes. If not using a sewing machine, stitch with small running stitches. After attaching design pieces, stitch around panel ¼″ from edges, through layers of backing, batting, and front.

Following Embroidery Stitch Details on page 186, use embroidery floss, gold lamé thread, and pieces of yarn to outline shapes. For outlining shapes, use stitches such as couching, whipped running stitch, buttonhole stitch, outline stitch, and chain stitch. For interior details on buildings, use stitches such as French knot (dots on pattern), straight stitch, chain stitch, outline stitch, and buttonhole stitch. Tree details are worked in olive green floss. Outline tree shapes in buttonhole stitch; work featherstitch down center of each. Sew on beads at random, if desired. Tack on bells at X's.

Border: From eight or nine colors of fabric, cut rectangles, each 1½″ wide and varying in length from ¾″ to 2″ (this includes ¼″ seams). With right sides together, seam one rectangle to another along the 1½″ sides to make four strips: two 16½″ long, two 28½″ long.

With right sides facing, place a 16½″-long pieced strip at top of embroidered panel; stitch together with ¼″ seams. Repeat with other 16½″ strip at bottom. Repeat for side pieces with 28½″ strips.

To make border for backing, cut and piece enough of one color to make two strips each 1½″ x 16½″ and two strips 1½″ x 28½″.

With right sides facing, sew back border strips to front border strips, making ¼″ seams. Fold to back and press so that backing strips do not show on front side. Turn backing strip edges under ¼″; slip-stitch around all edges to panel backing.

To make hanging loops: From border fabrics, cut rectangles, each 2″ wide, in various lengths. Seam pieces together as for border, until you have five strips each 6″ long. From one fabric, cut five strips 2″ x 6″ for linings. With right sides facing, place one pieced strip and one lining strip together for each loop; stitch along both lengthwise edges of each, making ¼″ seam. Turn right side out. Fold each strip in half crosswise with pieced side inside; stitch across ends with ¼″ seam. Place loops at even intervals along back top of panel, leaving about 1″ of each extending above. Slip-stitch loops in place.

To macrame fringe: To work macrame, read Macrame Instructions and refer to Figures on page 54. From rug yarn in four colors, cut fifty 16″ lengths. To attach to panel, thread yarn strand through large-eyed needle. From front of panel, insert needle at one edge, keeping it close to lower edge; pull needle through to back. Insert needle next to first stitch and pull yarn through to front, making yarn ends even and leaving a loop on back. Take both ends of yarn, insert them through loop at back and pull until loops show at lower edge of panel. Repeat across lower edge, alternating colors.

When all yarn lengths are mounted, use thumbtacks to firmly anchor panel on working surface. Entire fringe is worked in square knots, using four strands for each.

Row 1: Holding center two strands straight, tie square knot with outer strands as shown in Figs. 5A–D, page 54. Keep center strands taut, but tie rather loose square knot. Make 25 square knots across row, one with each group of four strands.

Row 2: Make alternate rows of square knots as shown in Fig. 6 on page 54: Leave first two strands free, redivide strands into groups of four, using two strands from adjacent knots of first row. Tie square knots across, spacing row evenly below first row.

Row 3: Use all strands and knot as for first row.

Row 4: Repeat Row 2.

Row 5: Repeat Row 1. Trim ends.

To hang, run wooden strip through loops.

Knitted Madonna

Inspired by a Christmas card, this appealing Madonna and Child design adapts beautifully to a knitted wall hanging. Needlepointers can use the same chart to work the design on canvas.

SIZE: 18″ x 23″, without frame.

MATERIALS: Medium weight yarns (sport yarn weight), 4 ozs. red, 2 ozs. turquoise and dark blue, 1 oz. or less of brown, pale blue, flesh tone, pale gray-green, beige, and gold (the gold should have a silken sheen or metallic glow). Knitting needles Nos. 5 and 3, circular or straight. 18 bobbins. Red lining material, ½ yard. Two dowels, ⅜″ diameter, 18″ long. Two brass upholstery tacks. For hanging panel, brass chain or gold cord.

GAUGE: 6 sts = 1″ (No. 5 needles).

Note: See Knitting Abbreviations and Stitches, page 184.

Pattern Notes: When changing colors, pick up new color from under dropped color. When carrying a color forward, loop it loosely every 3rd or 4th st around working color. Cut and join bobbins as necessary. Use a separate blue bobbin for each side of dress; do not carry across center green strip.

PANEL: Divide dark blue into 2 balls. Wind 18 bobbins loosely as follows: 1 red, 2 dark blue, 4 turquoise, 4 gold, 1 beige, 1 green, 2 flesh, 1 brown, 2 pale blue.

Double-knit Casing: With red and No. 5 needles, cast on 209 sts.

Row 1 (wrong side): * With yarn in front, sl 1 as if to p; with yarn in back, k 1; repeat

TOP

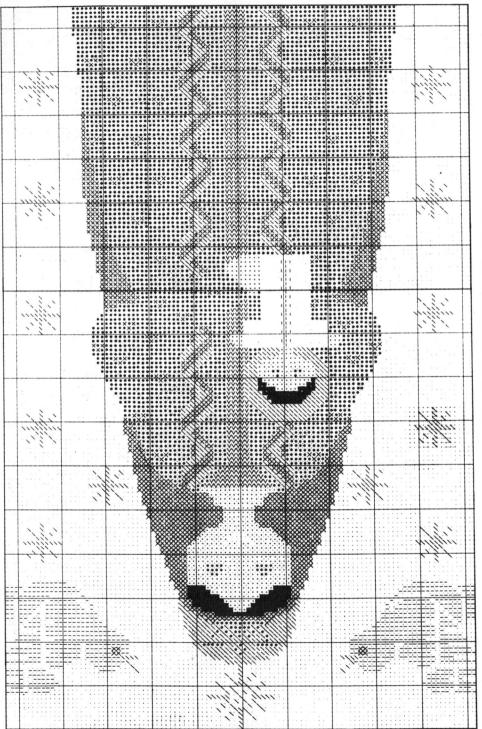

FLESH

BEIGE

GOLD

TURQUOISE

GREEN

PALE BLUE

DARK BLUE

BROWN

RED

BOTTOM

from * to last st; with yarn in front, sl last st as if to p.

Row 2: * With yarn in back, k 1; with yarn in front, sl 1 as if to p; repeat from * to last st; with yarn in back, k 1.

Row 3: Repeat row 1.

Row 4: Repeat row 2.

Row 5: Repeat row 1.

Row 6: Cast on 7 sts for side hem, k 6, sl 1 as if to p, place a marker on needle, k 1, * k 2 sts tog, repeat from * across.

Row 7: Cast on 7 sts for side hem, p 7, place a marker on needle; p across, slipping marker.

Row 8: K 6, sl 1 as if to p, sl marker; k 52 red, k 1 gold, k 52 red, sl marker, sl 1 as if to p, k 6.

Work in stockinette st, following chart for center 105 sts (1 row already worked) and working side hems in red as established, purling 7 sts each side on wrong side, knitting 6 sts and slipping 1 st for fold line on right side.

When 7 rows of chart remain, bind off 6 sts at beg of next 2 rows, finish rows in pat. Following chart, work next 4 rows of pat on 107 sts.

Next Row (right side): K 17 red, 73 blue, 17 red.

Lower Casing: Turning Row (right side): With No. 3 needle, k in colors established. Using No. 3 needles, work 5 rows in stockinette st in colors established. Bind off with No. 5 needle.

FINISHING: Turn under side hems; tack down loosely. Turn up lower casing on turning ridge; tack in place, leaving one end open. Block.

Cut lining material to panel measurements. Pin smoothly to wrong side; turn under raw edges to meet hems and casings. Sew three sides to hems; correct ease before sewing fourth side. Separate threads at one end of double-knit casing and insert dowel. Insert dowel in lower casing; sew open end. For hanging panel, tack cord or chain to upper dowel with upholstery tacks.

Latch-Hook Santa

Strawlike ribbon yarn is hooked into a 4-mesh-to-the-inch rug canvas to make this fluffy Santa wall hanging or floor mat, 17" by 20¼".

SIZE: 17″ x 20¼″

EQUIPMENT: Pencil. Ruler. Scissors. Latch hook. Small paintbrush. Lightweight cardboard.

MATERIALS: Rug canvas, 4-mesh-to-the-inch, 19″ x 22¼″. Straw-like ribbon yarn (rayon) in 24-yard skeins: matte-finish: 7 skeins white, 4 skeins bright red, 24 skeins medium green, 1 skein beige; shiny-finish: 2 skeins black, 1 skein yellow gold. All-purpose glue. Dowel, ¼″ diameter, 2′ long. Red enamel paint.

DIRECTIONS: Fold approximately 1″ on each long edge of canvas over to front, matching holes of mesh; glue. Fold up approximately 1″ on what will be bottom edge;

cut away inside corners of fold to last vertical row before fold; glue in place.

Cut cardboard into 1¼″ wide, 12″ long strip. Wind yarn crosswise around cardboard strip. Insert scissors and cut along one 12″ edge, making yarn pieces 2½″ long. Cut pieces of yarn in all colors.

Work from left to right or right to left, whichever seems more convenient. **Note:** To cover canvas with the straw yarn, it is necessary to work over horizontal threads of canvas and also over vertical threads between horizontal rows, turning canvas to side to work vertical threads. Repeat, alternating vertical and horizontal rows.

To work latch hook, fold yarn over shank

FIG. 1

FIG. 2

FIG. 3

FIG. 4

of hook (Fig. 1); hold ends with left hand. With hook in right hand, hold latch down; push hook down through mesh under two horizontal threads and up (Fig. 2). Draw hook toward you, placing yarn ends inside hook (Fig. 3). Be sure yarn is completely inside hook when latch closes. Pull hook back through canvas, drawing yarn through loop; tighten knot by pulling ends (Fig. 4).

Follow chart and color key starting at bottom. Work across in rows on horizontal and vertical meshes. Work approximately 2″ with green strands to bottom of Santa. Continue following chart up to within 13 horizontal rows from top of chart. Cut off excess canvas beyond 13 horizontal rows. To form casing for dowel, turn canvas over to back. Skip top three horizontal rows at edge of canvas; hook on next eight vertical and horizontal rows. Matching unworked meshes, fold the eight hooked rows to front. Hook over vertical and horizontal meshes of unworked area on front through both layers of canvas, leaving casing open. Paint dowel red and let dry. Insert dowel through casing.

Crewel-Embroidered Christmas Creatures

Amusing embroidered animals in assorted yarns share in the good cheer. A fluffy, turkey-worked mane brings a lifelike dimension to the lion, resting peacefully with the little lamb; the smug cat sits under the mistletoe, daring a mouse to come for a kiss; and the dapper French-knotted snowman wears a big holiday smile and a holly-trimmed hat.

EQUIPMENT: Tracing paper. Dressmaker's tracing (carbon) paper. Pencil. Ruler. Embroidery needles. Embroidery scissors. Tweezers.

MATERIALS: Dark green linen or homespun type fabric 8″ x 11″ for Lion and Lamb. Red burlap or coarse linen 8″ x 12″ for Snowman. Red velvet 13″ x 16″ and white organdy 4″ square for Cat and Mouse. Small amounts of fine embroidery yarns, such as crewel wool, in colors shown. Heavy mounting cardboard: 4¾″ x 7″ for Lion and Lamb; 6″ x 10″ for Snowman; 11″ x 14″ for Cat and Mouse. Straight pins. Masking tape.

GENERAL DIRECTIONS: Illustrations are actual size. To make patterns, trace outlines of design and outline separate areas of design. Using dressmaker's tracing (carbon) paper, transfer all parts of design to fabric, leaving margins as shown. If necessary, mark over design lines with a sharp pencil to keep lines clear while embroidering. Follow color illustrations for yarn colors; follow individual directions for stitches used (see Stitch Details on page 186). Use single strand of yarn in needle for all embroidery.

Finishing: When embroidery is finished, press fabric with steam iron. Stretch smoothly and evenly over mounting cardboard, using straight pins pushed through fabric and into edges of cardboard. Begin pinning at center of each side and work toward corners. Bring excess fabric to back of mounting board and tape. Frame as desired.

Snowman: Fill body and head areas with French knots worked very close together. Make striped scarf in split stitch using three shades of yarn; work line of small outline

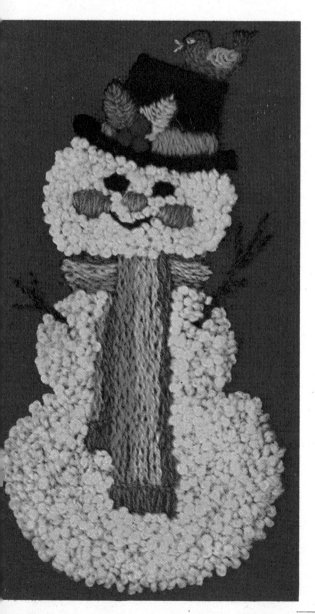

stitch across scarf ends, just above fringe; work fringe in vertical straight stitches. Embroider the branch hands as well as both arms and mouth in very small outline stitch. Work eyes, nose, cheeks, hat brim, and hatband in satin stitch. Work hat crown in split stitch, and make a line across top of crown in outline stitch. Work berries in satin stitch; work each holly leaf in fly stitch worked one under the other very close together. Work the bird body and tail in split stitch; the wing in fly stitch worked as for leaves; the beak in straight stitch; the eye in French knot.

Cat and Mouse: Pin the 4″ piece of organdy fabric over cat outline on red velvet; baste to velvet with very small backstitches along outline. This is to keep the red velvet from showing through the embroidery. Work the cat body, tail, and head separately as shown, through both organdy and velvet, using long and short stitch in white. Make lines marking forepaws, chin, and mouth in outline stitch. Work eyelashes in buttonhole stitch (turn upside down to work). Make nose in three tiny straight stitches. Make inner ears in straight stitch. Make bow in satin stitch worked in two sections as shown, using two shades of one color yarn; work center of bow separately in satin stitch; work outline stitch along top edge on one side and along bottom edge on other side of bow. With embroidery scissors, cut away organdy fabric close to stitching; pull out any protruding threads carefully with tweezers. Embroider whiskers in outline stitch. Make mistletoe stem in outline stitch. Work berries in French knots. Work leaves in satin stitch.

For **Mouse,** work body in two separate sections, head, and side ear in long and short stitch, using three shades of yarn for gradations in color as shown. Work five rows of outline stitch for tail, using three shades of yarn. Work five rows of outline stitch for outline of remaining ear; fill in ear with long and short stitch. Work nose and eye in satin stitch. Make whiskers in outline stitch.

Lion and Lamb: For **Lion,** work ears, nose, eyes, muzzle, and legs in satin stitch; remainder of face and body in split stitch; work mouth in outline stitch; pupils and toes in straight stitch; tail in buttonhole stitch; work mane in Turkey work loops (uncut), and tail tassel in Turkey work loops (cut).

For **Lamb,** work body, top of head and eyes in French knots; work face in split stitch with tiny chain stitch outline; work ears, feet, nose in satin stitch; mouth in outline stitch.

Work flowers in French knots, stems in outline stitch, and leaves in lazy daisy stitch.

CRÈCHES and RELIGIOUS FIGURES

Papier-Mâché Madonna and Child

*Inspired by El Greco's "The Adoration of the Shepherds,"
this serene Madonna and Child radiates the loveliest of holiday
themes from a mantelpiece or table. The graceful forms and
elegant drapery are created from papier-mâché built on
simple wire armatures.*

EQUIPMENT: Paper for patterns. Pencil. Scissors. Ruler. Compass. Wire-cutting pliers. Single-edged razor blade. Measuring cup. Mixing bowl and spoon. Paper cups for mixing paints. Camel's-hair paintbrushes, one very fine, one about No. 7, one wider (optional). Damp and dry cloths.

MATERIALS: Galvanized wire: 18-gauge, at least 5'; 20-gauge, at least 2'; 26-gauge, at least 3'. Newspapers. Single-ply paper toweling. Flour for paste. Paint: flat white; fire engine red enamel; white enamel; royal blue enamel; brown spray enamel. Lightweight cardboard. All-purpose glue. Masking tape. String.

DIRECTIONS: Enlarge patterns for garments and seat, on page 77, by copying on paper ruled in 1" squares. Complete half-patterns indicated by long dash lines. Use dimension patterns, Figs. 1 and 2, as guides for making wire armatures.

Armatures: Use pliers for shaping and twisting wires.

Madonna: Cut about 43" of 18-gauge wire. Following dimension pattern (Fig. 1), form oval for head at center of wire, and twist together for neck (Fig. 3). Cut 12" piece of 18-gauge wire for the arms; center it at bottom of neck and twist to form shoulder (Fig. 4); check with dimension pattern for accuracy, then twist other shoulder and measure again. Twist for waist (Fig. 5). Cut a 6" piece of 18-gauge wire. Follow dimension pattern and with one leg (Fig. 5) form hip; twist other side; check for accuracy against dimension pattern. If this twist comes out somewhat crooked, it will not matter.

Baby: Following dimension pattern (Fig. 2) and using 20-gauge wire, make armature in same manner as for Madonna, but without a waist or shoulders; for head and body, cut wire 15" long; cut arm wire 4" long and hip wire 2" long. Trim body wire, if necessary, after armature is formed.

While working with pliers, make a little tool (Fig. 6) with a 9" piece of 18-gauge wire, which will be useful for handling pasted paper later on.

To Form Shapes: For paste, mix about ½ cup flour and about ⅜ cup water in a bowl until smooth and consistency of cake batter. Make fresh batches of paste as needed. Keep damp and dry cloths on hand to wipe hands; wash hands whenever necessary. Tear a few pieces of paper toweling into strips roughly 1" x 5"; tear paper, do not cut it, because the ragged edges blend in better when pasted. Saturate paper towel strips thoroughly with paste.

Madonna: Tear a piece of newspaper roughly 15" square and crumple it (do not fold or roll) loosely into a ball. Fasten it on the upper front of armature with a few paste-saturated strips of paper towel (see Fig. 7). Next put a wad of newspaper on the rear of the lower torso and anchor with paste-dipped strips. Fill in the waistline with a small bit of crumpled newspaper, but keep waist very narrow; continue to cover the entire wire body with more crumpled newspaper and paste-dipped paper towel strips (Fig. 7). View body from all angles; if some part is too big, mash it down and put another paste-dipped strip of paper over it. If some part is too small, crumple more newspaper and add on with paste-dipped paper towel strips. Do not make body too tightly compact as you go along, or it will not bend into position later. Crumple more newspaper around arm and leg wires; anchor and fasten to body with paste-dipped strips. Taper to very thin wrists and ankles as shown in Fig. 7.

To make head, cut a piece of newspaper 12" square; crumple into egg shape with slight shaping for chin on one side of tapered end. Place inside the wire loop and cover with paste-dipped paper towel strips. Fill in neck with newspaper and wrap with paste-dipped strips (see Fig. 7), keeping it quite slender. Keep turning body to view from all sides, and refer to figure illustration for general feeling of form. When you have a satisfactory shape, check to see that all newspaper is covered with at least one layer of paper towel strips. After first layer of pasted paper has dried, smooth the face by shaving bad lumps off with razor blade and by pasting another strip of paper towel over it. Fill bad hollows with wads of paste-dipped paper towel and cover over with strips. Smooth the face and front of neck. Referring to Fig. 8, indicate features with pencil marks. For nose, make a very tiny wad of paste-saturated paper towel; stick in place and cover with bits of paste-dipped paper towel.

To make hands, cut ten 3″ pieces of 26-gauge wire. Tear paper towel into 1½″-square pieces; taper the width a bit so the fingers will be tapered at one end (see Fig. 9). Saturate the 1½″ pieces of paper with paste and roll around wire (Figs. 9 and 10). Exaggerate the length and slenderness of fingers, but do not make fingers spidery. With a little more paste, tuck in and taper ragged tip ends. Make ten fingers in this manner. Use the two slenderest fingers for the little fingers, the two fattest fingers for the thumbs. Lay four fingers together, making middle finger 1″ long; twist wires together at bottoms for wrist. Paste a small strip around lower portion, making palm 1″ long (Fig. 11). Add thumb at an angle (Fig. 12); twist thumb wire around other wires at wrist. Paste a small strip around thumb and palm (Fig. 13), and another small strip over space between thumb and index finger. Study figure illustration and Fig. 14 for positions of fingers; bend fingers and curl palm lengthwise. To fasten hands to wrists, slip wires of hand inside papier-mâché of arm end. Fasten by twisting a piece of fine wire around hand and arm wires (Fig. 15). Fill in wrists and cover with paste-dipped paper towel, anchoring hand to arm.

To Make Seat: Using patterns, cut seat sides and top in one piece, and cut separate base out of lightweight cardboard; cut out along solid lines; score with razor blade and fold along dotted lines. Shape seat (see Fig. 16) with top and base in place and hold together with masking tape. Trim base to fit if necessary. Cover with irregular pieces of paste-dipped paper towel, being sure to have at least two layers over the cracks where sides of seat come together (Fig. 16). Use straight, flat part of seat as front. See photograph on page 76.

Bend the Madonna to sit on seat (see illustration on page 76 for position). Check with dimension pattern for bending hips and knees.

Incline body to the side and forward, bending waist, neck, and shoulders. Bend arms halfway between shoulders and fingertips for elbows. Set one knee higher than the other. Study illustrations and bend figure to look as graceful and natural as possible. If papier-mâché cracks as you bend it, that does not matter.

Baby: Use crumpled paper towel instead of newspaper to cover armature, and shape body, head, and limbs. Study the illustration, (Fig. 17) to see how the plump tummy and hips and the narrow shoulders are exaggerated. Begin with first crumpled wad on tummy. Then do hips and legs, bending into final position as you mold (Fig. 17). Just indicate feet and hands by tapering. Make the face a little flat; do not bother with a nose. After the body has dried and stiffened, put a piece of pasted paper towel over top of head and push it around with wire tool into crinkles that look like hair. Mark features on face with pencil as for Madonna, following Fig. 8.

Clothing: Make one part at a time and put on the body before the pasted paper becomes dry. All clothing is made of three thicknesses. Cut first layer of newspaper, using pattern. Apply paste (with hands) to one side of newspaper shape and cover it with paper toweling. Tear towel paper to same shape as newspaper. Apply paste to other side of newspaper and cover with paper toweling; tear towel paper to same shape, but leave about 1″ larger at edges marked on patterns with dotted line. Apply paste to this 1″ and turn it over to make a hemmed edge. **Note:** To make hem of skirt a little stronger, lay a piece of string along fold when turning up the 1″.

To make sleeves, straighten out arms to put on sleeves. Follow the general directions for clothing above. Spread paste generously along the side and shoulder "seams" of the sleeve and overlap sides around arm. Position cuff and tie with string around wrist, about ¾″ above edge. Remove string when dry. Finish adhering sleeve sides and shoulder. Fasten shoulder with extra strips of paper towel, pasting to body and to sleeve. Bend arms back into position, and arrange folds while paper is still damp.

For skirt, follow general directions for clothing above. After skirt is hemmed with string, straighten legs and try skirt on the Madonna, arranging gathers at waist, with seam in center back. Squeeze the skirt at waist to set the gathers. Remove skirt and lay flat. Apply paste around waist and hips of Madonna. Apply paste inside skirt around top, and along back seam; lap back seam and press together to secure. Place Madonna inside skirt, feet first. Arrange gathers at waist and tie with string while drying. To drape the skirt, while it is still damp, rebend legs inside skirt to the seated position. Working with Madonna sitting on seat (but not pasted to it), arrange the skirt following illustration on page 72. The damp towel paper falls into beautiful shapes; you can arrange and rearrange until you are pleased with the effect. Be sure knees are far enough apart, the left lower than the right, so the blanket and Baby will be accommodated. See that the skirt is tucked close to the seat on both sides. Let dry overnight, so the skirt folds will stay where they have been placed.

Make blouse in three thicknesses as instructed above. Put paste around neck, on shoulders of blouse, and on Madonna. Paste blouse to Madonna, tucking it close around neck and tight at shoulder seams. Pat paste around top of skirt at waistline, and inside lower edge of blouse. Pull blouse around underarms and paste points to back. Arrange blouse in pleasing folds, and gather lower edge over pasted waistline; squeeze tightly to set gathers.

For cowl, cut newspaper 2½" wide, 17" long, allowing 1" extra towel paper on one long side for hem. Make cowl following general instructions for clothing above and hem along one long side. Place damp cowl around head of Madonna, hemmed edge toward face, with one end at shoulder length and other end long, to drape around neck. Practice draping down each side of head and arranging into folds around neck to get lengths right. Remove cowl. Apply a generous amount of paste on head at top, back, and sides, down back of neck, and around shoulders. Paste on the cowl, being sure that the edges come together down the back of neck. Drape cowl on both sides and arrange soft folds around neck as in illustration.

Cut mantle and make in three thicknesses, following general directions. Practice draping damp mantle, referring to illustration, with the Madonna on the seat. See that the mantle comes down close around the seat, so it can be pasted tightly to it. Remove mantle. Apply paste on Madonna body, head, shoulders, back, arms, and back of skirt. Paste on the mantle, beginning at top of head, and with body resting on seat. When the folds are arranged to your satisfaction, put paste on the seat and paste the whole dressed body to it. When the Madonna and seat are dry and can be handled again, cover the entire underneath part of the figure and seat with three

thicknesses of pasted paper, pasting carefully to bottom folds of skirt.

For blanket, use pattern and follow the general directions. Study illustration for draping. Place the most exaggerated corner of blanket in the Madonna's left hand, and arrange it with Baby in position. Paste blanket to lap and fingers, but leave Baby removable for painting.

Painting: When the figures are dry, give the Madonna and Baby one coat of flat white paint, using the No. 7 brush to reach inside the folds as far as possible. When the white paint is dry, use brown spray enamel on the deep interior folds of mantle and cowl; then spray the seat and base of figure brown.

Paint the dress red first. In a cup, mix some

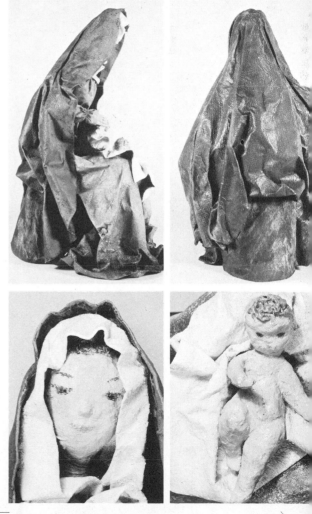

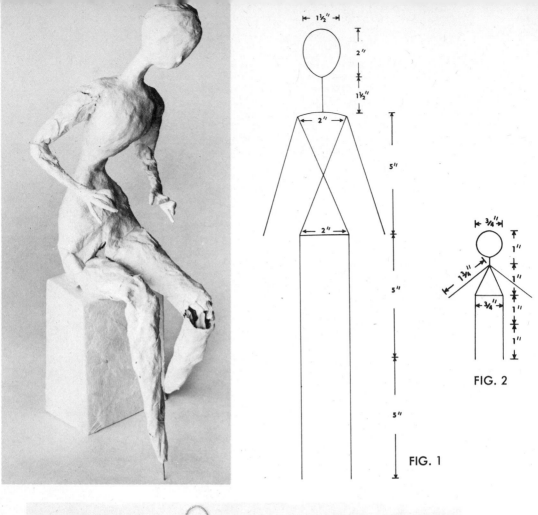

FIG. 1

FIG. 2

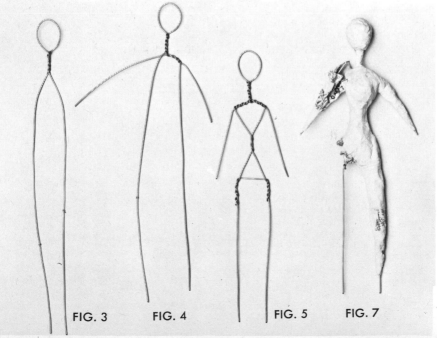

FIG. 3   FIG. 4   FIG. 5   FIG. 7

FIG. 6

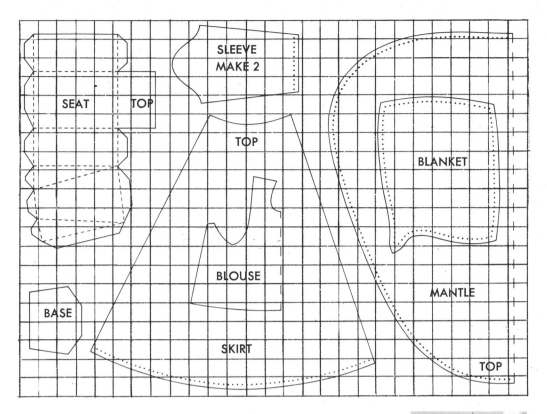

SLEEVE
MAKE 2

SEAT   TOP

TOP

BLANKET

BLOUSE

MANTLE

BASE

SKIRT

TOP

FIG. 9   FIG. 10   FIG. 11   FIG. 12   FIG. 13   FIG. 14   FIG. 15

MADONNA   BABY

FIG. 8

FIG. 16

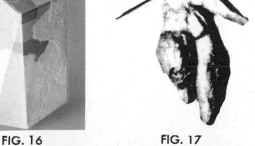

FIG. 17

red and a little white paint. Use No. 7 brush for the small and inside areas. Use the wider brush for larger areas if you wish. Wipe the paint off the folds with a rag or toweling for an interesting effect, if desired.

Paint the cowl and blanket white. To paint flesh-colored areas, put a little white enamel into a cup, add a tiny drop of red and stir; continue until you have a good flesh color. Be sure to paint under the chin and the neck as far down as you can inside the cowl, and paint the Madonna's hands. Paint the entire Baby flesh color. Let dry.

To paint the mantle, mix white with blue to soften. Paint outside and inside parts of mantle blue; let dry. When paint is dry, you can get an interesting effect by giving a light, quick spray of brown paint to the lower folds of the skirt and mantle, and up the folds of the back.

For the faces (see Fig. 8), put a little more red into the flesh color for the Baby's rosy knees, tummy and cheeks, and a spot for the nose, and the Madonna's cheeks; use a very small brush and fine, light strokes to make a blurry effect. For mouths, mix a drop of red with a touch of flesh color. Following Fig. 8 and referring to illustration on page 72, paint the mouths with tiny brush strokes: just a dot for the Baby; and for the Madonna, begin in the center, working out and very slightly up at the corners; keep it blurry. Paint Madonna's fingertips same red.

Spray a puddle of brown paint in a paper cup to use with a brush. Paint eyes, eyebrows, and hair brown. To make Madonna look downward, make the brush strokes more solid at the bottom of the eye ovals. For the Baby's hair, mix flesh color with a touch of brown paint used for eyes, brows, hair.

When all the paint is dry, glue the Baby to blanket, using all-purpose glue.

Crocheted Crèche Figures

A charming version of the Christmas story is re-enacted here in crochet. Worked up quickly using yarn scraps, each figure is about 7" tall. Standing figures have styrofoam bases. The curly sheep are worked in an easy loop stitch.

SIZE: Figures about 7" high.
MATERIALS: Knitting worsted in various colors for clothes, hair, sheep. Knitting and crochet cotton, ecru, and brown for heads and arms only. Steel crochet hook No. 4. Aluminum or plastic crochet hook size E. Chenille sticks 12" long. Cotton for stuffing. Embroidery floss for features. Beads from old jewelry. Fabric paint. Black glass-headed pins. All-purpose glue. Sheet of styrofoam ½" thick. Gold paper.
GAUGE: 6 sc = 1" (knitting and crochet cotton, double); 4 sc = 1" (knitting worsted).
Note: See Crochet Abbreviations and Stitches, page 184.

FIGURES (all figures except the Baby):
HEAD: Using knitting and crochet cotton double and No. 4 hook, ch. 2.
Rnd 1: 6 sc in 2nd ch from hook.
Rnd 2: 2 sc in each sc around.
Rnd 3: * Sc in next sc, 2 sc in next sc, repeat from * around—18 sc.
Rnd 4: Sc in each sc around.

Rnd 5: * Sc in each of 2 sc, 2 sc in next sc, repeat from * around—24 sc.
Rnds 6-11: Sc in each sc around.
Rnd 12: * Sc in each of 4 sc, pull up a lp in each of next 2 sc, yo and through 3 lps on hook (1 dec), repeat from * around—20 sc.
Rnd 13: Sc in each of 6 sc, dec 1 sc 4 times, sc in 6 sc—16 sc.
Rnd 14: Dec 1 sc, sc in each of 12 sc, dec 1 sc.
Rnd 15: Sc in each sc around. End off.
ARM AND HAND (make 2): Using cotton double and No. 4 hook, ch 6, sl st in first ch to form ring.
Rnds 1-5: Sc in each ch around, then sc in each sc around.
Rnd 6: (Sc in each of next 2 sc, 2 sc in next sc) twice—8 sc.
Rnds 7-11: Sc in each sc around.
Rnd 12: (Dec over next 2 sc) 4 times. End off.
ROBE: With knitting worsted and size E hook, ch 33, sl st in first ch to form ring.
Rnds 1-3: Sc in each sc around, then sc in each sc around—33 sc.
Rnd 4: Dec 3 sc evenly spaced—30 sc.

Rnds 5-7: Sc in each sc around.
Rnd 8: Dec 5 sc evenly spaced—25 sc.
Rnds 9-11: Sc in each sc around.
Rnd 12: Dec 5 sc evenly spaced—20 sc.
Rnds 13-17: Sc in each sc around.
Rnd 18: Dec 5 sc evenly spaced—15 sc.
Rnds 19-21: Sc in each sc around.
Rnd 22: Dec 5 sc evenly spaced—10 sc.
Rnd 23: Sc in each sc around. End off.
SLEEVES AND SHOULDERS: With knitting worsted and size E hook, ch 10, sl st in first ch to form ring.
Rnds 1-10: Sc in each ch around, then sc in each sc around.
Rnd 11: Dec 2 sc in rnd.
Rnds 12 and 13: Sc in each sc around (end of one sleeve). At end of rnd 13, ch 1, turn.
Row 14: Sc in 3 sc, ch 1, turn.
Rows 15-19: Repeat row 14. At end of row 19, ch 5, sl st to beg of row 19.
Rnd 20: Sc in each sc and ch around—8 sc. Work 1 rnd even. On next rnd, inc to 10 sc. Work 10 rnds even. End off.

TO VARY FIGURES: All figures have bands of crochet on bottom of robes. Use sc or dc bands of same color as robe or different colors to decorate robes and vary heights of figures. Sleeves can have edges or tops of different colors.
TO ASSEMBLE FIGURES: Fold 12″ chenille stick in half, insert fold end in head. Stuff head. Sew head to center of shoulders. Slip robe over chenille stick; sew around sleeves and shoulders, attaching to robe. For arms, cut 9″ piece of chenille stick; run through sleeves. Turn over ends to desired length. Slip hands over ends. Stuff figures lightly with cotton.

To make figures kneel, bend body wire. For standing figures, cut oval of styrofoam to fit bottom of robe, stretch bottom of robe over oval.

Trim robes with simple embroidery, beads, braids, etc. Halos for Holy Family and angel are circles cut from gold paper, pinned to head.

HAIR: Use worsted yarn. Comb out strands of yarn. Glue on for hair and beards.

ANGEL WINGS (make 2): With yellow yarn, ch 9.

Row 1: Dc in 4th ch from hook and in each ch across. Ch 3, turn.

Row 2: Sk first dc, dc in each of next 4 dc, 2 dc in next dc, 2 dc in top of ch 3. Ch 3, turn.

Row 3: Sk first dc, dc in each dc across—9 dc. Ch 3, turn.

Row 4: Sk first dc, dc in each of next 6 dc, 2 dc in next dc, 2 dc in top of turning ch. Ch 3, turn.

Row 5: Dc in first dc, 2 dc in next dc, dc in each dc across, dc in top of turning ch. End off. Inc edge is top of wing. Gather bottom of wing a bit. Sew wings tog part way up; sew to back of angel.

CAPE (black- and gray-haired kings): Ch. 14. Repeat row 1 of Angel's Wings. Work even on 12 dc for 2 more rows, inc 1 dc each side of next row. Work 2 rows even, inc 1 dc each side of next row. Work even for desired length.

HEAD CAPE (white-haired king): Ch 10. Repeat row 1 of Angel's Wings. Work 2 rows even. On next row, inc 1 dc at center; work 1 row even. Repeat last 2 rows until there are 12 dc. End off.

CROWNS:

Gray-haired King: Ch 15, sl st in first ch to form ring. Sc in each ch around. On next rnd, sc in first sc, dc in next sc, 3 tr in next sc, dc in next sc, sc in each sc to end. Join; end off. Sew to head.

Black-Haired King: Work as for gray-haired king, but make 3 points around ring; sew points tog at tips.

White-Haired King: Ch 12, sl st in first ch to form ring. Sc in each ch around. * Sc in next sc, ch 4, sk 1 sc, repeat from * around; sl st in first sc. For center of crown, ch 2, 6 sc in 2nd ch from hook. Work 2 sc in each sc around—12 sc. Work 2 rnds of 12 sc. End off. Sew into center of crown. Sew cape to crown; sew crown to head. For top ornament, press a pearl-headed pin through beads and through crown and head.

MARY'S MANTLE: Ch 59; work 1 row sc, 1 row dc, 1 row sc, 1 row dc. End off. With same color, ch 28; work 1 row dc. Ch 2, turn. Work first 15 sts in dc, last sts in sc. Sc around tip of piece to starting ch. Work sc in each ch to last 15 sts, dc in each of last 15 ch. End off. (This piece is for center back of mantle.) Fold mantle in half, insert center back piece, with narrower end at fold. Sew center back piece to back edges of mantle, forming a cap for head at top fold. Make a ch of white to fit around face; work 1 row sc. Sew to front of mantle to frame face. Sew mantle to head.

SHEPHERDS' HEADCLOTHS: Ch 16. Work 6 rows of 14 dc. End off. Fold over a bit at top to fit head; sew sides. Gather and sew to head. Tie a ch of yarn around head.

SHEPHERDS' CROOKS: Cut chenille sticks to desired lengths; turn ends over. Make ch same length as stick; sc 1 row in ch. Sew piece over stick; bend stick into shape.

MANGER: Cut a chenille stick in fourths; cover same as for crooks. Sew 2 pairs tog in crosses.

Sides (make 2): Ch 19. Work 6 rows of 18 sc. End off. Sew sides tog on one long edge. Set into top V's of crosses; sew in place. Place straw-colored yarn in manger.

BABY: HEAD: Using cotton double, ch 2.

Rnd 1: 6 sc in 2nd ch from hook.

Rnd 2: 2 sc in each sc around.

Rnd 3: Sc in each sc around—12 sc.

Rnd 4: * Sc in each of 2 sc, 2 sc in next sc, repeat from * around—16 sc.

Rnds 5-7: Work even.

Rnd 8: (Pull up a lp in each of 2 sc, yo and through 3 lps on hook) 4 times, sc in each of 8 sc—12 sc.

Rnd 9: Work 6 dec's as in rnd 8—6 sc.

Rnd 10: Work even. End off.

HAND: Using cotton double, ch 4. Sc in 2nd ch from hook and in next 2 ch. Work 2 more rows of 3 sc. End off. Sew into shape.

SLEEVES: With yarn, ch 6. Work 4 rows of 5 sc. End off. Sew edges tog. Slip on 4″ chenille stick; slip hands on ends.

BODY: With yarn, ch 12. Sl st in first ch to form ring. Work even on 12 sc until piece is 2″ long. End off. Sew starting edge closed in flat seam. Stuff body, sew top over neck edge and to top of sleeves.

FACES: All faces except Mary's and Baby's have embroidered eyes and mouth. Mary's and Baby's are paint. Eyes are outlined in paint, brows and noses are paint.

SHEEP: BODY: Ch. 13. **Note:** Directions are for small sheep. For larger sheep, inc 1 or more sts on body and head.

Row 1: Insert hook in 2nd ch from hook, catch strand of yarn at back of left index finger, pull through st, dropping lp from index finger, leaving small loop at back of work; complete sc—1 loop st made. Work loop st in each ch across. Ch 1, turn.

Row 2: Sc in each st across. Ch 1, turn.

Row 3: Loop st in each sc across. Ch 1, turn. Work sc and loop st rows alternately until there are 4 loop st rows. End off.

BODY ENDS (make 2): Ch 4. Repeat rows 1-3 of Body—3 loop sts.

TAIL: Work as for Body End for 4 rows.

HEAD-NECK: Ch 9. Work 1 row of 8 loop sts. Turn. Sl st to 3rd st, ch 1, sc in 3rd st, 2 sc in next st, sc in each of next 2 sts—5 sc. Ch 1, turn. Work 3 more rows of 5 sts as for body.

Next Row: Work in sc, dec 1 st. Work 1 row of 4 loop sts. End off.

FACE: Ch 2; 4 sc in 2nd ch from hook. On next rnd, 2 sc in each sc. Work 2 rnds even on 8 sc. End off.

EARS: Ch 2, sc in 2nd ch from hook. End off. Sew into ear shape. For larger ears, ch 3; sc in 2nd and 3rd ch.

TO ASSEMBLE SHEEP: Cut chenille stick in fourths (thirds for large sheep). Form 2 pieces in U shape. Sew up bottom body seam. Stick one U through back end, one through front end, forming 4 legs. Stuff body. Sew ends over openings (loops down on ends, toward back on body). Sew bottom of neck tog forming a circle. Stuff back of head and neck. Gather top of head a little, stuff face and sew in. Roll tail; sew up seam; sew on. Sew on ears. Cover legs as for shepherd's crook. Nose and mouth are straight sts; eyes, black glass-headed pins.

Mexican Crèche

*Tiny clay figures are easily molded by hand, fired or air-dried,
and then painted with charming folk-art motifs.*

EQUIPMENT: Oilcloth. Cutting wire. Sturdy flat working surface. Plastic wrap. Ruler. Pencil. Tracing paper. Scissors. Sharp knife. Sponge for smoothing. Rolling pin. Small flat and fine-pointed paintbrushes. Kiln with firing temperature for clay used.

MATERIALS: Almost any kind of un-grogged clay can be used, about 3 lbs. for all pieces (air-drying clay may also be used). Acrylic paints: white, beige, dark brown, gold-leaf.

DIRECTIONS: Cover working surface with

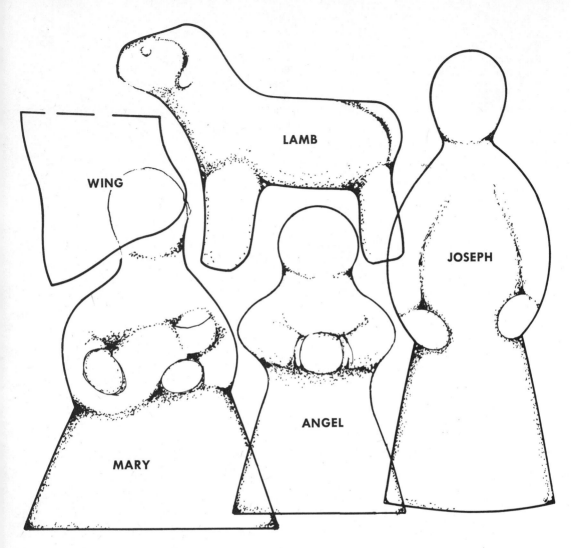

WING

LAMB

JOSEPH

MARY

ANGEL

oilcloth wrong side up. Wedge all the clay to be used at one time. To wedge, use wire to cut the mass in half. Throw one half down, then throw the other half on top of first. Then press clay with both hands, kneading it like dough until smooth and free of air bubbles when cut in half again (clay must be free of air bubbles or else it may explode in kiln or crack). Work with just enough clay needed at a time, keeping remaining clay moist in plastic wrap.

Following actual-size drawings, form basic shapes (all features, lamb's tail, ears, and hands are painted after firing). Smooth with hands and fingers as you work. Make figures a little larger than desired finished size, since clay will shrink in drying and firing.

For angel wings, roll out clay about ¼" thick; trace pattern and complete half-pattern. Place tracing on rolled-out clay. With a knife, cut out wings; crosshatch surface of angel where wings will be attached; wet one surface of wing and crosshatch area; press together. Shape wing to back; slightly bend wings toward front.

Set all pieces down on flat surface so bottom will remain flat. Insert pencil or dowel from the bottom of body, push up through body close to the top to make hole; remove. This hole will allow piece to dry from inside. Set pieces aside and let dry thoroughly (approximately three to five days). You can tell if piece is dry by touching it with a wet finger. If damp spot remains, it is not yet dry.

If using air-drying clay, paint at this point (see instructions below). If using regular clay, fire figures to required temperature.

Following illustration, paint figures mostly white. Paint heads and areas for hands beige or tan. Paint features and hair dark brown.

For decorations, use gold paint and a touch of dark brown. If necessary, trace a design; place design on area to be decorated, pencil side down; go over lines of design to transfer to figure. Paint in areas and lines.

For lambs, paint stripe of gold for tails and paint lines on each side of head to indicate ears.

Storybook Crèche

The story of Christmas is presented as a miniature book that opens up to reveal the Nativity scene. The "book" is a hinged wooden box painted and covered with felt; the tiny figures inside are made of felt and paper.

EQUIPMENT: Tracing paper. Pencil. Ruler. Small paintbrush. Scissors.
MATERIALS: Hinged wooden box, 4″ x 5¾″, 1½″ deep; 3½″ x 5⅛″—inside dimensions. Paint: yellow, red, purple, magenta. Scraps of felt: pale blue, turquoise, medium blue, gold, pink, magenta, dark green, bright green, dark gold, white, red, purple. Scraps of white, lightweight cardboard or sturdy paper. Small amount straw or dried grass. Gold paper

TURBAN

SLEEVE

SHEPHERD

CROOK

EAR

SHEEP

TAIL

MARY

SLEEVE

HAIR

JOSEPH

TURBAN

BACK

LIPS

HANDS

BEARD

TRIM

BABE

WING

BLANKET

edging. Scrap of paper. Two gold medallions. Gold letters: ½″ high; one 1″ letter "T". Yellow baby rickrack. Four small pompons from white ball fringe. Two black pipe cleaners. Ball-point pens: red, blue, black. All-purpose glue.

DIRECTIONS: Trace actual-size patterns. Dash lines on pattern show where pieces are overlapped.

Open box from side like book. Paint right inside magenta; paint left inside purple. Paint inside rims red; let dry. Paint outside edges (pages) yellow. Glue red felt on front cover, purple felt on back cover; cover spine (outside hinged area) in two strips of purple felt (on top and bottom of box). Glue narrow strips of red felt along yellow sides of box to give cover a look of thickness (see illustration on page 83). Glue two 1″-wide strips of red felt across spine as shown. Trim these felt strips and outline front cover with gold edging. Arrange lettering on front cover as shown; cut piece of magenta felt 1″ x 1½″; glue large "T" on it and glue all letters on cover. Glue nine rows of yellow rickrack all around book to simulate pages.

Using patterns, cut star of gold paper; glue in corner; cut gold paper rays; glue around star. Cut shepherd, Babe, Joseph's head and hands, and Mary of pink felt.

Cut shepherd's robe and sleeve of turquoise felt. Cut turban of light blue and strip of magenta: cut crook of paper; mark with black pen. Glue parts together. Mark eye with blue pen, mouth with red pen. Glue in left side of box. Glue straw along bottom. For sheep, glue two pompons together; cut two ears and two tails of white felt; glue in place. Bend short pieces of pipe cleaners into small leg shapes and short extension for each nose. Mark with black pen; mark dots for eyes with pens. Glue legs and noses in place; bend to adjust. Glue in box as shown.

For right side, cut Joseph's back and front turban pieces of dark green felt. Cut turban strip and robe of medium blue felt. Cut two robe trims of bright green felt. Cut beard of dark gold felt. Cut crook (same as for Shepherd) of paper; mark with black pen. Glue Joseph's pieces together. Mark eyes with blue pen; nose with red pen. Cut mouth of paper; color with red pen; glue on beard.

Cut Mary's robe and sleeve of blue felt. Trim sleeve and robe with strips of white felt as shown. Cut hair of gold felt. Glue Mary's pieces together. Glue very narrow pieces of turquoise felt to outline inner edge of hood and end of sleeve. Glue gold medallion on back of her head. Mark eyes and mouth in blue and red pen.

Cut Baby's blanket of light blue felt; cut strips of white felt. Cut hair of gold felt; glue pieces together. Mark eye and mouth in blue and red pen. Glue medallion to back of head. For manger, cut piece of paper 1″ square; fold in half. Cut two strips of paper ⅛″ x 1¼″. Fold each into "M" shape. Fit and glue "M's" under square to make legs. Cover one side with strips of gold felt. Glue Baby in manger. Glue Joseph, Mary, and Baby in box with straw along bottom.

To make stable, cut piece of cardboard 3⅝″ x· 1¼″. Cover completely in gold felt. Glue inside box for loft at a slight slant. Cut piece of cardboard 2¼″ x 3⅝″; fold in half lengthwise. Glue one half inside top edge; cut remaining cardboard to taper slightly at outer edge. Cover this part with dark gold felt. Then cut strips of gold and glue on vertically. Cut three strips of cardboard for beams: one to fit from top to bottom inside of box; two to fit from loft to bottom. Cover one side of each with dark gold felt; glue strips in place. Cut small strip of cardboard to connect two beams; cover one side with dark gold felt; glue. Cut two birds and two wings of white felt; glue wing on each; mark each eye with red pen. Glue birds on loft with straw.

DECORATIVE CRAFTS

Apple-Head Christmas

Here is The Night Before Christmas in miniature! As Santa arrives upstairs, Grandma and Grandpa are busy downstairs in this 30" tall, easily constructed chipboard house. The unusually expressive faces are carved dried apples.

Note: Dolls, as well as complete set-up, are sturdy and longlasting and are designed to hold up for many years.

Before starting house, make up apple doll heads.

EQUIPMENT: Paring knife. Sharpened dowel sticks. Jar.

MATERIALS: Four medium-sized, hard, late fall apples. Six whole cloves for eyes. Lamb's wool for hair.

DIRECTIONS: Peel each apple carefully. Cut one apple into slices approximately ⅛" thick for hands and ears. For other three apples, decide which end is best for bottom of head. Cut out core at bottom and insert a sharpened dowel stick. Smooth apple with knife, taper narrower at bottom. Cut features deeply into apple: cut triangle for eyes with slits above that will form lids; carve out sides to shape nose, cheeks, and chin; cut out small amount under chin; cut curved grooves at sides for ears; cut slit for mouth. For wrinkles, score with thumbnail on forehead and chin. Stick a whole clove in each eye. Set apples on dowel sticks; set sticks in a jar with apples above rim; place on radiator or stove to dry for about three weeks. Set apple slices aside to dry.

DOLL HOUSE:

SIZE: Approximately 30" high x 30" wide.

EQUIPMENT: Mat knife, with extra blades. Ruler with steel edge, 24" long. T-square and triangle. Large and small paintbrushes. Pencil. Paper for patterns.

MATERIALS: Four sheets 3-ply chipboard, each 30" x 40". Wooden canvas stretcher, 20" x 30". One piece ¼" plywood for base, 15" x 30". Decorative trim, 44" long x ½" wide. All-purpose glue. Masking tape, 1" wide. Flat varnish, small can. Poster paint: red, yellow, blue, white, and black. Pale yellow wall paint (any kind in flat finish). Small amount of red and yellow cellophane. One facial tissue. Eight twigs, approximately 2½"-3" long for fireplace. Toy andirons.

Additional accessories shown, for which directions have not been given, can be purchased in a variety store.

Note: Make patterns for items as required, using measurements indicated. Use mat knife and steel-edge ruler to cut chipboard.

HOUSE DIRECTIONS: Step 1: Cut a 15" x 30" piece of chipboard; glue on top of plywood base; place heavy weights on top until glue is dry.

Step 2: Assemble and align 20" x 30" wooden canvas stretcher; place on a flat surface. Measure and cut a 20" x 30" piece of chipboard. Mark a window on this piece of chipboard 4¾" x 8½", approximately 2" down from top 20" edge and 4" in from left longer side (see Fig. 2, page 89). For light to come through to simulate glowing fireplace, at center of panel, 2" up from bottom edge, cut a triangle, 2½" wide x 2" high.

Apply glue to slightly raised portion of the canvas stretcher around all four sides. With window at left, triangle at bottom, place chipboard panel on stretcher; weight down with heavy object until glue is thoroughly dried (at least three hours).

Step 3: Apply glue to bottom wooden edge of canvas stretcher; with back edges flush, center stretcher upright on rear of plywood base.

Step 4: Cut two chipboard side panels, each 10" wide x 30" high. On each panel, draw a line from top to bottom, ¾" in from one 30"-long edge. To score, go over this line several times with a mat knife; bend back to make a ¾" flap. To form side of house, glue the ¾" flap of each side panel to opposite sides of the wooden stretcher edges of back panel (see Fig. 2). Tape in position to hold; remove tape when dry. For each side, push front of panel outward until it is ¼" in from side edge of floor. Apply glue along bottom of front and back of panel, where it meets the floor. Tape in position to hold; remove tape when dry.

Step 5: Cut two panel supports, each 14¼" x 30". On each, draw a line from top to bottom, ¾" in from one lengthwise edge; draw another line 4½" in from first line; then another line 8¼" in from second line, leaving ¾" remaining. Score all three lines heavily; bend back (see Fig. 1). Apply glue to entire length of ¾″ flaps of each support, and on the exposed triangular corners of floor. Glue and tape panels to each side, and floor corners; remove tape when dry.

Step 6 (See Fig 2): To construct beams for floor of second story, cut two strips of chipboard, each ½″ x 20″; glue together for double thickness. Cut two strips ½″ x 9″. Glue the double strip across the back wall 12½″ down from top edge. Glue the 9″ strips to each side wall 12½″ down from top. Cut a strip ½″ x 25¼″; score across strip ¼″ from each end; fold back and glue flap to center of each side wall strip, forming a beam from wall to wall. Tape in position; remove tape when glue dries.

Step 7: Place a chipboard sheet on top of model; mark inside back and side walls of model along underside of board for second story floor. Cut out along marked lines; rest on wall strips to check fit. Remove. Paint inside of set and underside of floor pale yellow

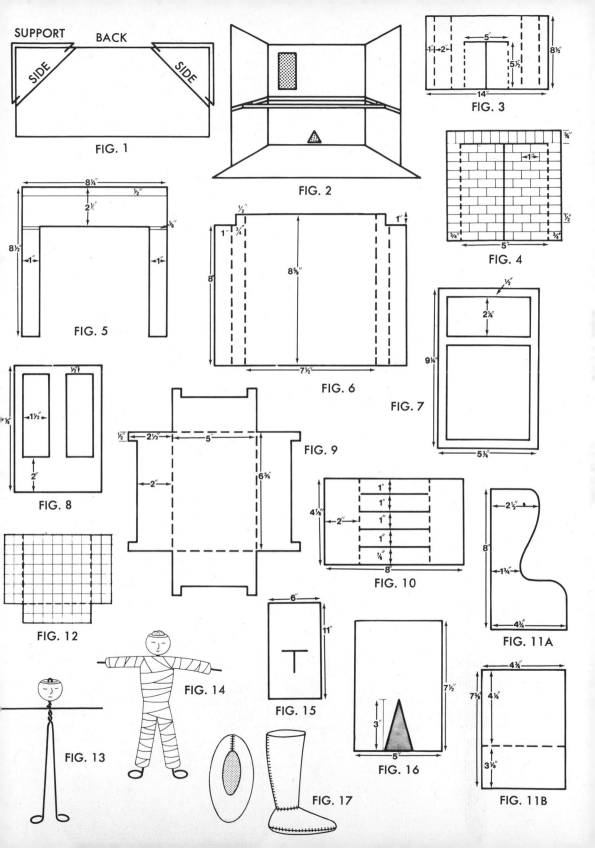

SUPPORT   BACK

SIDE   SIDE

FIG. 1

FIG. 2

FIG. 3

FIG. 4

FIG. 5

FIG. 6

FIG. 7

FIG. 8

FIG. 9

FIG. 10

FIG. 11A

FIG. 11B

FIG. 12

FIG. 13

FIG. 14

FIG. 15

FIG. 16

FIG. 17

as shown, or as desired. Set floor aside to dry.

Fireplace (See Fig. 3): Cut a piece of chipboard 14″ x 8½″. Mark off and score on dash lines; cut on solid lines as indicated. Draw a line ¾″ away, around fireplace opening. Paint within this ¾″ area and inside of fireplace with brick red color (mix about a teaspoon of red paint, 1 teaspoon of yellow, a drop of blue, a drop or two of white); let dry.

Mark out bricks by ruling pencil lines lengthwise, ½″ apart (see Fig. 4): rule off 1″ segments along each line to create brick pattern. To simulate mortar lines between the bricks, lay ruler on pencil lines; cut along lines with mat knife just deep enough to cut through paint surface. Move ruler 1/16″ below each cut line; cut another line. When brick area has been doubly lined and cut, gently peel away area between the two cut marks to expose the gray unpainted cardboard.

Fireplace Facing (See Fig. 5): Using measurements indicated, cut out facing from a piece of chipboard. Paint sides, front, and edges white; also paint white the 2″ sides of fireplace shown in Fig. 3; let dry. Glue facing to front of fireplace over edge of brick area. Weight down until glue dries.

Bend sides of fireplace back and apply glue to 1″ flaps at each side of fireplace opening; bend back and fasten to center back wall.

Push in the two brick panels of fireplace opening until they touch back wall on either side of cut-out triangle; glue and tape in position; (put a heavy object in front to hold in place while glue dries). When dry, remove tape gently.

Mantelpiece Top: Cut two pieces of chipboard, each 9″ x 2¾″; glue together for double thickness. Paint top and edges white; let dry. Glue to top of fireplace; weight down. Cut two small pieces of chipboard, each 1″ long x ⅛″ wide; paint sides and edges white. Glue on each side of fireplace facing as indicated (see Fig. 5). Cut a strip ½″ x 8¼″; paint white; glue across, just below mantel top.

Use brick-colored paint to paint hearth area in front of fireplace 1″ wide x 6″ long. Mark, cut, and peel to form brick pattern as for fireplace.

Paint rear fireplace wall around triangle cut out solid black. Add a small amount of white paint to black paint; smudge onto brick sidewalls and bottom of fire chamber. Leave brick color showing toward front of opening.

Stuff a bit of red and yellow cellophane into triangular opening. Place andirons in fireplace opening. Dip a facial tissue into a thin mixture of very liquid gray paint; squeeze out moisture; shred tissue; let dry. Pile twigs on andirons. Place shredded gray tissue in bottom of fireplace and among twigs, to simulate ashes.

Overmantel Chimney Piece (See Fig. 6): Using measurements indicated, cut, mark, score, and bend a piece of chipboard. Paint same color as walls; let dry. Apply glue to 1″ flap at each side; fasten to wall above mantel, over fireplace.

From chipboard, cut two strips, each ⅛″ x 6⅝″; two strips ⅛″ x 5⅝″. Paint white; glue to wall over fireplace, 1″ in from edges of overmantel piece, to form a panel.

Decorative Wall Strip: From chipboard, cut two strips, each ⅛″ x 9⅛″; cut two strips, each ⅛″ x 5⅝″; paint white; let dry; glue to side walls and back wall, approximately 4¾″ up from floor.

Floors: Paint both bottom and second story floors brown; let dry.

Baseboards for Downstairs Room: From chipboard, cut two strips, each ½″ x 9⅛″ for side walls; cut two strips, each ½″ x 5⅝″ for back wall; paint white; let dry; glue in position around base.

Second Story: Apply glue along top edge of side and back wall beam strips, along top of wall to wall beam, and top edge of overmantel piece. Lay floor on top of glued surfaces; gently press down into position.

Baseboard for Upstairs Room: From chipboard, cut two strips, each ½″ x 9⅛″ for side walls; cut one strip, ½″ x 20″ for back wall; paint white; let dry; glue in position around base.

Baseboard moldings may be needed, if floor does not fit tightly against walls. Cut two strips, each ⅛″ x 9⅛″ for side walls; cut one strip ⅛″ x 20″ for back wall; paint white; let dry; glue strips in position where bottom of baseboard and floor join.

Second Story Decorative Trims: From chipboard, cut a strip ½″ x 30″ for front edge; score ⅜″ from each end; bend back lightly. Paint white; let dry; decorate as desired, or with swag and pendant design as shown. Glue to edge of floor across front; glue tabs to edge of side walls.

Top of Bedroom Walls: From chipboard, cut two strips, each ½″ x 9½″ for side walls; cut one strip ½″ x 20″ for back wall; paint white; decorate same as front edge; glue in position.

Window Frame (See Fig. 7): Using measurements indicated, cut out window frame from chipboard. Paint white; glue in position around window opening. Cut a strip ½″ wide x 4¾″ long; paint white; glue in position for window sill.

Glue a strip of decorative trim around the three sides of plywood base extending out from house walls.

FURNITURE:

Additional Materials: Eight white-headed straight pins. ½ yard slipcover fabric. 20″ piece of decorative braid trim. Fiberfill for stuffing. Thread. Lightweight sheer curtain fabric, ¼ yard. White lightweight fabric or men's handkerchiefs: two pieces, each 8″ x 8″; two pieces, each 5″ x 3″.

Headboard (See Fig. 8): Cut out from chipboard, using measurements as indicated; paint dark tan.

Bed (See Fig. 9): Mark on chipboard, cut out and score, using measurements as indicated. Fold legs and sides down along score lines. Glue inside edges of legs together where they join; tape to hold; leave tape on. Paint bed same color as headboard.

Glue headboard to right wall about ¼″ away from corner on top edge of baseboard. Place bed in front of headboard, on the diagonal across the floor; glue legs to floor.

Dresser (See Fig. 10): Mark on chipboard, cut out and score as indicated. Paint dark tan. To simulate drawer indentations, cut a line ¹⁄₁₆″ under each line at 1″ intervals; peel paper away, as for fireplace bricks. Paint indentations dark tan. For drawer pulls on each drawer, push one white-headed straight pin into chipboard on each end of drawer, ¾″ from edge of score marks.

Fold back side panels along score marks. Apply glue to panel edges and along base of dresser; glue in position on left wall approximately 2″ from corner. Place heavy object in front of dresser, while glue dries.

For dresser top, cut chipboard 2¼″ x 4½″. Paint same as dresser; glue on top of dresser.

Note: Apply a coat of flat varnish to painted furniture, floor, and white trim.

Wing Chair (See Fig. 11A): Make a pattern following dimensions in Fig. 11A. Use pattern to cut two side-wings from chipboard. Cut out back panel 4¾″ x 8″. Cut out seat 4¾″ x 7⅜″; score as indicated in Fig. 11B. Tape side-wings to back along each 8″ side; leave tape on.

To cover outside of chair, open out chair so it is flat; place on wrong side of fabric; cut out cover, allowing ½″ around perimeter of chair. Slash into ½″ allowance around curves. Apply glue around chair edges; fold slashed fabric over glued chair edge; let dry.

To cover inside of the three chair pieces, use pattern for side-wing and measurements for back. Cut fabric ½″ larger all around than each piece. Slash into ½″ allowance, turn under allowance and glue. Apply glue to inside edges of chair; pat each inside cover piece into position; let dry.

For seat, cut fabric slightly larger than seat and area below scored lines; apply glue along edges of underside of seat. Slash fabric as required; mold around seat and bottom piece. Apply glue to side and back edges of covered seat; place in position. Turn chair on side; weight down to hold seat in place; let dry. Glue a strip of decorative braid trim around base of chair.

For back cushion, cut a piece of fabric 5″ x 8½″. With right sides facing, fold in half crosswise. Sew together around three sides of pillow, leaving small opening; turn to right side; stuff; turn in open edges and slip-stitch closed. Glue pillow to chair back.

Curtains and Valance: Cut two pieces of sheer curtain fabric, each 5″ x 11″; pleat one 5″ end of each panel; glue one to each side of top window frame edge. Cut a strip of chipboard ½″ x 5¾″; paint white; glue over curtains at top of window frame to form valance.

Pillow: Cut a piece of white fabric (or handkerchief) 4½″ x 3″. With right sides facing, fold in half crosswise. Sew together around three sides, leaving a small opening; turn to right side; stuff. Turn in open edges; slip-stitch closed.

Sheets: Cut two pieces of white fabric (or handkerchief), each 8″ x 8″ for sheets. Make narrow hems around all sides.

Quilt or Coverlet: Make as desired, or as shown. Quilt shown in photograph is made of 91, 1″ squares sewn together (see Fig. 12); corners are sewn together and edges are bound with bias tape.

PEOPLE: (Figs. are on page 89)

Additional Materials: Stiff wire for armatures of bodies and arms: three pieces, each 24″ long; three pieces, each 8″ long. Rag strips 1″ wide to cover three dolls. Lamb's wool for hair.

For Little Girl: Square of fabric approximately 5″ x 5″ for head. About twenty strands of yellow yarn for hair. Piece of cord approximately 5″ long. Red and brown felt-tipped markers. Cotton or fiberfill for stuffing. Narrow red ribbon, 2″ long.

For Santa: Red flannel, ¼ yd. for jacket and trousers. Scraps of white flannel. Scraps of black fabric. 8″ x 7″ piece of tan cotton for toy sack.

For Grandma and Grandpa: Two pieces of very fine wire, each about 6″ long for eyeglasses. Blouse and Shirt: Two pieces of different colors, each approximately 8″ x 8″. Trousers: One piece of dark colored fabric, 10″ x 8″. Black yarn, about 6″ long for bow tie. Skirt: One piece of dark color fabric, 7″ x

12". Man's handkerchief or scraps of white fabric for apron, collar, and cuffs.

Little Girl: Purchased doll may be used, or just fabric head may be made. For head, stretch a 5" square of fabric over a 1"-diameter ball of stuffing. Tie piece of cord around neck about 1¼" down from top to shape head. Paint on features with felt-tipped markers. Arrange yellow yarn strands over top and sides of head; divide at each side and braid ends. Tie a red bow at one end of braid. Place doll under sheet and coverlet, with head on pillow and braid falling over onto coverlet.

Adults (See Fig. 13): Remove wooden dowels from dried apples. For each body, double a 24"-long piece of wire; push the two cut ends through the apple head from top down, leaving a small portion of the folded end showing. Twist wire once at base of apple. For arms, place an 8" piece crosswise under first twist; twist body wire again, securing arm wire; twist arm wire around body wire. Turn ends of long body wire to form feet (approximately 1¾" long). Figures should be about 9" tall.

Apply glue along arm wires. Wrap arm wires with fabric strips until padding is about ¼" thick (see Fig. 14). Leave ¼" unpadded at each end of wire. Apply glue along body and leg wires. Pad chest area well; continue padding body and legs. Put glue on inside top of head; stuff with cotton or rags to round top portion of head.

Santa: From red cotton flannel, cut two sleeves, each 3" x 4½". With right sides facing, fold each sleeve in half lengthwise; sew close to raw edges along lengthwise side; turn to right side. Slip over arms; stitch top edges to padding.

Make jacket pattern using measurements in Fig. 15. Cut jacket from red flannel using pattern; cut "T" shape slit as indicated. With right sides facing, fold in half crosswise. Starting at open bottom edges, sew sides together close to edge, leaving ½" from fold open for arms. Turn to right side. Stitch a white flannel strip, 1" x 12", around bottom of jacket. Slip jacket over Santa's head, with descending part of "T" to back; fold under raw edges; stitch closed.

Cut hands approximately 1" wide x 1¼" long from dried apple slices. Apply glue to ¼" exposed hand wire; slip apple hands onto wire. Wrap each sleeve tightly around wrist with red thread. Wrap a ¼"-wide strip of white cotton flannel around each wrist; tack or glue to jacket.

Make pattern for trousers using measurements in Fig. 16.

Cut two trousers from red flannel using pattern. With right sides facing, sew front to back, close to edge along each outside edge and along inner leg "V"; turn to right side. Slip trousers on Santa. If Santa looks too thin, stuff additional padding in midsection; stitch pants to padding. For belt, cut a ½" strip of black fabric long enough to fit around Santa's waist; stitch ends together at back.

Boots (See Fig. 17): Cut two pieces of black fabric, each 2" x 2". Wrap around each lower leg over trousers for boot tops; sew together from knee to ankle at back of leg. Use pattern to cut four ovals of black fabric. In two ovals, cut a slit and a small round area out of center, as indicated. For each foot of boot, sew one cut-out oval to one solid oval around edges. Slip over wire foot; sew upper boot to oval around ankle area.

Face: Cut two small ear shapes from dried apple slices; glue to side of head; let dry. Apply glue along chin and jawline, up to ear; put a dab of glue under nose. Twist a bit of lamb's wool into a moustache about 2" long; glue under nose. Spread lamb's wool along jaw and chin to make Santa's beard. Apply glue to padding on top of head and along forehead; place bits of lamb's wool along forehead in a "bangs" effect; place lamb's wool over top of head and down back.

Cap: Cut two triangles from red flannel, each approximately 3½" at base and 4" high. With right sides facing, sew together close to edge, along lengthwise edges; turn to right side. Glue a ¼"-wide strip of white cotton flannel around base of cap; glue cap onto head.

Bend Santa into position in window. Fold 8" x 7" piece of tan fabric in half crosswise to make toy sack 7" long; stitch sides and one end together; turn right side out. Fill bottom with cotton or rags; put over Santa's shoulder; glue small section of bag to hand. Place miniature toys in bag, gluing to hold in place if necessary.

Grandma: Make body and assemble same as for Santa. From fabric as shown or as desired, make blouse same as for Santa. From contrasting fabric, cut skirt piece 7" x 12". Turn under ½" at top and bottom along lengthwise sides; hem. With right sides facing, fold in half crosswise; stitch ends together. Turn to right side. Sew a double row of long running (gathering) stitches along top of skirt. Put skirt on Grandma, with blouse tucked in; pull threads to gather to fit waist; tack to blouse. Make apron and collar and cuffs from man's handkerchief or scraps of lace or white fabric.

Glue lamb's wool hair to head. Pull bits up to top of head to make small topknot as shown. Twist a small piece of thin wire into eyeglasses; position on nose.

Place Grandma in Wing Chair. Glue bottom of skirt to floor.

Grandpa: Make body and assemble same as for Santa, with less padding. For shirt and trousers, use same patterns as for Santa; make shirt slightly smaller. Tuck shirt into trousers. Tack a small black yarn bow under chin for bow tie.

Make and attach shoes same as Santa's boot bottoms.

Twist wire into eyeglasses; position on nose. Glue short pieces of lamb's wool neatly across head as shown; add a small moustache, about ¾" long.

Decorate a small artificial Christmas tree with beads, matchsticks (painted white for candles), and bits of tinsel, as shown or as desired. Place tree in corner, on one side of downstairs room.

Glue Grandpa in place.

Felt Vignettes

Five charming felt scenes recapture the magic of Christmas Eve in any child's house—from trimming the tree to dreaming sweet dreams. Glue the simple cutouts onto a felt background and mount on a styrofoam base. Display the scenes on mantel or wall, or arrange them on a table in joyful sequence.

EQUIPMENT: Paper for patterns. Pencil. Ruler. Regular and embroidery scissors. Sharp serrated knife or saw.

MATERIALS: Sheet styrofoam 2″ thick (see

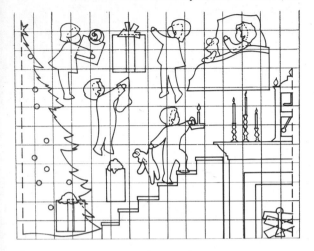

directions for sizes). Felt in colors shown or desired. All-purpose glue. Yellow rug yarn, 1½″ yds.

DIRECTIONS: Enlarge patterns by copying on paper ruled in 1″ squares; complete half-patterns indicated by long dash lines. Short dash lines indicate where pieces are over-lapped.

Mark and cut eight pieces of styrofoam as follows: 9″ x 10″ for mantel; 2¾″ x 4½″ for child with stocking; 2¼″ x 2¼″ for boxes; 10″ x 4¼″ for children with gift boxes; 8¾″ x 7½″ for children climbing stairs; 7″ x 12″ for tree; 8¾″ x 4½″ for children decorating tree; 8¾″ x 4¾″ for children sleeping.

Cut pieces of felt for each styrofoam block to cover front, top, bottom, and sides; spread glue on felt; press to styrofoam to adhere. Trim felt if necessary. Using patterns, cut separate pieces of felt; use embroidery scissors for delicate cutting. Cut necessary pieces in triplicate as illustrated. Glue in place on each block. Glue yarn in place as illustrated.

Calico Swag

"Gingerbread" men, each 7″ tall, are easy to sew, stuff, and link hand-in-hand over doorway or on wall.

EQUIPMENT: Paper for pattern. Pencil. Ruler. Scissors. Straight pins.

MATERIALS: Red and green calico cotton fabrics: Approximately 8″ x 16″ for each of twelve dolls; ½ yd. of each for end loops.

Red, green, and white sewing thread. White rickrack, ⅜ yd. each. White shank buttons, ⅜″, 3 each for eyes and noses. Polyester fiber-fill for stuffing.

DIRECTIONS: Enlarge pattern by copying

on paper ruled in 1″ squares; complete half-pattern indicated by dash lines. From double fabric, cut two dolls for each doll. Pin rickrack to right side of one doll piece as indicated by dash lines on pattern, and down center front of body. With white thread, stitch rickrack to doll piece.

With right sides facing, pin two doll pieces together. Stitch all around, ¼″ in from edges, leaving an opening at inner part of leg. Clip into seam allowance at curves. Turn to right side. Push out corners and curves smoothly. For eyes and nose, tack on buttons to front of doll as indicated by dots on pattern. Through opening, stuff doll fully. Turn in edges of opening; slip-stitch closed.

Repeat for eleven other dolls.

With matching thread, stitch dolls together at arm ends, alternating red and green fabrics.

For loops, cut two pieces of red and two pieces of green calico, 7″ wide, 28″ long each. With right sides facing, fold each strip in half lengthwise; cut off one end slightly at an angle. Stitch together along edges and diagonal end, ¼″ in from edges, leaving straight end open to turn fabric. Turn to right side.

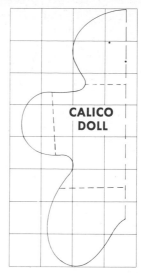

CALICO DOLL

Turn in open edges and slip-stitch a red and a green strip together at ends. Place the red and green halves together by folding about 1″ from joining making uneven ends. Bend folded end down to form loops about 6″ long; wrap end around the two halves tightly and tack together. Tack arm of each end doll to each looped piece.

Christmas Doves in Felt

Bringing their own special message of peace and good will, this beautiful pair of white felt doves is equally effective as a mantel decoration or elegant table centerpiece.

SIZE: 11″ long.

EQUIPMENT: Scissors. Pencil. Paper for patterns. Large-eyed embroidery needle. Sewing needle.

MATERIALS: White felt, 34″ x 22″. Two pieces stiff but bendable wire, 20″ and 9″. Small amount white six-strand embroidery floss. White sewing thread. Dacron-polyester or cotton batting for filling. All-purpose glue.

DIRECTIONS: Enlarge patterns by copying on paper ruled in 1″ squares. Dash lines indicate stitching lines. Add ¼″ seam allowance all around bird body pattern only.

For body, cut two pieces from white felt. Embroider eye on both pieces, using outline stitch around edge, and filling in with satin stitch. (See Stitch Details on page 186.) Sew bodies together all around with ¼″ seam, leaving about 3″ open at bottom. Clip into seam allowance at curves. Turn to other side

and stuff tightly. Turn under ¼″ seam allowance at opening; slip-stitch closed.

For tail, cut two bottom tail pieces, one middle tail, and one top tail. Shape 9″ piece of wire as indicated by finer solid line, between stitching lines on bottom tail pattern

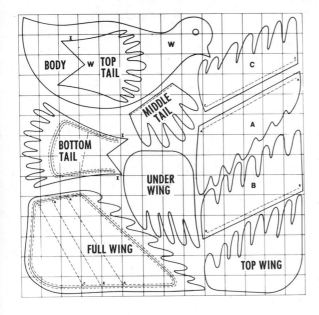

piece. Tack wire to one bottom tail. With wire between, sew the two bottom tail pieces together along stitching lines on both sides of wire. Stitch middle piece to bottom tail along stitching line. Center tail on bird's back, matching X's at either side of body to X's on tail; slip-stitch to body along V-shaped edge. Tack back tip of bird's body to center underside of tail. Center top tail piece over attached tail, covering stitched "V" edges; glue.

For wings, cut four full wing pieces. Shape two pieces of wire as indicated by finer solid line, between stitching lines on pattern. With shaped wire between, sew two wing pieces together for each wing, in same manner as for tail. For wing feathers, cut two of each piece marked, Top Wing, A, B, C, and Under Wing. Assemble to make a right and a left wing. Starting at feathered end of each full wing, match corresponding letters of each wing piece to full wing; stitch each in turn, A, B, then C, along stitching lines. With curved edges flush, glue one top wing to each wing, covering edge of last stitched wing piece. With feathered side of wing against body, tack one wing to each side of bird at points marked "W." Glue under wing to underside of each wing, front curved edges matching and bottom of under wing overlapping wing edge about ⅝″ on body. Bend wings outward.

Winter Panoramas

The sparkling painted New York skyline and quaint European village painted on corrugated paper bring around-the-world charm to the mantel or base of the tree.

EQUIPMENT: Paper for patterns. Tracing paper. Soft and hard-lead pencils. Ruler. Small flat and pointed paintbrushes. Large straight pin or fine nail. Scissors.
MATERIALS: Corrugated paper 10½″ x 48″ for each panorama (it comes in long rolls and is used for packing). Poster paints (or felt-tipped pens) in black, blue, white, and a variety of colors as illustrated or desired.
For Mantel Decoration: One string of white Christmas lights. Silver self-adhesive stars. Long nails. Artificial snow. Silver textured gift-wrap paper. Rubber cement.
DIRECTIONS: For Tree Base Cover: Enlarge patterns by copying on paper ruled in 1″

squares. Trace pattern. Go over lines of tracing on wrong side with soft pencil. Place tracing, right side up, on smooth side of corrugated paper. Go over lines of traced design on right side with hard pencil to transfer lines. Repeat design across as many times as necessary to fill corrugated strip of paper.

Mark all outlines (heavier lines on pattern) and fill in all black areas with black paint or ink. Fill in other areas with paint or ink as illustrated or as desired; let dry. For snow, paint areas indicated by finer lines on pattern and where illustrated with white paint. Fill in area below buildings (foreground) with white paint for snow. Fill in area above buildings with blue paint or ink for sky; let dry. Wrap around tree base; secure.

For Mantel Decoration: Paint as for above,

then poke holes with pin or nail along outlines and in centers of some buildings as shown. Cut off part of sky area to outline skyline.

Place scene on mantel with string of lights behind it. Secure silver stars to wall behind if desired.

Enlarge **Mantel Tree** pattern by copying on paper ruled in 1″ squares; complete half-pattern indicated by dash line. Cut eight trees out of silver textured paper; fold each in half with silver sides facing. Cement folded centers together (back side) and cement adjacent sides (backs) of tree pieces together, making an eight-sided tree. Glue two silver stars together with top of tree between. Repeat for second tree. Place a tree at each side of scene on mantel. Sprinkle artificial snow on mantel in front of scene.

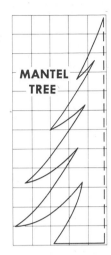

MANTEL
TREE

Stained-Glass Panel

The story of Christmas is told on this stunning, jewel-toned hinged screen, aglow with candlelight. Simple copper stencils are soldered to rich stained-glass panels, about 7¼″ high.

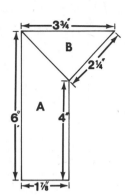

**DIAGRAM FOR
END PANELS**

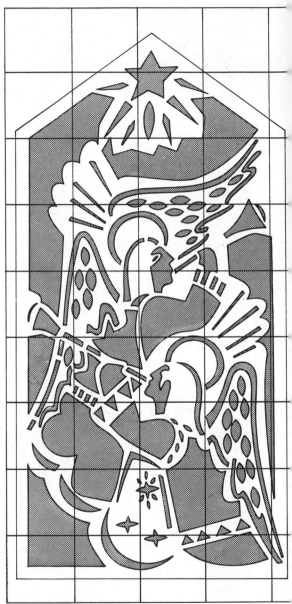

Note: Refer to Equipment, Materials, and General Directions for Stained Glass on pages 28–29.

ADDITIONAL MATERIALS: Antique glass: Blue, one sheet 8″ x 10″; red, two sheets, each 8″ x 10″; yellow, one sheet 8″ x 10″. Adhesive-backed foil sheet 15″ x 10″. Muriatic acid antique solution. Five 2′ pieces of ¼″ brass U channel. Eight small pin hinges.

DIRECTIONS: Follow General Directions for cutting, preparing, and soldering glass. Follow diagram for end panels to make patterns for pieces A and B. Use pattern A to cut four pieces from yellow glass; use pattern B to cut two pieces from blue glass. Use outline of the three design panels to cut one panel from blue glass and two panels from red glass.

Trace each stencil design on tracing paper. Cut 15″ x 10″ foil into three pieces, each 5″ x 10″; place one piece on each of the three solid-colored panels, adhesive side down. Place appropriate pattern design on foil-covered glass, as shown. Trace all pattern lines with ball-point pen or pointed pencil to imprint design lines on foil. Remove pattern. Use stencil knife to carefully cut out design; cut out all shaded areas shown on pattern. Leaving a ¼″ border beyond glass panel edges, trim foil on each side; fold this ¼″ around each side; burnish foil to glass.

To form end panel, solder two A panels together along 4″ side; solder one blue B piece to top to complete panel.

With cotton swab, apply muriatic acid solution to antique cut-out foil on three panels and soldered end panels. Rub with cloth until

solder and foil sheet become a dull, mottled silver. Let dry; wash with soapy water; rinse; dry again.

Use 2′ piece of brass U channel for each panel. As channel is molded around perimeter, insert edge of glass into channel. Use glass pliers to clip into corners; miter to fit; clip off excess brass channel.

Attach panels to each other by soldering two small pin hinges between each panel, one approximately ¾″ up from bottom and the other ¾″ down from top side edge.

BAKER'S CRAFT

Alpine Ornaments in Cookie Clay

*Made to last year after year, merry "cookie clay" ornaments
are simple to mold, bake, and paint in colorful folk-art motifs.
Coats of clear varnish give them a glossy finish.*

EQUIPMENT: Large bowl. Plastic bag. Small knife. Cookie sheet. Toothpicks. Small flat and fine-pointed paintbrushes. Brush for varnish.

MATERIALS: Cookie clay recipe (see below). Fine wire for loops. Tempera or poster paints. Clear high-gloss varnish or gloss wood finish.

Cookie Clay
4 cups flour
1 cup salt
2 teaspoons mustard powder
1¼ cups water

Using fingers, mix ingredients together in a large bowl. If clay is too stiff, add a little more water. When thoroughly mixed, lift from bowl and knead for five minutes. To prevent drying, put clay in a plastic bag and keep closed until needed.

DIRECTIONS: Pinch off a piece of clay; reclose plastic bag. Roll the clay into a ball in the palm of your hand. Following illustration, form the basic body shapes. Form separate heads, hats, arms, pompons, and shoes, using smaller amounts of clay. Some shapes may be formed with just one piece of clay (see illustrations, which are about one-third smaller than actual size). Make shapes about ⅜" to ½" thick. Use small knife and small tools such as manicure equipment. To join pieces, dip fingertips in water; moisten edges of pieces; press together. Pieces added on front surfaces, such as figures on tree and heart, are about ⅛" thick.

Place pieces on cookie sheet for final shaping. When ornament is completed, form short piece of wire into loop; insert wire ends into top piece for hanging.

Prick shape with a toothpick in three or four places to prevent uneven rising. Bake at 300° F. for 2 to 3 hours, depending upon thickness of ornament. Ours are approximately ⅜"-½" thick. Test with a toothpick; if still soft, bake a little longer. Let shapes cool completely.

Paint shapes as shown or as desired; leave tan areas in natural cookie color. When paint is completely dry, brush on the varnish or gloss finish as a protective coating. Give ornaments two or more coats, drying between each, depending on amount of glossiness desired.

Bread Dough Wreath

A festive wreath, complete with fruit ornaments, is molded from bread dough, baked in the oven and then varnished for permanent shine.

EQUIPMENT: Mixing bowl. Plastic wrap. Cookie sheet. Aluminum foil. Rolling pin. Toothpicks. Fork. Knife. Wire rack. Paintbrush for varnish or shellac.
MATERIALS: "Bread" Dough (see recipe below). Whole cloves. Varnish or shellac. Epoxy cement.

"Bread" Dough

4 cups flour
1 cup salt
1½ cups warm water
1 teaspoon instant tea (heaping)

Mix the flour and salt together. To the 1½ cups warm water, add 1 heaping teaspoon of plain instant tea. Dissolve well; let cool. Add liquid tea to flour mixture; mix very well with hands. Knead until smooth. Roll into ball; cover with plastic wrap.

DIRECTIONS: Cover cookie sheet with aluminum foil. Preheat oven to 300° F.

Pinch off a large piece of dough; roll into a long sausage shape, then shape into a circle on cookie sheet. Wet ends and press together. Circle may be any size you desire, but keep in mind how much dough you have left with which to add ornamentation. Our wreath, without decorations, has approximately an 8″ outer diameter with a 5″-diameter center opening, and is about ½″ thick.

To decorate wreath, pinch off pieces of dough and roll out with rolling pin or flatten with hands to about ¼″ thickness. Cut out leaf shapes with knife. Score each leaf with knife to mark the vein lines. Moisten back of each leaf with a little water; press on wreath. Make the largest fruit next (apples, pears, peaches). Press whole cloves into dough for stems and core ends of fruit: for stems of apples and pears, push clove bud into dough, leaving the stem end out; for the core ends of fruit, press in the stem end of the clove, exposing just the bud from which the ball of clove has been removed. Wet the wreath circle and attach the fruit pieces. Fill in spaces with clusters of grape, strawberry, nut, and a few plum shapes. Imprint texture and lines with toothpick or fork.

To make bow, roll out dough to ¼″ thickness; cut a long strip (20″-24″) about 1¼″ wide. Fold and pinch strip into bow; cut away ends as illustrated. Place bow separately on foil-covered cookie sheet.

Bake wreath and bow in preheated 300° F. oven for 3 hours or until completely dry and hard (if bow is done before wreath, tear foil and remove bow from oven). Place on wire rack and let cool. Peel off foil. Leave on rack for several days in dry place.

Coat wreath and bow separately with varnish or shellac. When dry, cement bow to wreath, using epoxy cement as directed on package.

Angel Ornaments

Make three heavenly "baker's clay" angels to hover 'round the tree. Their bodies are formed, then "dressed" with gowns cut from extra-thin dough. Each is 3½" tall. (Shown on next page.)

EQUIPMENT: Measuring cup. Mixing bowl. Mixing spoon. Breadboard. Rolling pin. Aluminum foil. Plastic wrap. Tracing paper. Pencil. Ruler. Compass. Grater with small holes. Small kitchen knife. Cookie sheet. Small, fine-pointed paintbrush for painting. Small, flat paintbrush for varnish. Sewing needle.

MATERIALS: Flour and salt (see directions for amounts). Fine wire for hangers. All-purpose glue. Acrylic paints (see illustration for colors or use desired colors). Gloss polyurethane varnish. Narrow velvet ribbons. Sewing thread to match velvet.

DIRECTIONS: To make dough, mix together 4 cups of flour and 1 cup of salt; add 1⅞ cups of water. (**Note:** For smaller portions, use ½ cup flour, ⅛ cup salt, ¼ cup water.) Mix ingredients thoroughly; finish with your hands if necessary. Knead dough on a generously floured board until it is very smooth and has a good consistency with which to work. You will be able to determine the right consistency as you work with this dough; it is easier to knead more flour into dough that is too moist than it is to knead water into dough that is too dry. Be sure to keep unused portion of the dough covered with plastic wrap. If dough becomes too sticky before you are through with it, knead more flour into it.

Trace pattern for each part of angel separately; complete half-pattern indicated by dash line. Form parts of angel on a piece of foil. Each angel is approximately 3½" tall and is an assembly of several dimensional shapes of dough.

To make ball or oval shape, roll balls of dough in palms of hands and flatten slightly according to specifications. For head, make ball shape ¾" thick; for body, make oval ¾" thick.

For legs and arms, roll coils between palms of hands, each ⅜" thick. For collar, make very narrow coil long enough to fit around neck area.

For dress and wings, roll out dough with rolling pin to thickness required and place tracings on dough; cut out dough around tracing. Cut two wings ½" thick and one dress ⅛" thick.

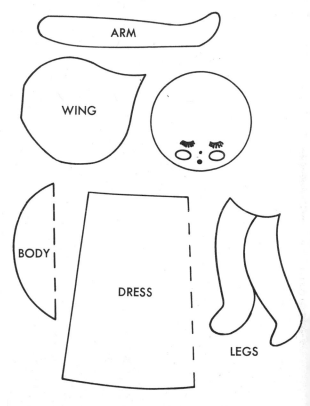

Assemble the parts of angel following the color illustration; moisten dough wherever pieces are joined. First place head and wings together, then place top half of body over wings, letting lower half drape down. Secure legs in place. Curve them as illustrated; pinch ends to form feet. Drape dress over body, gathering dress along top as shown. Place collar coil around neck; ruffle collar if desired.

For hair, force dough through small holes in grater and arrange around sides and top of head; secure by moistening dough. Make indentations in wings with pencil point.

For hanger, cut a 1½" piece of wire; bend it into a U-shape; dip ends into glue; insert ends into top of head.

Place foil with figure onto cookie sheet;

bake in oven at 275° to 300° F. about 3 hours. If you do not bake immediately, cover with plastic wrap while you assemble another. Never leave figure unbaked for more than 1½ to 2 hours.

Let figures cool; paint hair, dresses, and arms for "sleeves"; decorate as illustrated or as desired. For faces, use brown for lashes, pink for cheeks, red for mouths and noses.

When paint is dry, varnish completely with two or three coats; let dry between coats.

For hanging ribbon, cut 10″ and 6″ lengths of ribbon. Fold shorter length into thirds to form bow. Insert longer length through wire in head; bring ends together and overlap. Insert bow between ribbon at top; with matching sewing thread, tack through center of bow to secure.

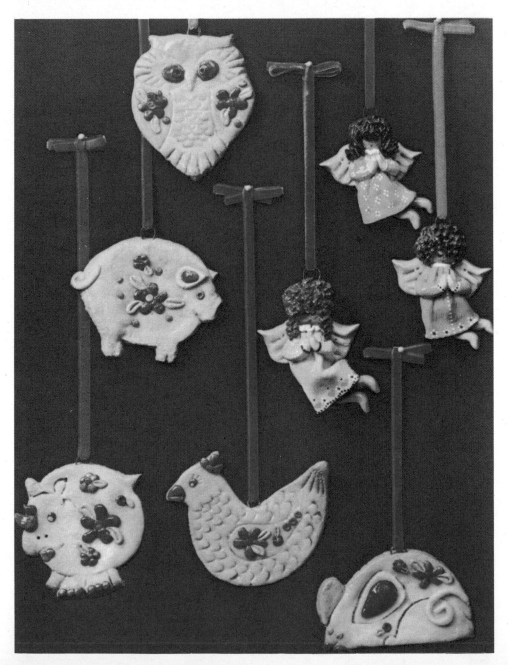

Bread Dough Animals

Five flowery baker's clay animals are molded, trimmed and painted, ready to hang from the tree.

EQUIPMENT: Paper for patterns. Tracing paper. Pencil. Ruler. Mixing bowl and spoon. Measuring cup. Breadboard. Rolling pin. Aluminum foil. Plastic wrap. Small kitchen knife. Spatula. Toothpicks. Cookie sheet. Potato peeler or any tool with U-shaped scoop end. Small, fine-pointed and small flat paintbrush. Sewing needle.

MATERIALS: Flour and salt (see directions for amounts). All-purpose glue. Wire for hangers. Acrylic paints: Pink, orange, and green. Gloss polyurethane varnish. Narrow velvet ribbon. Sewing thread.

DIRECTIONS: Enlarge patterns by copying on 1″ squares; complete owl half-pattern indicated by dash lines. Trace patterns. The heavier lines indicate outlines and separate dough pieces placed on shape. The finer lines indicate markings which are to be made with toothpick.

For making dough, follow the first paragraph of directions for Angel Ornaments on page 105.

Roll out dough to ⅜″ thickness on floured breadboard. Place pattern tracings lightly on dough; mark around tracing with toothpick. Remove tracing. Using knife, cut out outline of each shape. With spatula, place shapes on foil-covered cookie sheet. With toothpick, make all the fine lines within the outline (go deep into the dough but be careful not to go all the way through), such as lines for some ears and mouths, owl's body lines and chick's wing and tail. To mark feathers on chick, use U-shaped potato peeler end. Make thin dough shapes for owl's and chick's beaks, mouse's inner ear, pig's ear, rhino's horn, rhino's toes, and for all flowers and leaves and flower centers. Use toothpick to make holes in eye centers. Make narrow coils by rolling between palms for mouse's tail and pig's tail. Stick all pieces in place, being sure to moisten dough on touching surfaces so they will adhere securely. Cut pieces of wire 1¼″ long; bend and put glue on ends; insert one into top of each ornament for hanger (see illustration for placement).

Bake pieces within one hour after making them. If you do not bake shapes immediately, cover with plastic wrap while assembling others.

Bake shapes at 300° F. for 4 hours. Cool. Paint flowers, leaves, eyes, and other features as illustrated; let dry. Seal pieces on both sides and edges with two coats of varnish; let dry between coats.

Make ribbon hangers (see last paragraph of directions for Angel Ornaments, page 106).

Ginger Santa

Here is a roguish, edible Santa to center your party table. His curly beard and fur trim are frosting and flaked coconut.

SIZE: 17½" tall.

EQUIPMENT: Paper for patterns. Pencil. Tracing paper. Ruler. Scissors. Thin cardboard. Aluminum foil paper. Saucepan. Large bowl. Measuring cup and spoons. Mixing spoon. Pastry board. Rolling pin. Sharp knife. Large lightly greased cookie sheets or aluminum oven liners (at least 15" x 19" for Santa). Wire rack. Pastry tube with fine and medium tips (or paper rolled into cone shape with tip cut off).

MATERIALS: Gingerbread dough and icing (see recipes below). For trims: flaked coconut, peppermint striped candies (one ball and three wheel shapes), tiny red heart candy, pink jelly bean, tiny piece of licorice.

DIRECTIONS: Enlarge pattern for Santa on page 109 by copying on paper ruled in 1" squares; complete half-pattern as indicated by dash line. Santa pattern is given half-size; if desired you can make cookie half-size by simply tracing pattern. Cut pattern out of cardboard and cover the back with foil paper. Make cookie dough, bake, and ice as indicated below.

Cookie Dough

¾ cup water
2 cups sugar
⅓ cup dark corn syrup
1½ teaspoons ginger
1½ teaspoons cinnamon
1 teaspoon cloves
1½ cups melted butter

1½ teaspoons baking soda
6 cups flour

Icing (basic recipe)
1 cup confectioners' sugar
1 egg white
½ lemon

Combine water, sugar, syrup, and spices in saucepan and bring to boiling point. Remove from heat; add melted, but not hot, butter and mix it in. Chill by placing saucepan in pan of cold water. Then add baking soda mixed with small amount of water. Gradually stir in flour until dough is very soft. Refrigerate overnight. Next day, turn dough onto pastry board. Add flour slowly as needed to get a consistency that will roll out smoothly. Make dough firm, but not hard. (If dough is not firm enough to hold shape, add about one cup or more of flour until firm.)

Roll dough out to about ⅜″ thickness. Place dough on greased cookie sheet or oven liner before cutting. Place pattern over dough; roll over pattern lightly so it will stay on while cutting. Cut around pattern with sharp knife to make shape; remove excess dough. Bake in moderately hot oven (400° F.) for 8-10 mins. Cool. Remove to rack.

To make icing, beat sugar, egg white, and juice of ½ lemon together until smooth. Mix additional icing in same proportion as needed.

Fill pastry tube with medium tip with white icing. With icing, fill in areas indicated by dotted lines on pattern. Cover these areas with coconut to simulate fur and hair. With fine tip, make lines for eyebrows. Using icing as glue, secure three wheel peppermint candies down front for buttons and secure

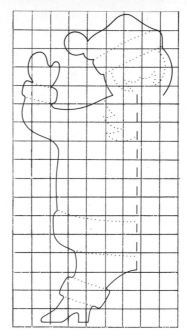

one ball candy at hat tip for pompon. Secure tiny curved slices of licorice for eyes with icing. Invert red candy heart; secure for nose. Cut tiny slice of jelly bean; secure for mouth.

Angel Cookies

A heavenly host of cookie angels, decorative and delicious, are assembled from simple cookie shapes. White frosting "enamels" the surface, food coloring provides a palette for painting. Hang them on the tree—or serve them to your guests.

EQUIPMENT: Cookie cutters: 1″, 2″ and 2½″ round; 3½″ star-shaped; and 2½″ and 3″ scalloped. Paring knife. Cookie sheets. Drinking straws. Pastry brush. Small water-color brush. Plate. Electric beater.
MATERIALS: Liquid food coloring, in assorted colors. Metallic cord (optional).

Cookie Dough
2 cups sugar
1 teaspoon baking soda
½ teaspoon salt
4 cups flour (sifted)
1 cup butter (or other shortening)
2 eggs
4 tablespoons cream
grated rind of 1 orange (grate very fine)
1 teaspoon almond flavoring
1 teaspoon vanilla

Mix dry ingredients as you would mix pie crust with the shortening. Beat eggs and cream together; add to dry ingredients. Add grated orange rind and mix well. Add almond flavoring and vanilla. Mix lightly and roll dough thin on lightly floured board. Cut as directed on page 110. Place and assemble, ½″ apart, on lightly greased cookie sheet, dampening areas to be covered by other pieces with fingers dipped in warm water. If metallic cord hangers and bows are desired, punch holes in cookies with drinking straw. Bake 11 or 12 minutes at 300° F, or until cookie layers are baked through without browning too much.

Frosting
2 egg whites
2 cups confectioners' sugar
1 teaspoon almond flavoring
1½ tablespoons water

Mix well with electric beater, adding water slowly as you beat. Consistency should be same as thick enamel or paint.

TO CUT AND ASSEMBLE COOKIES (see illustration above; angel heads from left to right across top row; angel figures from left to right across bottom row):

First Angel Head: Center 2"-round cookie for face over star-shaped cookie.

Second Angel Head: Cut 2½" scalloped cookie for wings; cut out a wedge from bottom. Place 2" round cookie for halo over top of wings. Place 1" cookie for face over halo.

Third Angel Head: Cut as for second angel head, but do not cut away wedge from wings. Add a bit of dough for hands.

Angel Figures: Roll a large thin sheet of cookie dough on floured board. With paring knife, cut dough into strips, about 4½" wide, across entire sheet. Divide each strip into triangles for angel bodies, as shown in Diagram. Cut halos with 2" round or scalloped cookie cutter. Cut faces with 1" round cutter or bottle cap. Cut wings (wing pieces also form arms) with 2½" round or scalloped cutter. Use bits of dough for hands.

First Angel Figure: Place halo on top of triangle, covering about 1" of point. Place face over halo, bottom curve of circles meeting. Cut deep wedge from wings; place wings over triangle, wedge opening up and touching sides of halo (section that covers triangle is for arms). Place bit of dough over bottom of this piece for hands.

Second and Third Angels: Place halo on top of triangle. Place face over halo, face extend-ing beyond halo at right or left. Cut wings in half; place cut edge of one half under one side of triangle; place second half over triangle, for arms. Add a bit of dough for hands.

Fourth Angel: Place halo and face as for first angel. Center wings over triangle. Add a bit of dough to center of wings for hands.

TO DECORATE COOKIES: Place drops of assorted food colorings 2" apart on a plate; allow to dry while frosting is being mixed. With pastry brush, paint surface of each baked cookie with frosting (recipe above). Allow frosting to harden before applying color. With water-color brush, paint frosted surface as illustrated by rubbing wet brush over desired dry color. Keep a container of hot water near for rinsing color from brush as you decorate. By keeping the brush wet with water, you will be able to use very small amounts of color, thereby obtaining pastel shades. (Test colors on sample cookie.) Dark shades for eyes and hair are made by mixing colors together: green and blue plus a touch of red will make brown; a mixture of a bit of each color will make black. Add cord hangers and bows after colors are dry.

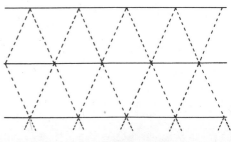

DIAGRAM FOR CUTTING ANGEL COOKIE BODIES.

Gingerbread Crèche

*A cookie-shingled stable, complete with a coconut "straw"
floor, is fashioned from gingerbread and embellished with
other edibles to make this delightful crèche. The figures, stable
sections and crèche base are cut from ¼"-thick sheets of
gingerbread dough and then baked. Details are drawn with
white and colored icing. Pieces are assembled with melted
sugar glue.*

EQUIPMENT: Tracing paper. Pencil. Ruler. Lightweight cardboard. Scissors. Aluminum foil. Sifter. Large saucepan. Mixing spoon. Three cookie sheets (or use one three times). Rolling pin. Sharp knife. Pastry brush. Tea strainer. Paper toweling. Bowls for icing. Electric beater. Pastry tube with tips for fine writing and making small circles. Toothpicks.

MATERIALS: Gingerbread Dough and Decorating Icing (see recipes, page 113). Tea. Package of flaked coconut. Instant coffee. Vegetable food dyes. Silver dragées.

DIRECTIONS: Trace patterns on page 112, omitting decorations; complete half-patterns

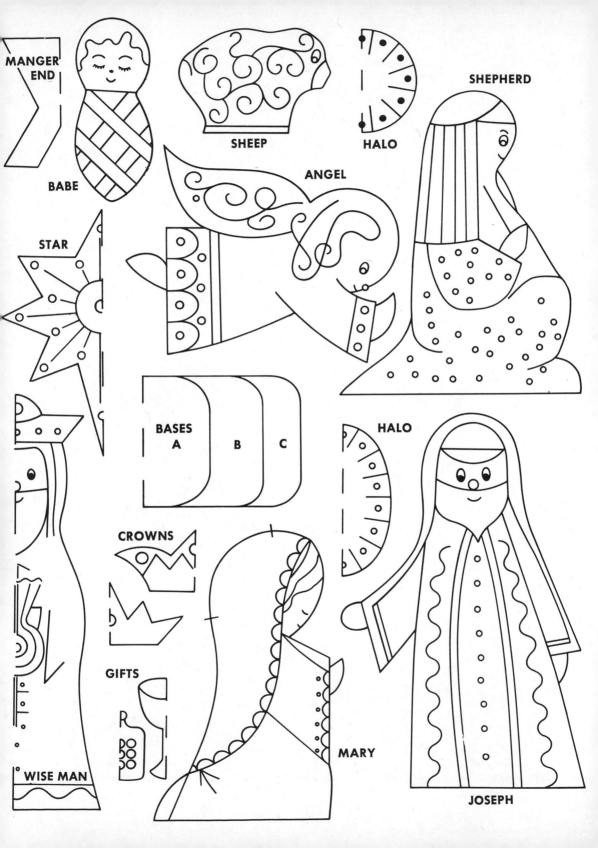

MANGER END

BABE

SHEEP

HALO

SHEPHERD

ANGEL

STAR

BASES
A   B   C

HALO

CROWNS

GIFTS

MARY

WISE MAN

JOSEPH

indicated by dash lines. Cut patterns out of cardboard. Cut three wise men, each with a different crown. Make patterns for stable of cardboard as follows: For sides, cut piece 4½″ x 13″; for back, cut a triangle with 5½″ base, 13″ tall; for large shingle, cut piece 1½″ square; for small shingle, cut piece ¾″ x 1⅝″; for top, cut piece ½″ x 4¾″; for loft, cut piece 2½″ x 4¼″. For manger side, cut piece 1¾″ x 1″. Cover patterns with foil.

Make Gingerbread Dough as follows:

Gingerbread Dough

5 cups sifted all-purpose flour	1 teaspoon nutmeg
1 teaspoon baking soda	3 teaspoons ginger
	1 cup shortening
1 teaspoon salt	⅔ cup sugar
	1 cup molasses

Sift together flour, baking soda, salt, nutmeg, and ginger. Melt shortening in large saucepan over moderate heat (about 250° F.). Add sugar and molasses; stir well. Remove from heat. Gradually stir in 4 cups of flour mixture until thoroughly combined. Work in remaining flour mixture with hands. Chill overnight.

The next day, preheat oven to 375° F. Place ⅓ of dough on ungreased cookie sheet. Roll dough into ¼″ thick rectangle on cookie sheet. Place pattern pieces on rectangle of dough and, using sharp knife, cut around patterns carefully. Cut one of each piece except for the following: cut two sheep; cut two manger ends and two manger sides. Cut two of base A; cut five of base B; cut one of base C. Cut two large side pieces; cut 50 large shingles; cut 20 small shingles. Remove excess dough. You will need three cookie sheets with rectangles of dough rolled out on each to make all these pieces. Place cookie sheets with cutouts in oven and bake 13-15 minutes or until lightly browned. Do not remove pieces from cookie sheets until completely cooled.

Make a sugar glue to hold pieces together as follows. Put sugar in saucepan and melt over low heat. Using pastry brush, brush one edge of back triangle with sugar and very quickly place one side on and hold for a couple of seconds (it hardens very quickly). Dip inner surface of each shingle in melted sugar and, working from bottom up, quickly press onto side of stable to form roof. Alternate large and small shingles as desired and make them overlap each preceding row. Repeat with other side and remaining shingles. Put melted sugar on the two side edges of loft piece and quickly slide it in place. Brush bottom surface of rooftop piece with melted sugar and place on top. With melted sugar,

secure manger sides to end pieces, star to stable top.

To make floor for entire crèche, cut piece of heavy cardboard 10½″ x 16½″. To simulate straw, make a strong blend of tea; place package of coconut in tea and let steep about 15 minutes; strain; dry on paper toweling. Thin sugar glue with a little water and spread on floor cardboard. Sprinkle floor with coconut-tea mixture; add instant coffee for dirt. Glue coconut-tea mixture on loft and manger bottom.

Make Decorating Icing as follows:

Decorating Icing

2½ cups confectioners' sugar	2 egg whites
¼ teaspoon cream of tartar	½ teaspoon vanilla

Sift together sugar and cream of tartar in large bowl. Add egg whites and vanilla. Beat until very stiff. Cover with damp cloth until ready to use.

When ready to decorate, place amounts of icing in individual bowls (one for each color); leave icing in one bowl white and add food dyes, small amounts at a time, to other bowls of icing until desired shades are blended. With knife, carefully spread icing to cover areas such as faces, hands, beards, crowns, star, and Babe's clothing. With icing in tube with fine writing tip, make lines of design as shown in illustration and as indicated on patterns. Make dots of icing by dabbing icing (with circle tip) where indicated by circles on patterns. For the smallest details, such as the mouths and Babe's facial features, dip toothpick directly into food dye and paint. Work carefully. Decorate each wise man as illustrated. Secure silver dragées to star center and to wise men's crowns and to one gift as shown with white icing. Add green icing to floor to simulate grass.

When figures have been iced and are dry, dip bottom of each figure into melted sugar and press immediately onto base. The largest base is for the kneeling shepherd; the two small bases are for the sheep; the remaining bases are for the remaining figures (except for angel and Babe). Spread melted sugar on top of each base and sprinkle the coconut-tea mixture on it. With melted sugar, secure halos to Mary and to Babe. Place Babe in manger. Spread melted sugar on back surface of angel and press onto front top of stable; hold until secure.

To make staffs for Joseph and the shepherd, dye piece of thin spaghetti for each in tea; secure in place with melted sugar.

Gingerbread Village

Recreate one or all four sections of this fantasy village for the most unusual, lasting centerpiece ever! Simple shapes are cut from gingerbread dough, then baked before assembling. Creamy white icing blankets the ground and covers the roof of each tiny building; gingerbread townsfolk and trees and sugary candies add the magical details. The entire village measures 3'x5'.

SIZE: 3' x 5', approximately 13" high.

Note: The village is made up of four separate sets: 1. Bakery and Sweet Shop; 2. Toy, Barber, Ski, and Antique Shops; 3. House; 4. Inn, pond, gingerbread people, and trees.

EQUIPMENT: Pencil. Ruler. Scissors or single-edged razor blade. Lightweight cardboard for patterns. Cellophane or masking tape. Saucepan. Double boiler. Wooden mixing spoon. Large pastry board. Large baking sheets. Small cookie sheet. Sharp pizza cutter. Electric mixer. Damp cloth. Rosette decorating tubes: #18, #14 and #11; #4 for lines and writing. Small bowls. Spatula.

MATERIALS: Four pieces of cardboard (see individual directions for size of each). Plywood surface 3' x 5', ½" thick for village base. (If you make just a portion of the village, use smaller surface.) Gingerbread and frosting (see recipes). Ten sour balls for skating pond. Small pieces of candy-coated chocolate or licorice for pebbles and chimneys, seven 8-oz. packages. One jar of candy red hots. Vegetable food coloring: Red, green, blue, yellow. Multicolored sprinkles. Three pieces of candy cane, each 2½" long. One cup granulated sugar.

Note: Enlarge patterns to actual size on cardboard, following graph; each square represents 1". Complete all half-patterns indicated by dash lines; trace same size patterns. Label all pattern pieces and cut out. Tape all pattern pieces together to make a model of the village. Read through all directions carefully before taking apart cardboard models. Set patterns aside until gingerbread is baked.

Gingerbread Dough (one batch)

4½ cups flour	1 cup margarine
1 teaspoon ginger	1 teaspoon baking
1½ teaspoons	soda
allspice	½ teaspoon salt
1 cup molasses	1 egg
1 cup brown sugar	

Mix flour and spices together, set aside.

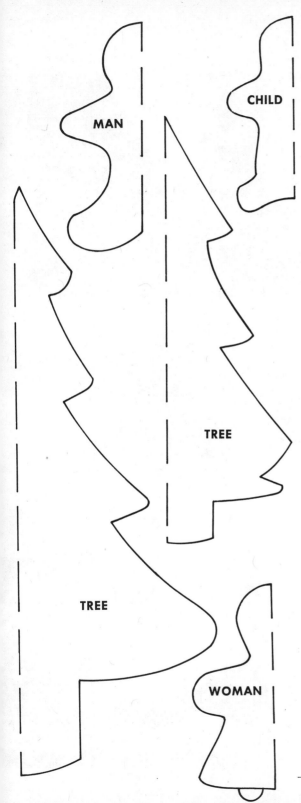

Combine molasses, sugar, margarine, and baking soda in saucepan. Bring to a boil, stirring constantly for five minutes. Cool until just warm.

Add salt and egg to molasses mixture. With wooden spoon, gradually stir in flour mixture until thoroughly combined. Leave in bowl and refrigerate about two hours.

Roll out mixture on floured board to about ¼" thickness, unless otherwise specified. Place on lightly greased baking sheet. Before baking see General Directions. Bake at 375° F. for 8-10 minutes.

You will need nine batches for entire village: Each set-up needs two batches; gingerbread people, trees, trims, need one batch.

Frosting (one batch)

1 lb. confectioners' sugar	¾ teaspoon cream of tartar
3 tablespoons meringue powder	½ cup less 2 tablespoons water

If meringue powder is not available, substitute three egg whites; omit water.

Combine all ingredients in bowl of electric mixer; beat at high speed for five minutes. Keep covered with a damp cloth until ready to use.

You will need twelve batches for entire village: Each set-up needs 2½ batches; "snow" on ground needs 2 batches. Frosting is used for snow, decorations, to hold building pieces together, and to attach all external pieces. For thinned-down frosting, add a few drops of water.

Skating Pond: Crush about ten sour balls; melt in double boiler. Pour freely on cookie sheet; candy will harden to form pond; set aside.

GENERAL DIRECTIONS: For building sections, roll out large piece of dough. Place dough on large greased baking sheets with pattern pieces for building sides and roofs on top; cut out line of sections and doors (all doorways are 1¼" x 3"). Remove and save excess dough. Bake sections and doors. When done, place patterns on sections again, cut out all windows carefully; for shutters, cut windows in half lengthwise. Remove from baking sheet to flat surface; air-dry overnight.

Beams and Roof Trims: Roll out and bake two pieces of dough, each 12" x 8". For beams, cut strips ½" wide. Using pizza cutter, cut into lengths required for each building as shown in illustrations. For roof trims, cut 1"-wide strips. Using pizza cutter, cut design in strips as shown for each building, or as desired. See individual directions for trim lengths; cut ends of each piece on the diagonal so that they fit together at peak and sides of buildings.

Chimneys: Roll out and bake dough. For each building (except Barber Shop): See Figs. 1 (right). Cut one piece "A," 1½" x 3½"; one piece "B," 1½" x 1¾". (Step 1) Cut two pieces "C," 1¼" x 3½"; cut off shaded area. (Step 2) Assemble chimney pieces. Use frosting to hold pieces together. Let dry. Apply frosting to chimneys; while still moist, cover with candy pebbles. Set aside to dry until ready to attach roofs.

Signs: Cut from baked gingerbread in sizes given in individual directions. Use decorating tube #4 for printing as pictured.

People: Cut from baked gingerbread. Using patterns on page 116, cut out about eight children, six men, six women. Use #4 decorating tube to decorate as pictured, or as desired.

Christmas Trees: Cut from baked gingerbread. Using patterns, cut out about seven large and four small trees. Cover front of each with thinned-down green frosting; while still moist, distribute sprinkles over surface.

To Assemble Buildings: See individual directions for assembling. Coat inside of all large sections of buildings with thinned-down frosting. Buildings that have a stucco effect should be covered with tinted frosting before building is put together. Use small spatula to apply frosting freely to give rough stucco effect. While frosting is still wet, place beams in position, as pictured. Let dry until frosting becomes firm.

Put together buildings of each set-up on individual pieces of cardboard about 3″ larger than building area. For each building, with #14 or #18 decorating tube, put frosting along bottom edge of front section; place on cardboard. Frost side and bottom edges of each side section; attach to front. Frost bottom of back section; attach to sides. Frost bottom and sides of support section; attach between front and back of building matching points marked "a" and "b" on diagram. Put frosting on top and bottom of doors; place in openings from inside of building. Apply frosting along inside and outside of bottom of building. This will secure it to the cardboard.

Lattice-Work Windows: Use #4 decorating tube to make evenly spaced vertical "strings" of icing across window opening from top of window to bottom; when dry, make evenly spaced horizontal "strings" from side to side.

Paint shutters with thinned-down frosting; color and decorate as pictured, or as desired.

Apply frosting to back of beams and back

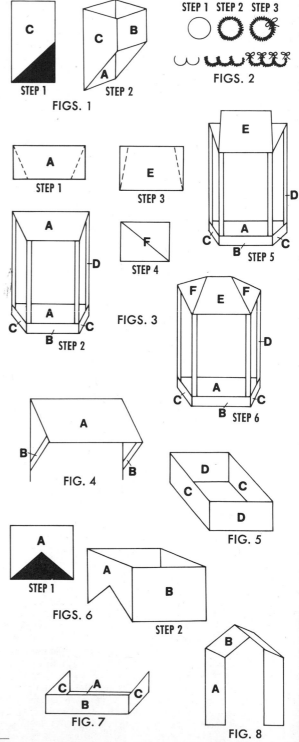

STEP 1   STEP 2   STEP 3

FIGS. 2

C
STEP 1

C   B
A
STEP 2

FIGS. 1

A
STEP 1

E
STEP 3

A
A
C   C
B   STEP 2

FIGS. 3

F
STEP 4

E
A
C   C
B   STEP 5

D

F   F
E
A
C   C
B   STEP 6

D

A
B   B
FIG. 4

D
C   C
D
FIG. 5

A
STEP 1

A
B
STEP 2

FIGS. 6

C   A   C
B
FIG. 7

B
A
FIG. 8

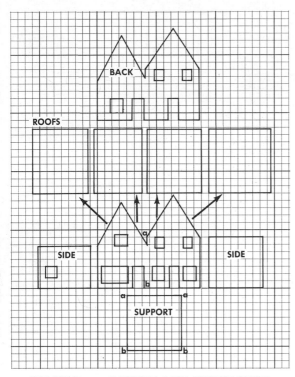

BACK

ROOFS

SIDE   SIDE

SUPPORT

SET-UP 1   BAKERY AND SWEET SHOP

of shutters; attach to buildings as pictured. Complete each building, including decorations, before putting on roof.

With #14 or #18 decorating tube, apply frosting to top edges of building sections; place each side of the roof in position. Put additional frosting where top of roof joins building. Hold for a few seconds to secure. Put a coat of frosting on roof. Place roof trims in position on front edges of roof. Place chimneys in position. Apply additional frosting to roof. Sprinkle with granulated sugar.

Christmas Wreaths: See Figs. 2, page 117. (Step 1) Working directly on doors and large windows, with dark green frosting, use #11 decorating tube to make a circle; let dry. (Step 2) Go over circle with zigzag motion. (Step 3) Use #4 decorating tube and red tinted frosting to make bows. Follow same procedure for garlands. Decorate buildings with garlands as shown.

To Create Village: Arrange the four building set-ups as pictured; staple each cardboard base to plywood. Make roads by coating with frosting and covering with candy pebbles.

Frost entire board right up to the buildings, making snow drifts here and there. Put pond in place on top of frosting; add frosting around perimeter of pond; add frosting on chimney tops, shutters, signs, beams; while still moist, sprinkle granulated sugar on pieces for snow. Place trees and people in place, as pictured.

Set-Up 1—Bakery and Sweet Shop. (See patterns at left.)

Cardboard base is 14″ x 20″.

Bakery: Stucco front, back and side sections with yellow tinted frosting.

Roof Trim: Cut two pieces, each 7¾″ long; two pieces, each 6½″ long; one piece 8¾″ long. Attach to front edges of roofs and side of Bakery roof.

Door: Cut in half crosswise; leave top open slightly to give effect of Dutch door.

Sign: Cut piece 2″ x 1″. Attach one short end, 4″ up from base, to beam that separates Sweet Shop from Bakery; sign will extend out from building. For support, cut one beam 1½″ x ¼″. Cut ends diagonally; attach one end flush against same beam as sign, directly below roof trim; attach other end to middle of top edge of sign.

Bay Window: See Figs. 3, page 117. (Step 1) Cut two pieces "A," each 3¼″ x 1″. Cut ½″ triangle from each end of "A." (Step 2) Cut two pieces "B," each 2¼″ x ¾″; two pieces "C," each 1″ x ¾″; four pieces "D," each 2¼″ x ½″. To make bottom of window, attach one "B" to front of one "A," one "C" to either side of "A." Center second "B" to back of "A"; attach. Let dry. Attach to building, under window opening. Attach other "A" piece to building above window opening. Place four "D" pieces in place between.

Roof of Window: (Step 3) Cut one piece "E," 2¼″ x 1¼″; cut ¼″ triangle from each end. (Step 4) Cut one piece "F," 1″ x 1¼″; cut "F" in half diagonally. (Step 5) Attach "E" to window and building. (Step 6) Attach one "F" piece to either side of "E" and building. Cover window roof with two rows of shingles. (See Toy Shop for directions for making shingles.) "String" icing across to make window panes.

Sweet Shop: Stucco all building sections with pink tinted frosting. Attach one piece of candy cane to building on either side of doorway, ½″ up from base of building.

Roof Trim: Cut two pieces, each 7¼″ long; two pieces, each 8½″ long; one piece 8¾″ long. Outline trim with pink tinted frosting. Attach to front and side of roof.

Awning: See Fig. 4, page 117. Cut one piece "A," 6″ x 2″; cut two support pieces "B," each

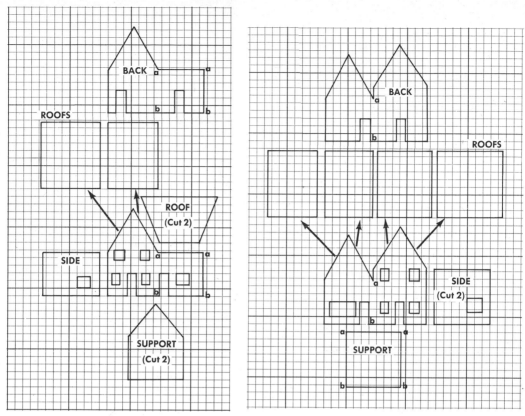

TOY AND BARBER SHOP   SET-UP 2   **SKI AND ANTIQUE SHOP**

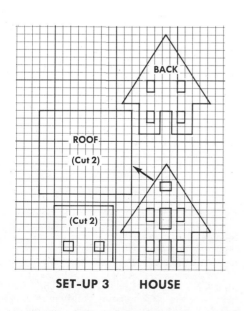

SET-UP 3   **HOUSE**

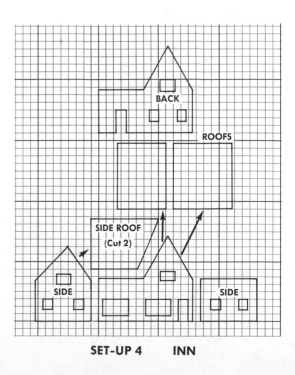

SET-UP 4   **INN**

3″ x ½″. Attach awning "A" over windows and doorway at an angle; place one "B" support at each side of awning.

Two Window Boxes: See Fig. 5. Cut four pieces "C," each 2″ x 1″; cut four pieces "D," each 1″ x ½″. Join two "C's" to two "D's" to form each box; attach one under each window. With frosting, make red and white stripes on awning. Cover side awning supports and window boxes with red frosting.

Sign: Cut piece 3½″ x 1″. Center above awning; attach to building.

Set-Up 2—Toy, Barber, Ski, and Antique Shops. (See page 119.)

Cardboard base is 32″ x 14″.

Toy Shop: Shingles: Roll out dough to ⅛″ thickness; cut into ½″ strips. From strips, cut ½″ and ¾″ pieces. Coat front and side of store with frosting; place alternating sized shingles in rows across entire front and side of building, leaving 1½″-wide space free for side chimney, approximately 1½″ in from back edge of building.

Trim: Make green garlands with red bows (Figs. 2, page 117) along front edge of each side of roof.

Shutters: Cover with yellow frosting.

Door: Cover with red frosting.

Sign: Cut piece 1″ x 1¾″. For sign hanger, cut one beam piece 1¾″ x ¼″. At point where Toy Shop meets Barber Shop, 5″ up from bottom, attach one end of hanger, extending it horizontally from building. Attach top of longer end of sign to bottom of hanger.

Barber Shop: Stucco front with pink tinted frosting.

Roof Trim: Attach two rows of shingles to edge of roof front. (See Toy Shop shingle directions.)

Barber Pole: Attach 2½″ long piece of candy cane to building approximately 1″ up from base of building, between entrance and window.

Sign: Cut piece 2¼″ x ¾″. Attach to center of building, directly below shingled edge of roof.

Chimney: See Figs. 6, page 117. Cut two pieces "A," each 1″ x 1¼″; two pieces "B," each 1″ x 2½″. (Step 1) Cut shaded area from each "A" piece. (Step 2) Attach "A" piece to each "B" piece to form oblong chimney. Coat with frosting; cover with candy pebbles; let dry.

Barber Shop roof is put in place after other buildings in this group are completed and their roofs are in place. Put chimney of Barber Shop in place, as pictured.

Ski Shop: Coat entire front of building with frosting; cover with candy pebbles.

Roof Trims: Cut two pieces, each 6½″ long.

Sign: Cut piece 1¼″ x 2¼″. Attach one shorter end to building, 3¾″ up from bottom where Ski Shop meets Antique Shop. For support, cut one beam 2¼″ x ¼″ with two diagonally cut ends. Attach one end to building, extending out directly under roof trim. Attach other end of support to top of sign.

Antique Shop: Coat bottom half of shop front and side with frosting; cover with candy pebbles.

Roof Trim: Cut one piece 7¼″; one piece 8½″; one piece 8¾″. Cover with yellow tinted frosting; outline with green. Attach to front and side of roof.

Sign: Cut piece 3½″ x 1″. Attach to center of beam connecting top and bottom of building.

Shutters: Cover with yellow tinted frosting, outline with green.

Set-Up 3—House. (See page 119.)

Cardboard base is 13″ x 14″.

Roof Trim: Cut four pieces, each 12″ long; outline with white frosting.

Shutters: Decorate with candy red hots.

Doors: Cover with red frosting.

Balcony: See Fig. 7, page 117. Cut one base piece "A," 5¾″ x 1″. For Railing, cut one piece "B," 5½″ x ¾″; cut two pieces "C," each 1″ x ¾″. Attach one long edge of balcony base "A" to building, across front under upper door; let dry. Attach one, 1″ edge of railing piece "C" to either side of balcony base "A"; attach one side to building. Attach railing piece "B" to base "A" and side pieces "C."

Set-Up 4—Inn. (See page 119.)

Cardboard base is 19″ x 14″.

Stucco all sections with white frosting. Cover beams with light blue frosting.

Roof Trim: Cut two pieces, each 6½″ long; two pieces, each 7¾″ long; two pieces, each 6¼″ long; two pieces, each 6¾″ long; one piece 8¾″ long. Outline trim with blue frosting. Attach.

Front Entrance: See Fig. 8, page 117. Cut two pieces "A," each 3″ x ¾″; two pieces "B," each 1″ x ¾″. Attach one short end of each "A" piece to one short end of each "B" piece for each side; attach the free ends of both "B" pieces to form peak of entrance. Attach to outside of doorway.

Shutters: Decorate with blue frosting.

Sign: Cut piece 2″ x 1″.

Cut sign hanger beam 2¾″ x ¼″. Attach one end of hanger under peak of entrance, having it extend out from building. Attach top of long side of sign to hanger bottom.

CARDS and TAGS

General Directions for Mounting and Matting Needlepoint, Cross-Stitch, and Batik Christmas Cards and for making Envelopes for the cards.

EQUIPMENT: Ruler. Pencil. Square. Single-edged razor blade. Steel-edged ruler for cutting guide. Scissors. Clean cardboard for cutting surface.

MATERIALS: 2-ply bristol board for cards. Brightly colored heavy paper for mat paper. Masking tape, at least ¾″ wide, double-faced and single-faced.

DIRECTIONS: Determine size of opening needed for mat. For needlepoint, make this slightly smaller than finished size of worked portion of canvas; for cross-stitch and batik,

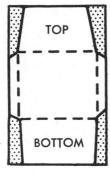

ENVELOPE

make opening size desired. For outside dimensions of mat paper, add 1½″ all around the opening size. Using square and ruler, draw guidelines for opening on wrong side of mat paper. Make sure opening guidelines are in center position. Using steel-edged ruler and single-edged razor blade, cut along guidelines, being careful especially at corners of opening. Cut bristol board so that when folded, it is exactly the same size as outside of mat. Trim needlepoint canvas or fabric, making margins about ¼″ larger all around than mat opening. Extend a small piece of single-faced masking tape across wrong side of each corner of fabric, so sticky side is up when work is face up. Place mat in desired position over work, and press down corners. The tape will hold the work in place temporarily. Being careful that position does not shift, carefully turn matted work wrong side up. Tape all around fabric edges and press securely to mat. Apply strips of double-faced masking tape all around the wrong side of mat, making the strips same length as side of mat and applying them as close to the outside edge as possible. To apply tape, peel both layers together off the roll for the required amount. Press sticky side to mat paper, and slowly peel off backing layer beyond edge of paper. Trim backing, then cut sticky layer close to edge of paper. Always leave backing peeled off a bit at the beginning of the roll so that separation of the two parts is easier. When all four edges of mat are taped, carefully place the taped mat on top of folded card; press down all around.

To Make Envelopes: Refer to diagram at left. Mark outline of card (dash lines on diagram) on piece of paper same color as card. Mark off side, top and bottom flaps. Cut away shaded areas. Fold side flaps in, bottom flap up. Trim bottom flap away from fold of top flap. Glue bottom flap to side flaps. Fold top flap down.

Needlepoint Cards

Four stunning designs to work in a variety of stitches— concentric squares; a glowing bargello pattern; snowflakes; a single tree, with padded satin pears and a partridge. (Shown on page 121.)

EQUIPMENT: Ruler. Pencil. Tapestry needle. Scissors. For partridge card: Embroidery needle. Tracing paper for patterns. **For Blocking:** Soft wooden surface. Square. Brown wrapping paper. Rustproof thumbtacks.

GENERAL DIRECTIONS: Materials are given in individual directions. Bind canvas edges with masking tape to prevent raveling. Work designs following charts as directed, stitch details opposite, and directions below. **Half Cross-Stitch:** This stitch is used because it produces less bulk on the back of the canvas, which makes mounting flatter.

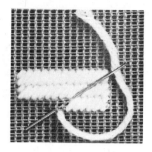

| HALF CROSS-STITCH | CASHMERE STITCH VARIATION | CHECKERBOARD STITCH |

Penelope canvas is used when working this stitch. Because selvages must be kept at the sides when working, mark them with thread before cutting canvas to required size. To work stitches, start at upper left corner of canvas. Bring needle to front of canvas at point that will be the bottom of first stitch. The needle is in a vertical position when making stitch (see detail). Always work from left to right; turn work around for return row.

Cashmere Stitch Variation: Work rows of stitches from right to left. Bring needle up at bottom of row, take a diagonal stitch to the right over two vertical and two horizontal meshes. Rows may be squared off by taking a diagonal stitch over one horizontal and one vertical mesh, at each end of row.

Checkerboard Stitch: Starting in the lower right corner, work diagonal stitches from left to right over first one mesh, then two meshes, three meshes, two meshes and one mesh, forming a square. Make succeeding squares in the same manner, alternating direction of stitches and making ends of stitches of adjoining squares in same meshes of canvas.

Blocking: When needlepoint is completed, block as follows: Cover wooden surface with brown paper. Being sure corners are square, mark canvas outline on paper. Mark center of each side of canvas and centers of guidelines. Place needlepoint, right side down, over guidelines. Match center marks of canvas and guidelines; tack canvas to board at these points. Stretch corners to match guide; tack. Working from center of each side toward corners, tack canvas to board all around. Wet thoroughly by sponging cold water over needlepoint and canvas. Let dry thoroughly in horizontal position.

For mounting and matting, see page 122.

Concentric Squares: Materials: Penelope canvas 10-mesh-to-the-inch, 7¼" x 7¾". Tapestry yarn: 1 skein each red-orange, bright orange, fuchsia, light pink.

At center of canvas, mark area measuring 9 meshes square. Using orange yarn, fill this area with nine checkerboard squares. Work stitches all around center square, forming concentric squares, as follows: Using fuchsia, work a row of half cross-stitch. Then work a row of half cross-stitch using pink, and another row of half cross-stitch with fuchsia. Using red-orange yarn, work a row of single checkerboard squares. Using pink, work a row of half cross-stitch. With orange, work a row of cashmere stitch variation. Using fuchsia, work a row in half cross-stitch all around. Using orange, work a row of half cross-stitch along each side only; then work a row of fuchsia half cross-stitch along each side. Using red-orange, work a row of single checkerboard squares along top and bottom. Using orange, work a row of half cross-stitch along top and bottom only. Block as directed.

Partridge in a Pear Tree: Materials: Penelope needlepoint canvas, 10-mesh-to-the-inch, 7¼" x 9". Tapestry yarn: 1 skein each chartreuse and deep turquoise; 2 skeins ecru. Six-strand embroidery floss, 1 skein each gold and deep pink. Scraps of felt (gold and deep pink are desirable, but not necessary).

With pencil and ruler, mark a 3¼" x 5" area in center of canvas. Following chart and Color Key given, work design in half cross-stitch throughout (each square on chart represents a stitch). When needlepoint is completed, trace the actual-size patterns for pear and partridge. Using patterns, cut out one partridge from pink felt and six pears from gold felt. Arrange felt cutouts on tree as shown or as desired; tack down in position with tiny stitches in matching color embroidery floss. To embroider, refer to Embroidery

Stitch Details on page 186. Thread embroidery needle with four strands of floss. Work several long vertical straight stitches over the felt shape, going through needlepoint and canvas; this holds the felt edges in place.

Using the outline of the felt as a guide, work satin stitch horizontally across pears, diagonally across partridge. When finished, block right side up as directed in General Directions.

Bargello: Materials: Needlepoint canvas 14-mesh-to-the-inch (single mesh), 7½" square. Tapestry yarn: 1 skein each red-orange, orange, forest green, chartreuse, and magenta.

With pencil, mark a 3½" x 3⅝" area in center of canvas; turn canvas so longer edges are at sides. Bargello stitches are worked vertically on the canvas. The vertical and horizontal lines of the chart represent vertical and horizontal threads of the canvas. Following chart and Color Key given, work stitches vertically over one to seven threads as indicated on chart.

The top of each succeeding row of stitches is worked in the same mesh as the bottom of the stitches of the last row. Beginning at

upper right corner of chart and marked area of canvas, work entire chart as given. Then work from row A to row B in a mirror image for lower portion of design. You now have the right half of the design completed. For left half, repeat entire right half, omitting the starred row. Block as directed.

Snowflakes: Materials: Penelope needlepoint canvas 10-mesh-to-the-inch, 7⅝" x 9½". Tapestry yarn: 1 skein white; 2 skeins each bottle green and dusty pink.

With pencil and ruler, mark a 3⅝" x 5½" rectangle in center of canvas. Mark a horizontal line down the center of area. Then divide rectangle crosswise into thirds. You will have six squares measuring about 1⅞". Work design in half cross-stitch throughout (each square on chart represents a stitch). Following chart, work a snowflake in each of five squares using green and pink; reverse the color relationships for adjacent squares (see illustration page 121). Work the sixth snowflake in white, and use green for the background. Then work one row of stitches all around, matching the color to previous row. Block as directed.

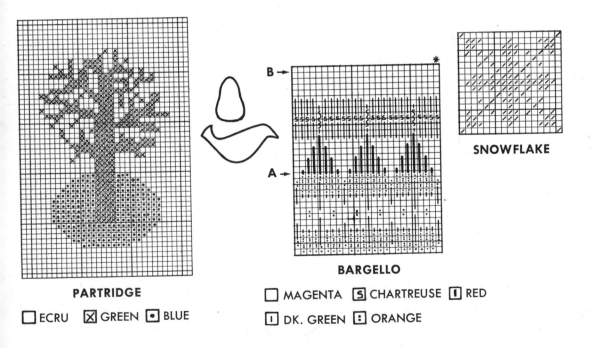

PARTRIDGE

☐ ECRU ☒ GREEN ⊡ BLUE

BARGELLO

☐ MAGENTA ⑤ CHARTREUSE ① RED

① DK. GREEN ⑧ ORANGE

SNOWFLAKE

Cross-Stitch Cards

A red reindeer, "Peace," and a partridge with a single pear are worked in embroidery floss on counted-thread cloth. (Shown on page 121.)

EQUIPMENT: Ruler. Pencil. Scissors. Embroidery hoop. Embroidery needle.

MATERIALS: Even-weave cloth in off-white. Six-strand embroidery floss (see below for colors and amounts). Masking tape.

GENERAL DIRECTIONS: Design will be distorted unless embroidery is worked on an even-weave cloth. This is fabric which has the same number of threads per inch, counted vertically and horizontally. Finished size of each is given for the embroidered area worked on a fabric with the thread count specified in directions. If fabric with this thread count is unavailable, determine the finished size of embroidery when worked on your fabric as follows: Count the number of stitches vertically on chart; multiply by the number of threads over which each cross is worked (1 or 2). Then divide the total by the thread count per inch. Repeat for horizontal measurement. Cut fabric finished size, plus about 2" margins all around. Bind all raw edges with masking tape. Find center of fabric; mark with pin. Insert cloth in hoop. Follow chart and Color Key; each symbol on the chart represents one cross-stitch (when working with one color only, all symbols are X's). Find center point of chart, and begin working from the center. Working from right to left, make one-half of all stitches in a row in one direction. Then work back in other direction, completing crosses. Be sure the ends of all crosses meet, and make all crosses the same, with the bottom stitches in one direction, top stitches in opposite direction (see detail, page 186). Work over one or two threads of cloth for each cross, as specified in individual directions. Secure the ends on the wrong side by running them under the back of the stitches. When finished, steam-press lightly.

For mounting and matting, see page 122.

Reindeer: Embroidery floss required is one skein red. Finished size is 4" x 2¾" on cloth with a thread count of about 22 threads per inch. Using three strands of floss in needle and working over two threads for each cross, embroider following chart and General Directions.

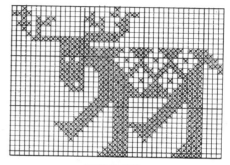

REINDEER

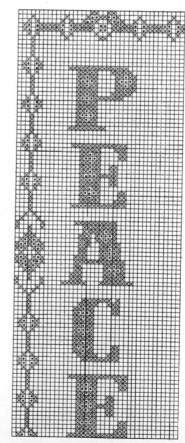

PEACE

⊠ BLUE

⊡ ORANGE

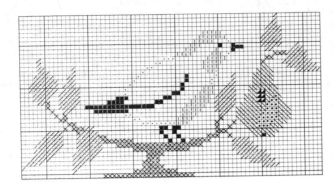

PARTRIDGE

- ☑ DK. GREEN
- ◨ LT. GREEN/TAN
- ☒ BROWN
- ⊡ ROSE
- ⊙ ROSE/TAN
- ◪ WHITE
- ⊡ TAN
- ▨ DK. BROWN

Peace: Embroidery floss required is one skein orange and two skeins blue. Finished size is 2¼" x 6¼" when worked on fabric with a thread count of about 18 threads per inch. Using two strands of floss in needle and working over one thread for each cross, embroider following chart and General Directions. Complete the border design in a mirror image all around.

Partridge: Embroidery floss needed is one

skein of each of the following colors: dark brown, dark green, light olive green, medium brown, rose, tan, and white. Finished size when worked on cloth with a thread count of about 26 per inch is 5¼" x 3". Using two strands of floss in needle, and working each cross over two threads, embroider following chart and Color Key, and General Directions. (**Note:** The combination colors are one strand of each color.)

Batik Cards

A pair of landscapes in blue and white share a winter mood.
(Shown on page 121.)

EQUIPMENT: Paper for patterns. Tracing paper. Soft pencil. Charcoal pencil. Ruler. Scissors. Thumbtacks. Small canvas stretchers (two pairs) or a soft wooden surface. Waxed paper. Electric hot plate. Two saucepans. Aluminum foil. Sticks for stirring. Teaspoon. Immersible thermometer. Flat, stiff brushes: one about ⅛" wide; one about ½" wide (make sure they will hold their shape and not get singed in hot wax). Small porcelain or plastic bowl. Container for measuring liquid. Rubber gloves. Apron. Iron. Ironing board. Paper toweling. Newspapers. Bleaching cleanser (to clean bowl).

MATERIALS: White 100% cotton or linen fabric. Paraffin wax and beeswax. Cotton fabric dyes. Non-iodized salt.

GENERAL DIRECTIONS: Wash fabric to preshrink and remove sizing which may cause uneven coloring; let dry; iron smooth.

Work out your design on paper. If using our designs, enlarge patterns by copying on

1. Plan and then trace pattern designs. Lightly transfer desired design to the fabric, marking with charcoal.

2. Melt the wax in top of double boiler. The aluminum foil between the pans will catch the drippings of wax.

3. Tack the fabric to canvas stretcher. Wax all the areas that are to retain the existing colors. Repeat for each dye.

4. Slowly and gently immerse the waxed fabric into the dye bath; leave fabric in the dye bath for 20 minutes.

5. Rinse the fabric in warm water (cold water will cause excessive crackle). Hang up the fabric straight.

6. Iron both the right and the wrong sides of fabric between paper towels to remove all wax from the fabric.

paper ruled in 1″ squares. Make final version of design on tracing paper. Center design on fabric (work on flat surface), leaving at least 1″ of fabric all around.

Transfer pattern to fabric using carbon paper (Illus. 1). If working without pattern, mark design directly on fabric with charcoal pencil. Assemble canvas stretchers and stretch fabric on the frame or on a soft wooden surface covered with aluminum foil (Illus. 3). Cover working surface with aluminum foil, waxed paper, or newspapers. Cover floor with newspapers.

To prepare wax: Use equal proportions, or 60% beeswax and 40% paraffin wax. If you do not wish crackle effect, use mostly beeswax.

Cut hole in sheet of aluminum foil to fit bottom of the top saucepan. Place the two saucepans on hot plate, one atop the other, with cut-out aluminum foil between to make double boiler (Illus. 2). *Do not melt wax directly over flame!* The foil is used to catch the wax drippings and avoid fire. Put water in bottom pan, wax in top. Heat wax to at least 170° F. and stir occasionally to hasten melting. Keep wax from overheating. After wax has melted, allow it to cool a little before applying to fabric. Turn heat off while working to keep wax from getting too hot; reheat if necessary. Take great precautions not to spill or get water even near the pot of hot wax. Water will cause splattering and you can be severely burned! *If fire occurs, extinguish flame with salt, not water.*

To Paint with Wax: Use small brush for delicate parts of the design and larger one for background. Work close to where the hot plate is. Make sure wax reaches 170° F. Dip brush in wax. Brush will fan out at first, so press out air and moisture against side of pan until it is flat again. Test first on fabric scraps. If wax spot on fabric is dark, wax is ready for use; if not, wax needs to be heated some more.

With full brush and even strokes, apply wax to fabric on the areas that are not to be dyed with the first color; use long strokes for large areas and short daubs for small areas. Since hot wax will run somewhat, be sure to work within the outlines of your design. Be careful not to drip wax on fabric. Do not leave brush in pot of wax after waxing of fabric is finished.

Mix dye with 1 pint of water in bowl, following manufacturer's directions for maximum depth of color. Add ½ teaspoon of non-iodized salt to each pint of liquid (this acts as a color fixative); stir to mix thoroughly. Paraffin wax must not be immersed in solution hotter than 90° F. Beeswax mixture will withstand dye bath up to 110° F.; let solution cool before using if necessary.

Start with lightest color dye first. Follow color illustrations on page 121 in applying wax on areas for each dye bath. Before placing fabric in dye bath, immerse it in lukewarm water to insure even penetration of dye.

Slowly and gently immerse waxed fabric into dye bath (Illus. 4); be careful to avoid cracking wax if crackle effect is not desired. Leave fabric in dye bath for approximately 20 minutes (Illus. 4); remove fabric from dye bath; rinse in clear, lukewarm water (Illus. 5). Remove excess water with paper towels, and hang fabric up straight and smooth to dry. Remember that color will lighten as it dries. If color is too pale when dry, fabric can be dyed again.

Clean bowl with bleaching cleanser before preparing next color dye. For second color, secure fabric to frame or wood surface as before. With wax, paint areas and lines which are not to be in second color dye. Soak in lukewarm water. Immerse in dye bath, rinse, and hang to dry. Repeat dyeing process for as many colors as you wish to use.

To Remove Wax: Cover ironing board with newspaper to protect it. Place fabric on ironing board between layers of paper towels (Illus. 6). Set iron for cotton, making sure iron is never too hot. As the heat of the iron is applied, the wax will melt and be absorbed by the paper. As the paper becomes saturated, replace it with fresh paper toweling. Repeat until all wax is absorbed and no wax shows on papers.

TREES: Cut fabric 7″ x 9″. Enlarge and transfer design as directed in General Directions. Apply wax to background areas, which will remain white. Immerse in royal blue dye bath for 20 minutes; rinse, and dry. Apply wax to unwaxed areas; entire fabric should be covered with wax. After wax has hardened, crush lightly to form cracks. Immerse in dye bath of scarlet for 20 minutes; rinse, dry, and remove wax as directed above.

VILLAGE: Cut fabric 8″ x 10″. Enlarge and transfer design to fabric as directed in General Directions. Apply wax to areas which are to remain white. Immerse in sky blue dye bath for 20 minutes; rinse, and let dry. Apply wax to areas which are to remain sky blue; only the areas which will be royal blue will remain unwaxed. Immerse in royal blue dye bath for 20 minutes; rinse, let dry, and remove wax.

See page 122 for mounting and matting.

Quick-Stitch Cards

Simple designs in quick cross-stitch make Christmas card gifts that can be used for decorations in years to come. Each is worked with embroidery floss on linen.

EQUIPMENT: Embroidery hoop. Embroidery needle. Ruler. Pencil. Scissors.

MATERIALS: Heavy linen or cotton fabric, about 14 threads per inch, see directions for amounts; fabric may or may not be even-weave; ours is 14 vertical threads per inch by 18 horizontal threads per inch. Embroidery floss, 7-yd. skeins: **Partridge,** one each of gold, orange, green, and a bit of brown. **Gingerbread man,** one each of brown, green, and orange. **Santas,** one each of black, red, and green. **Star,** one each of green and red. (If embroidering all designs, one skein of each color is sufficient.) Sewing thread to match fabric. Thick, smooth cardboard; see individual directions for amounts. Colored paper to coordinate with designs. Rubber cement.

GENERAL DIRECTIONS: On 14 x 18-thread count fabric, working crosses over two threads, our designs measure approximately as follows (including fringe): partridge, 6¼″ x 4¼″; gingerbread man, 6½″ x 5″; Santas, 5½″ x 7″; and star, 6¾″ x 8¼″. Designs may be enlarged or reduced by thread-count of fabric. If using a higher count, the design will work out smaller; if using a lower count, it will work out larger. If your fabric is even-weave, the designs will be slightly wider than shown. Charts can also be followed on finer thread-count fabrics without altering the finished size; vary the size of the cross-stitch by making crosses over three or four threads depending upon the fineness of the fabric.

From fabric, cut a piece larger than the above measurements, allowing enough excess to fit firmly in embroidery hoop. Secure center of fabric in hoop without distorting threads. Throughout embroidery, use three strands of floss cut into 18″ lengths.

Follow chart and Color Key on following page to cross-stitch design. See Cross-stitch detail on page 186. For star, chart is quarter of design; skip one thread of fabric and reverse and repeat chart to complete upper half. Then reverse and repeat for lower half. Secure ends of floss in stitches on underside; do not make knots. Work all cross-stitches over two threads horizontally and two threads vertically. To cross-stitch, work first half of all crosses in one direction; then cross them with a stitch in the opposite direction. Keep the stitches even and be sure ends of all crosses touch by using the same hole as used for the adjacent stitch. Work design as charted, beginning with main color area and doing smaller areas last. For partridge, the brown end of the pear is made by crossing two gold half-crosses in opposite directions (ends of two stitches meet at lower edge) with two brown half-crosses (ends of two stitches meet at upper edge). For stocking held by ginger-

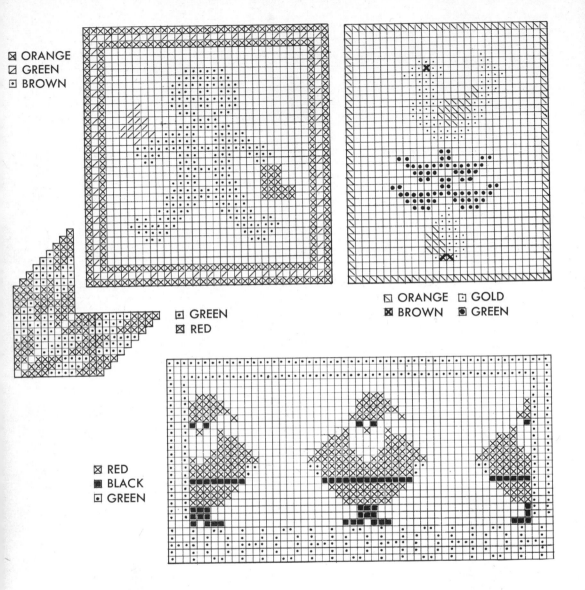

☒ ORANGE
☑ GREEN
⊡ BROWN

⊡ GREEN
☒ RED

☒ ORANGE ⊡ GOLD
☒ BROWN ◉ GREEN

☒ RED
◼ BLACK
⊡ GREEN

bread man, work two end toe stitches on chart as half cross-stitches to form point of toe.

When design is completed, work cross-stitch border as charted around all sides. There is no border for the star; instead, machine stitch around all sides about ½" out from the points. Machine stitch across lower edge of Santa cross-stitch.

For all, trim fabric to within ½" of cross-stitch or machine stitch borders. Pull out threads to make ½" fringe up to borders.

Cut one piece of colored paper and cardboard to measure about ¼" larger all around than fringed size of each cross-stitch piece. (Partridge, 6¾" x 4¾"; gingerbread man, 7" x 5½"; Santas, 6" x 7½"; and star, 7¼" x 8¾".) Cement colored paper to one side of cardboard; let dry. Then cement cross-stitch design to colored paper with even margins all around. If desired, cover back with colored paper and print holiday greeting.

Make envelopes following directions and diagram on page 122.

Machine-Embroidered Cards

Stitch this year's cards on your sewing machine, frame them with a bright band of construction paper. Each greeting is worked on crisp white organdy with mercerized cotton sewing thread.

EQUIPMENT: Sewing machine with zigzag setting. Tracing paper. Dressmaker's tracing (carbon) paper. Pencil. Scissors. Embroidery hoop, 8″ diameter. Mat knife or single-edged razor blade.

MATERIALS: Fabric: White organdy or crisp polyester-cotton lining fabric, 36″ or 45″ wide, ½ yd. #50 mercerized cotton thread, one spool each of the following colors: Yellow-green, olive green, bottle green, gold, brown, tan, bright red, yellow, bright blue, orange, hot pink, dark red, light blue, white, black, gold metallic. Five pieces of firm construction paper in assorted colors for "frames," each 13″ x 8¼″. Five pieces of lightweight white cardboard for backing, each 6¼″ x 8″. All-purpose glue. Scraps of fabric for practice.

DIRECTIONS: Prepare sewing machine for free-motion embroidery: Remove presser foot; lower or cover feed dogs (teeth); slightly loosen top tension; keep bobbin tension as for regular sewing.

Before working on actual fabric, practice on scraps of similar fabric.

Trace patterns on page 132. Transfer designs to fabric with dressmaker's carbon. For Christmas Bell Card, write greeting in your own handwriting. Place larger part of embroidery hoop on table; place fabric, right side up, with design in center, over embroidery hoop. Push smaller part of hoop into larger part, creating a well. (The position of the embroidery hoop for machine embroidery is the opposite of that for hand embroidery.) Slide hoops under the needle; lower the presser bar; bring bobbin thread up through fabric holding both thread ends; position needle to start stitching.

Use colors as shown or as desired. Follow

numbers on patterns for stitch to be used. Additional instructions are given below for each design. Check individual sewing machine instruction booklet for stitch-width setting.

1. Straight Stitch: Use straight stitch setting to make small stitches. Move hoop to follow design outline. (Outline design before filling in background.) To thicken script letters, make several rows of straight stitches close to each other.

2. Zigzag Stitch: Use wide stitch setting to make single long stitches; go over each single stitch back and forth. Move hoop to follow design outline.

3. Satin Stitch: Use wide or medium zigzag stitch setting to fill areas. To give close, even stitch, move hoop slowly from side to side, following shape of design. For lettering, set machine for monogramming and work large letters in satin stitch.

4. Solid Fill-In Embroidery Stitch: Use wide zigzag setting. Turn the hoops so that the design is on its side rather than facing you. Move hoop rapidly from side to side, allowing some stitches to overlap as needle is zig-zagging. Guide fabric in hoop to follow shape of design, filling in entire area. The side-to-side motion will make the needle swing the way the pattern lines are drawn.

5. Light Fill-In Embroidery: Use straight stitch setting. Move hoop with circular motion, following shape of design. Fill area, but allow fabric to show through somewhat.

Reindeer: Outline antlers and body with brown thread after filling areas. Use yellow-green and olive green for branches, working olive green over yellow-green.

Candle: Outline candle with dark red after filling area. Outline candlestick and all dividing lines with brown.

Bow Design: Work berries first. Then work bow in bright red, shading with dark red. Work branches and fill around berries last.

Tree: Work ornaments first. Fill in tree and work around ornaments to round them. Outline tree in straight stitching.

Bells: Work bells in bright red, with dark red shading. Outline bells with dark red straight stitching. Work berries in metallic gold. Work leaves; then outline and work veins in straight stitching. Outline ribbon and

separation line between bells with black straight stitching.

To Make Cards: Press each embroidered piece on wrong side. Trim to fit lightweight cardboard backing; glue to backing around outer edges.

For "frames," fold each piece of construction paper in half crosswise, with fold to the left. Open out flat; on front of folder, mark 5½" x 4" for opening, leaving a border measuring 1¼" all around. Using mat knife or razor blade, cut out. Spread glue along outer edges of cardboard and embroidered pieces. Place each, face up, under opening of folders. Make envelopes following directions and diagram on page 122.

Ad-Lib Cards

Personalized greetings start with a colorful traced outline of the design motif, then await the personal touch—squiggles, stripes, curlicues and dots placed at whim—to complete these distinctive, inspired holiday cards.

EQUIPMENT: Tracing paper. Soft and hard lead pencils. Ruler. Compass. Scissors.

MATERIALS: Stiff, smooth white paper. Colored construction paper. Felt-tipped ink pens with fine points, in variety of colors. All-purpose glue.

GENERAL DIRECTIONS: Trace patterns; complete half-patterns indicated by dash lines. Go over back of tracing with a soft pencil; check illustration for placement; go over lines of pattern with a hard pencil to transfer pattern to white paper as indicated below.

Outline, fill in and complete design, and draw borders with dots, lines, loops, chains, etc., with pens as illustrated. Mount on construction paper; see sizes below. Make envelopes following directions and diagram on page 122.

Bird: Cut out white paper 3¼" x 3½". Cut construction paper 5¾" x 8"; fold paper in half crosswise.

Flower Tree: Cut white paper 2½″ x 4¼″. Cut construction paper 5½″ x 7″; fold paper in half crosswise.

Horizontal Trees: Repeat large and small trees as shown. Cut white paper 2½″ x 5½″. Cut construction paper 5½″ x 8″; fold paper in half crosswise.

Vertical Trees: Repeat tree design as illustra-ted. Make border lines on each side in two colors as shown. Cut white paper 2¼″ x 5¾″. Cut construction paper 5¾″ x 9″; fold in half crosswise.

Flower: Mark two circles on white paper: 1″ and 1¾″ diameters. Mark over with pen in chain pattern. Make simple loop design in center and two on each side. Mark triangular

points along outer circle. Make border lines with chain pattern. Cut white paper 3¼" x 6¼". Cut construction paper 6¼" x 8"; fold in half crosswise.

Ornaments: Mark five 1" diameter circles in a row with ¼" diameter circles between and at top as shown. Make three-part leaves at each side of small circles. Make border lines of chains. Cut white paper 1¾" x 6¾". Cut construction paper 6¾" x 8½"; fold in half crosswise.

Star: Mark 1" diameter circle; add eight evenly spaced star points around it as shown. Make small flowers around star with simple straight lines intersecting as shown. Cut white paper 3¾" square. Cut construction paper 5¼" x 7½"; fold crosswise.

Greetings: Using pattern, copy design as shown. Make a three-line border on top and bottom. Cut white paper 2" x 6¾". Cut construction paper 6" x 6¾"; fold paper in half lengthwise.

Felt Silhouettes

Scraps of felt and glue are all you need to create the cards shown here. Trace the patterns (dash lines show where the pieces overlap), cut separate pieces from felt, and glue in place on a felt base. To finish, mount the "appliqués" on a card of colored paper. Make envelopes following the diagram on page 122.

Printed Cards

In this easy printing process, traced designs are placed over a sheet of aluminum (cut from pie tins or frozen food containers) and then scribed into the surface with a hard pencil point to make the "printing plates." Oil-based ink is spread on the plates, paper pressed on top.

EQUIPMENT: Tracing paper. No. 2 pencil. Brayers (three are needed for Three Kings Card, two for all others). Aluminum from frozen-food containers, pie plates, or heavy-gauge tinfoil. Old scissors. Glass or other non-absorbent surface for rolling inks. Thick pile of newspapers. Cleaning fluid. Clean rags.

MATERIALS: Paper for printing, unsized, such as construction paper, charcoal drawing paper, or Japanese block-printing paper. Paper for mounting: art paper, construction paper, gold gift-wrap paper (Three Kings Card), or any other suitable paper. Oil-base block-printing inks. (Linseed oil, light machine oil, or printing ink reducer for thinning inks, if necessary.) All-purpose glue.

GENERAL DIRECTIONS: Note: Print on unsized paper, then fold for card; or cut out printed design; trim and mount on other types of paper. Make envelopes following directions and diagram on page 122.

Trace actual-size patterns on page 138; complete half- and quarter-patterns indicated by dash lines. (The star design we used was already embossed in center of a pie plate.) Place aluminum or tinfoil on pile of newspapers; place traced pattern over it. Go over lines of pattern with pencil, using uniform pressure. With scissors, trim metal pattern close to edge.

Mix inks to obtain desired colors. If ink seems stiff, thin with a drop or two of oil or ink reducer; inks from freshly opened tubes are of proper consistency. Spread ink on glass, not more than 3″ at a time; dip brayer into ink and move back and forth on glass until ink has a smooth texture and makes a snapping sound and brayer is covered, evenly but not heavily. Place metal pattern on newspapers; roll inked brayer over pattern, re-ink brayer and roll over pattern again. Repeat until pattern is evenly inked.

Pick up pattern without touching inked surface by sliding top sheet of newspaper to edge of pile and placing hand under pattern; place on single clean sheet of newspaper. Place paper to be printed, untrimmed and unfolded, over inked pattern. Roll a clean brayer slowly over paper from center out, while holding paper down with palm of other hand (not fingertips). Roll again, then lift corners of paper and examine print made; roll once or twice more if necessary. Do not let paper shift. Carefully pull printed paper from pattern. Continue inking and printing,

using clean newspaper each time for both procedures. Let prints dry at least 24 hours before trimming and folding. Clean brayers, glass, and foil patterns with cleaning fluid, carefully removing all traces of ink.

Deer Card: Orange design is printed on off-white paper, trimmed to 7¾″ x 9¼″ and folded for card.

Three Kings Card: Metal pattern is inked half blue and half fuchsia, using two brayers; colors are overlapped at center with final stroke of either the fuchsia or the blue. Design is printed on white paper, trimmed to 5″ x 6″ and mounted on gold paper 5½″ x 6½″. Gold paper is mounted on white paper

7⅛″ x 11¾″, folded for card. For deckled edge, use sheet from spiral-bound sketch pad; cut along holes.

Star Card: Fuchsia design is printed on green paper, trimmed to 5¾″ x 6¾″. Green paper is mounted on pink paper 7″ x 12″, then folded for card.

Tree Card: Navy blue design is printed on green paper, trimmed to 5¼″ x 13¾″ and folded for card.

Angel Card: Blue design is printed on black paper (use charcoal sketching paper for textured effect shown), trimmed to 4¼″ x 5¼″. Black paper is mounted on fuchsia paper 6″ x 10″, folded for card.

Felt Gift Tags

Felt-on-burlap Yuletide designs are embellished with simple embroidery stitches and mounted on wrapping paper to create these festive gift tags. Use them again by gluing the designs to new tags.

EQUIPMENT: Tracing paper. Pencil. Ruler. Scissors. Embroidery needle.

MATERIALS: Gift-wrap paper in assorted colors, about 3″ x 5″ for each. Scraps of burlap and felt, and small amounts of six-strand embroidery floss in desired colors. All-purpose glue.

DIRECTIONS: Fold paper in half crosswise. Cut burlap the size of front of card. Trace patterns. Using patterns and referring to illustrations for colors, cut parts of design from felt. Arrange and glue pieces of felt on burlap; short dash lines on patterns indicate where pieces are overlapped. Work embroidery following stitch details shown on pages 186; see the individual embroidery directions below. Use three strands of floss in needle. Dots on patterns are French knots. To fringe, pull away one or two threads of burlap on all edges. If desired, outline burlap at edge of fringe with embroidery floss in running stitch. Glue burlap to front of paper card.

Embroidery Directions: For Stockings, work holly leaves in straight stitch; branch in outline stitch. For Holly Leaf, make all lines in straight stitch. For Poinsettia, make petal

lines in outline stitch, leaf lines in straight stitch. For Tree, make line across bucket and lines on tree in straight stitch with metallic thread. For Gingerbread Boy, make all lines in outline stitch. For Angel, fill in hair area with long and short straight stitches. Make eyes and mouth in tiny straight stitches. For gown design, make straight diagonal lines in one direction, then overlap with diagonal stitches in opposite direction. For Bird, make wing in chain stitch, tail in lazy daisy stitch. Make outline stitch branch and straight stitch leaves. For Santa, make eyes and lines on hat in straight stitch. Make Turkey work loops over beard and moustache area and center of hat as shown.

Crackled Glue Cards

These one-of-a-kind cards are easy to make in an unusual technique—the designs are outlined on paper in liquid paste and left to dry; the paper is bent slightly to crackle the glue before the oil-paint backgrounds are rubbed on.

EQUIPMENT: Scissors. Pencil. Tracing paper. Clean cloths. Fine paintbrush.

MATERIALS: Good quality white water-color paper. White drawing paper. Oil paints in desired colors. Liquid paste.

DIRECTIONS: Enlarge patterns to desired size (see page 183) and trace. Rub soft pencil on back of tracing; place on water-color paper a little larger than size illustrated and retrace design lightly. With paintbrush and paste, slowly and carefully paint design on paper. Let dry, then apply a second coating of paste. When thoroughly dry, bend the paper a little to make cracks in the paste. Squeeze oil paint onto a cloth and rub paint over paper and drawing. With a clean cloth, polish well over drawing until cloth is quite clean and paint no longer rubs off. Cut water-color paper with design to size illustrated. Mount by pasting onto drawing paper folded into card.

Make envelopes following directions and diagram on page 122.

GIFT WRAPS

Stick-Ons

"Print" your gift wraps with stick-ons from the dime store. For the most effective placement, wrap your presents first, then press the trims in place—centered on the package top or encircling the entire box.

Accordion Wraps

*Perfect for hard-to-wrap shapes or gifts from your kitchen,
wallpaper is folded like an accordion and closed with a bow
or drawstring to make these festive "lantern" packages.*

EQUIPMENT: Ruler. Scissors. Hole punch.
MATERIALS: Wallpaper samples. All-purpose glue. Decorative cords. Rubber cement.
DIRECTIONS: Cut paper to size indicated in individual directions. Fold in accordion pleats the number (an odd amount) and width indicated in individual directions. Then, keeping paper folded, crease the folded paper by folding it diagonally (follow diagram for each). Unfold complete piece and reverse the direction of some folds; follow pattern for each (solid lines fold out, dash lines fold in). In doing so, you will be refolding the paper back along some accordion folds and some diagonal folds. When all folds are completed, carefully open out, retaining all new folds. Overlap end panels and glue them together to form package.

With hole punch, punch hole near the edge at the top and bottom of each panel. Insert piece of cord through holes at bottom; tie it tightly, knotting ends securely; cut off ends. At top, make drawstring by cutting two lengths of cord. Insert one end of one through all holes; end by coming out through same hole in which you started. Do the same with other length of cord, but start and end at hole directly opposite from start and end of first cord. Knot ends of each cord length together. Pull drawstring to close package, and tie into bow.

Small Green Package: Cut paper 7″ x 23″; make 23 accordion pleated panels each 1″ wide. Then fold following Diagram A. Open and refold following Pattern 1.
Silver Packages: Cut paper for each 9″ x 27″. Make 27 panels each 1″ wide. Fold each as for Small Green Package, using Diagram A. Open and refold following Pattern 1.
Large Red Package: Cut paper 14″ x 28½″. Fold into 19 panels each 1½″. wide. Use Diagram B and make all four folds. Open and refold following Pattern 2.
Multicolored Package: Cut paper 14″ x 24¾″. Using rubber cement, line wallpaper with tissue paper. Fold paper into 33 panels each ¾″ wide. Fold following Diagram C, making three folds. Open and refold following Pattern 3. Do not punch holes in top, but just tie cord around top fold of package.

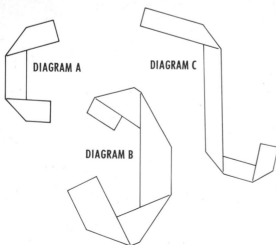

DIAGRAM A

DIAGRAM C

DIAGRAM B

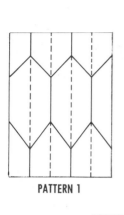

PATTERN 1

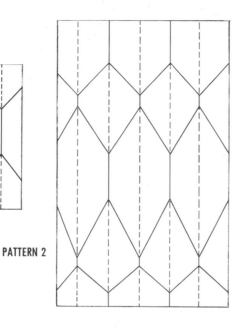

PATTERN 2

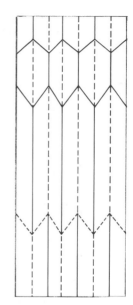

PATTERN 3

Basket Gift Wraps

Paint a pretty basket to use as "wrapping" for your gifts from the kitchen. The idea is simple—just buy a basket, paint and decorate it with sprays and dabs of enamel or acrylic or dots from a felt-tipped pen. Add a fabric lining or a drawstring or tie, and you have a two-fold gift that can be used all year 'round.

EQUIPMENT: Scissors. Tape measure. Straight pins. Pointed paintbrush (optional). Safety pin.

MATERIALS: Wicker baskets of various shapes and sizes may be used. Cotton fabrics (amounts depend upon size of basket and style of lining used), less than one yard. Thread to match fabric. Ribbons. Bias binding tape. Muslin or scrap fabric. Spray paint in desired color. Enamel paints or felt-tipped pens in one or two contrasting colors.

DIRECTIONS: Be sure basket is cleaned thoroughly and is dry. Spray paint basket inside and out. When dry, decorate with dots of one or two colors using enamel paints or felt-tipped pens.

Linings may be made in various ways: Complete separate pieces, or partial attached pieces in different widths. Choose the type that seems best for the basket style and intended contents.

Separate Square Lining: Measure depth and width of basket. Add the width and twice the depth to get an approximate size. Cut muslin to this size for trial. When size has been corrected, cut a piece from two contrasting fabrics, adding ¼″ all around for seam allowance. With right sides facing, stitch the two pieces together, making ¼″ seams; leave an opening on one side for turning. Turn right side out; push out corners; slip-stitch opening closed; press. For ties, cut two strips 1″ wide and approximately 15″ long from one of the fabrics used. With right sides facing, fold each in half lengthwise; stitch together along long edges. Turn right side out, using a safety pin to pull one end through the fabric tube.

Turn in ends of each strip. Stitch one end of each to opposite corners of square 2″ in from edges.

Separate Round Lining: Measure depth of basket and largest width (if oval). Add width and twice the depth. This will give the minimum diameter of circle to cover inside of basket. To this circle, add 2″ (or desired width) all around for ruffled edge. Test size with muslin piece before cutting fabric. Cut a bright print fabric to corrected circle size. Bind edges of circle with double-fold bias tape. Use opened bias tape to make a casing for drawstring. Pin tape to fabric about 2″ in from edges, all the way around circle; turn in and overlap ends. Stitch tape to fabric circle along both edges; leave overlapped ends open. Cut narrow ribbon about 5″ longer than circumference of casing. Draw ribbon through casing at overlapped opening.

Attached Partial Linings: Linings may be attached to inside around top or bottom of basket sides. Measure the circumference of basket and add a few inches for gathering. Cut a strip of fabric to this length, making it the width desired for extra puff above basket. Turn up one long edge ¼″; stitch hem. Along opposite long edge, turn down ¼″ and press; turn down again ¾″ and stitch hem close to edge to make casing. Fold strip in half crosswise with right sides facing. Stitch ends together, leaving open at casing edges. Run a ribbon or fabric tubing through casing at opening.

Attach hemmed bottom edge inside basket at bottom or top of sides by either sewing or stapling, depending on texture of basket.

Napkin Wraps

Big, bright napkins in cotton fabric of your choice make fabulous gift wraps that become part of the gift. Just tuck your present inside, then close it up with a ribbon, tape measure or drapery ring.

EQUIPMENT: Tape measure. Scissors. Straight pins. Sewing needle. Sewing machine for straight and zigzag stitch.

MATERIALS: Cotton fabric: ¾ yard 45″ wide for two napkins 22″ square, or ½ yard 36″ wide for two napkins 17½″ square. Sewing thread for fabric and trims (see individual directions for colors). Trims: ⅞″ wide grosgrain ribbon, 3⅓ yards; 1 package each of

jumbo and regular rickrack; ruffle trim, 2⅔ yards.

DIRECTIONS: Cut 45″-wide fabric into two 22½″ squares; cut 36″-wide fabric into two 18″ squares.

Solid Green Napkin: Set machine for close zigzag and stitch around napkin ¼″ in from raw edge, using white thread. Cut away fabric close to stitching. Baste ribbon (shocking pink with white polka dots) ⅝″ in from zigzag edge, mitering corners by folding ribbon (not cutting). Stitch down along both edges of ribbon and diagonally on mitered corners with shocking pink thread. Use same ribbon to tie bow around "package."

Green Print Napkin: Round off corners by placing jar lid at corners and marking around curves; cut away corners. Zigzag stitch along edges of fabric as for napkin above. Stitch jumbo red rickrack around edge on right side of fabric with red thread.

Solid Red Napkin: Fold raw edge under twice to make narrow hem. Press. Stitch regular white rickrack around edge on wrong side of fabric, with red thread, so that points of rickrack extend beyond edges of napkin.

Red Pin-Dot Napkin: Make as for solid red napkin, stitching edge of white ruffled trim to edge of wrong side of fabric with red thread.

Package Characters

Youngsters and adults alike will love these endearing wraps as much as any present they hide. Whimsical trims are cut from cardboard, felt and yarn scraps to create animal features on gift-wrapped packages. Patterns can be enlarged for almost any size gift.

EQUIPMENT: Paper for pattern. Pencil. Ruler. Scissors. Compass.

MATERIALS: Boxes. Gift wrapping papers in desired patterns. Lightweight cardboard. Scraps of felt and yarn (see illustration for colors). Shiny paper gift-wrapping ribbon. Rubber cement. All-purpose glue.

GENERAL DIRECTIONS: Wrap boxes in papers selected or suggested in individual directions. Patterns for package designs on page 146 are given on squares so that you can enlarge them to the size appropriate for your particular boxes. For packages approximately the size illustrated, enlarge patterns

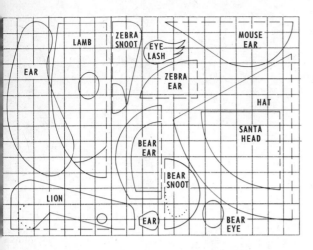

on ½″ squares. For large boxes, enlarge them on 1″ squares, and for small packages, trace the patterns. Measurements in individual directions are for designs enlarged on ½″ squares. Complete all half and quarter-patterns indicated by dash lines. Cut each piece out as indicated in individual directions. For making pompons, see directions and illustration on page 184.

Santa: Wrap box in patterned paper. Cut head from pink felt and cardboard. Glue felt to one surface of cardboard. For each eyelash, cut piece of black felt ¾″ x ⅜″; slash along ¾″ edge to make individual lashes. For nose, make a ¾″-diameter pompon of red yarn. Cut hat of cardboard and patterned paper to match package; using rubber cement, adhere paper to cardboard. Glue features on head and glue head on box, curving it slightly. Overlap and glue straight edges of hat together, so that base of hat fits on head. Glue the hat on head (top of box). From paper lace doily, cut pieces for beard and moustache; glue in place. Make six 2″-diameter pompons of white yarn. Glue one pompon to tip of hat. Glue remaining pompons around bottom edge of hat. Make a red ribbon bow and glue it under beard with a bit of holly.

Mouse: Wrap box in patterned foil. Cut two ears of cardboard; using rubber cement, cover both surfaces of each ear with same foil as box. Glue silver cord around edges of each ear. Make 1½″-diameter pompon of yarn for each ear and glue in center of one surface of each. Glue ears to one side of box as illustrated. Make two eyelashes as for Santa; glue in place as illustrated. Glue small black ball on for nose. For tail, cut an 8″ length of

bulky yarn (or long enough to reach bottom of box and curl up). Touch yarn with narrow stream of glue and curl to desired shape; let dry. Glue tail to top of package with ribbon bow glued over it.

Zebra: Wrap box in black-and-white striped "zebra" paper. Cut zebra snoot of white felt. Cut nose and two eyelashes of black felt. Glue directly on package as illustrated. Cut four ears of same paper as package; cement two together for each ear. Glue ears to package as illustrated. Glue lengths of black and white yarn strands between ears for mane. Glue ribbon bow to top of head as shown.

Lamb: Wrap package in a delicate patterned paper. Knot each end of 10″ length of white yarn; cut into one 3″ and one 4″ length. Glue to one end of box 1″ from edge, to make tail. Glue ribbon bow over top end. Cut head and two ears of white felt and cardboard. Glue felt to cardboard. Cut two eyes and nose of black felt; glue in place on head. Glue head on box with ears overlapping as illustrated. Make 2½″-diameter pompon of white bulky yarn; unravel yarn to fluff; glue to top of head. Glue another ribbon bow under head.

Bear: Wrap box in a geometric patterned paper. Cut four ears of same paper and two of cardboard; using rubber cement, adhere paper to both surfaces of cardboard. Cut two inner ears and snoot of green felt. Cut two eyes of black felt. For nose, make 1″-diameter pompon of black yarn. Glue pompon to snoot and glue on black yarn to indicate line of mouth. Glue snoot on package, and glue ears on top. Glue on felt eyes with pieces of black yarn to indicate lashes. Make 2″-diameter pompon of green yarn and glue between ears. Wrap wide ribbon around package near bottom and tie into bow as illustrated.

Lion: Wrap box in gold patterned foil. Cut face and two ears of gold-color felt. Cut a circle of gold foil large enough to extend beyond edges of box; slash all around circle to form fringe. Curl fringe over pencil. Glue to box and glue felt face over center of circle with ears glued on each side. Cut upper part of nose from gold foil paper. Cut lower part of nose and two eyes of black felt. Glue eyes and nose pieces to face. Cut four narrow strips of gold foil and glue on face for whiskers. Glue on black yarn to indicate mouth line. Add a shiny ribbon bow to top of package and under lion's mane. To make tail (not shown), cut length of yarn and glue to top of box opposite head; unravel end of tail for fluff.

Newspaper Trims

"Recycle" newspaper into delightful package stick-ons that add a special touch to shiny wrapping paper. Patterns can be easily enlarged to fit any box.

EQUIPMENT: Paper for patterns. Pencil. Ruler. Scissors. Paper punch.
MATERIALS: Boxes. Shiny, bright-colored gift-wrap paper. Newspaper. Rubber cement. All-purpose glue.
GENERAL DIRECTIONS: Enlarge patterns by copying on paper ruled in 1" squares; complete half- and quarter-patterns indicated by dash lines.

Use boxes large enough for designs given; or, if desired patterns can be made larger to fit boxes. Cover box with shiny, bright paper; fasten edges with cement. Cut decorations as indicated from newspaper and cement to the wrapped box.
Holly Wreath: Cut about 60 holly leaves and cement on front of box as shown. Cut four streamers; glue two together for each. Gather straight ends and cement at bottom of wreath. To make bow, cut piece of newspaper 5" x 12"; fold in thirds lengthwise; glue. Fold ends into center; glue a folded strip of paper over and around center. Shape into bow and cement to package.

Cat: Cut cat out of newspaper; cut out eyes. Cut bow out of shiny red paper; cement. Repeat design on other side of package.
Flowers with Bow: Cut eight flowers out of newspaper; cut out centers; cement down center of both front and back of package. For bow at top end, cut strip of newspaper 1⅞" x 10"; fold in thirds lengthwise; glue. Fold ends toward center; glue; cement this on box end. Repeat with second strip 8" long; cement on first strip. Glue 4½" strip into ring and cement over other strips.
Tree: Cut tree out of newspaper; punch holes out of tree as shown; repeat for back. Cut small circles out of newspaper to fill in front, back and side areas; cement in place as illustrated below.
Rosette: Cut rosette out for each side; punch out holes as shown; cement to box. For center, cut 1½" x 2" strip of newspaper; fold into

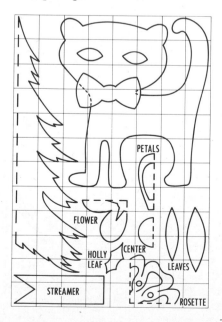

147

thirds lengthwise; glue. Glue ends together to form ring. Cement to center of rosette on each side. Cut long strip of newspaper 1½″ wide; fold into thirds lengthwise; glue. Cement strip all around edge of box.

Flower (page 147): Cut five large petals, six small petals, two centers, one large and eight smaller leaves of newspaper for each side; cement in place as illustrated on page 147, gluing centers over ends of petals.

Rippled Trims

Corrugated paper designs are cemented on paper-covered gift boxes in fanciful arrangements to make festive wraps.

EQUIPMENT: Paper for patterns. Pencil. Ruler. Compass. Scissors.

MATERIALS: Boxes. Shiny, bright-colored gift-wrap paper: enough for covering boxes; scraps for decoration. White corrugated paper. Rubber cement.

GENERAL DIRECTIONS: Enlarge patterns below by copying on paper ruled in 1″ squares; complete half-patterns indicated by large dash lines. Short dash lines indicate where pieces are overlapped.

Use boxes large enough to decorate with designs given, or if desired, patterns can be enlarged or reduced to fit larger or smaller box. Cover box with shiny, bright paper; fasten edges with cement. Cut decorations from corrugated paper and plain paper and cement them to wrapped box as indicated.

Lion: Cut mane, head, separate ears, outer eyes and two paws of corrugated paper. Cut pupils and nose of black paper; cement on front of package. For back of package, cut lion back, separate tail and tail end of corrugated paper; cement.

Candle: For each side of box—cut flame, strip for candle ⅝″ x 6⅜″, and four or five large and small circles of corrugated paper. Cut the candle glow and several small circles of shiny yellow paper; cement as shown.

Diamond Pattern: Cut as many diamonds as needed to cover front and two sides of box in arrangement shown; cement in place.

Tree: On front of wrapped box, mark a triangle, the base being the width of box and the height almost the length of box. From corrugated paper, cut small tree leaves and triangle to fit top of tree using pattern and variations. Fill in triangular area with leaves and cement as shown.

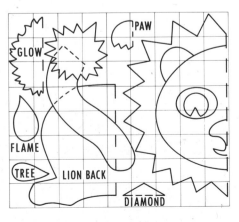

STOCKINGS, STUFFERS and SANTAS

*Lovingly stitched in knitting and crochet, these colorful
handmade creations assure a truly old-fashioned Christmas,
filling the home with cheer and amusement. Red
Candy-Striped Sock, page 150; Green Embroidered Stocking,
page 150; Crocheted Santa, page 153; Gingerbread Boy,
Santa, Snowman and Elf dolls, page 151.*

Red Candy-Striped Sock

Here is a large and roomy knitted sock to hold all the goodies that Santa will bring. (Shown on page 149.)

MATERIALS: Knitting worsted, 1 4-oz. skein red (R), 1 oz. white (W). Knitting needles No. 6; set of dp needles No. 6. Two stitch holders. Yarn needle.

GAUGE: 5 sts = 1".

Note: Top part of sock is worked back and forth; foot part is worked in the round on dp needles. See Knitting Abbreviations and Stitches, page 184.

SOCK: Beg at upper edge, with regular needles, cast on 68 sts. Work in stockinette st (k 1 row, p 1 row) for 6 rows.

Next Row (eyelet row): * Yo, k 2 tog, repeat from * across. Beg with a p row, work in stockinette st until piece measures 14" from eyelet row, end p row.

Divide for Heel: Place first 17 sts and last 17 sts on 2 stitch holders.

Instep: Join R at instep; k 2 tog, k across to last 2 sts, k 2 tog—32 sts. Working in stockinette st, work 21 rows, end p row.

Heel: Slip heel sts on one needle with back edges at center. Place instep sts on a holder. With wrong side facing, join W.

Row 1 (wrong side): With W, (p 2 tog, p 6) 4 times, p 2 tog—29 sts. Working in stockinette st, work 3 more rows W, (4 rows R, 4 rows W) twice, 1 row R, end p row. Cut W.

Turn Heel: Row 1 (right side): K 16, k 2 tog, k 1, turn.

Row 2: Sl 1, p 4, p 2 tog, p 1, turn.

Row 3: Sl 1, k 5, k 2 tog, k 1, turn.

Row 4: Sl 1, p 6, p 2 tog, p 1, turn. Continue in this manner, working 1 more st between decs until all sts have been worked and 17 sts remain, end p row.

From right side, with R, pick up and k 15 sts along side of heel, k across 17 heel sts, pick up and k 15 sts on other side of heel —47 sts.

Row 1: Purl.

Row 2: K 1, sl 1, k 1, psso, k to last 3 sts, k 2 tog, k 1. Repeat last 2 rows until 29 sts remain. P 1 row, k 1 row.

FOOT: Place 29 heel sts and 32 instep sts on 3 dp needles. First heel st is beg of rnd. Work around in stockinette st (k each rnd) on 61 sts for 40 rnds, dec 1 st on last rnd— 60 sts. Join W.

Shape Toe: Row 1: With W, (k 2 tog, k 26, k 2 tog) twice—56 sts. K 1 rnd W.

Rnd 3: With W, (k 2 tog, k 24, k 2 tog) twice —52 sts. K 1 rnd W. Repeat last 2 rnds, having 2 sts less between decs every other rnd until 20 sts remain; **at the same time,** work in following color sequence: (4 rnds R, 4 rnds W) twice. Weave toe sts tog.

FINISHING: Steam-press sock. Sew back and gusset seams. Turn hem to wrong side on eyelet row; sew in place.

Hanger: With W, cast on 30 sts. K 1 row, p 1 row. Bind off. Sew to inside top back.

Green Embroidered Stocking

Colorful embroidery stitches at the cuff, heel and toe of this knitted stocking add decorative touches. (Shown on page 149.)

MATERIALS: Knitting worsted, 1 4-oz. skein green (G); small amounts white (W), red (R), yellow (Y), blue (B), and lime (L) for embroidery. Knitting needles No. 6. Steel crochet hook No. 00. Two stitch holders. Yarn needle.

GAUGE: 5 sts = 1"; 13 rows = 2".

Note: See Knitting Abbreviations and Stitches, page 184.

STOCKING: Beg at top, with G, cast on 68 sts. Work in ribbing of k 1, p 1, for 14 rows. Work in stockinette st (k 1 row, p 1 row) for 78 rows. Cut yarn. Slip first 17 sts and last 17 sts on 2 stitch holders for heel. Join yarn at instep, dec 1 st each side of first row, work in stockinette st on 32 sts for 66 rows, end p row. Cut yarn.

Heel: Slip heel sts on one needle with back

edges at center. Place instep sts on a holder.

Row 1 (wrong side): Sl 1, p 2 tog, p across to last 2 sts, p 2 tog.

Row 2: * Sl 1, k 1, repeat from * across.

Row 3: Sl 1, p across. Repeat last 2 rows until there are 27 rows.

Turn Heel: Row 1 (right side): K 18, k 2 tog, k 1, turn.

Row 2: Sl 1, p 5, p 2 tog, p 1, turn.

Row 3: Sl 1, k 6, k 2 tog, k 1, turn.

Row 4: Sl 1, p 7, p 2 tog, p 1, turn. Continue in this manner, working 1 more st between decreases until all sts have been worked and 18 sts remain, end p row.

Sole: From right side, pick up and k 16 sts along side of heel, k across 18 heel sts, pick up and k 16 sts on other side of heel.

Row 1: Purl.

Row 2: K 1, sl 1, k 1, psso, k to last 3 sts, k 2 tog, k 1. Repeat these 2 rows until 30 sts remain. Work even on 30 sts until sole measures same as instep, end p row.

Shape Toe: Row 1 (right side): K 1, sl 1, k 1, psso, k to last 3 sts, k 2 tog, k 1.

Row 2: Purl. Repeat last 2 rows until 10 sts remain. Place sts on stitch holder. Slip instep sts from holder to needle, shape toe as for sole. Weave toe sts tog.

FINISHING: Steam-press stocking. Sew back and side seams. Crochet or braid a 6" chain with 1 strand each of R and W for hanger. Sew ends inside top back of stocking.

Embroidery: With 1 strand each of R and W, blanket st around top edge. With W, working below ribbing, work a row of coral sts; then, always working 2 rows below previous embroidery sts, work 1 row of R cross-sts, 1 row of Y chain sts. Working over and under 2 sts, work 1 row of W running st; fill in spaces with B running st. Work 1 row L chain sts, then 1 row R running st. With W, work a cluster of 4 lazy daisy sts over 5 G sts; skip 3 sts between each. Work 1 row Y running st, 1 row L chain sts. At start of toe shaping, work a row of R chain sts around toe. Working down and up toe along seam, work a row of Y chain sts; space rows of B and W, R and W running sts on sides of Y sts. Work clusters of 4 lazy daisy sts between sections. See illustration on page 149 and Stitch Details on page 186.

Knitted Dolls in Stockings

Here are four charming toys—Santa, elf, snowman and gingerbread boy—each in his own sock with room to spare for more goodies. (Shown on page 149.)

SIZE: Each doll, about 6" high plus hat.

MATERIALS: Knitting worsted, about 1½ ozs. main color (MC); small amounts other colors for trim (see individual directions for colors). Knitting needles No. 5. Two stitch holders. Cotton batting for stuffing. Yarn needle. All-purpose glue.

GAUGE: 5 sts = 1"; 7 rows = 1".

Note: See Knitting Abbreviations and Stitches, page 184.

GENERAL DIRECTIONS: STOCKING: Beg at top, with contrasting color (CC), cast on 24 sts. Work in garter st (k each row) for 7 rows. Change to MC and work in stockinette st (k 1 row, p 1 row) for 16 rows, end p row. Cut yarn.

Divide for Heel: Slip first 7 sts and last 7 sts on 2 stitch holders.

Instep: Join MC and work even in stockinette st on 10 sts for 20 rows, end p row.

Shape Toe: (For Snowman only, change to CC.) **Row 1:** K 1, sl 1, k 1, psso, k to last 3 sts, k 2 tog, k 1.

Row 2: Purl. Repeat last 2 rows once.

Row 5: K 1, sl 1, k 1, psso, k 2 tog, k 1—4 sts.

For Elf only, work on these 4 sts for 2¼", end p row. K 2 tog twice; p 2 tog—1 st remains. End off.

Heel: From wrong side, slip heel sts on one needle with back edges at center. Place 4 instep sts on a holder. Join MC on right side (for Snowman only, join CC).

Row 1 (right side): * Sl 1, k 1, repeat from * across.

Row 2: Purl. Repeat these 2 rows until heel measures 1¼", end p row.

Turn Heel: Row 1: K 8, k 2 tog, k 1, turn.

Row 2: Sl 1, p 3, p 2 tog, p 1, turn.

Row 3: Sl 1, k 3, k 2 tog, k 1, turn.

Row 4: Sl 1, p 3, p 2 tog, p 1, turn.

Row 5: Sl 1, k 4, k 2 tog, k 1, turn.

Row 6: Sl 1, p 5, p 2 tog, p 1—8 sts. Cut yarn.

151

Sole: From right side, join MC at top of heel, pick up and k 4 sts along side of heel, k across 8 heel sts, pick up and k 4 sts along other side of heel—16 sts.

Row 1: Purl.

Row 2: K, dec 1 st each side. Repeat last 2 rows until 10 sts remain. Work even until sole measures same as instep, end p row. Shape toe as for instep; work Elf toe as for instep.

Weave toe sts tog.

FINISHING: Steam-press stocking. Sew back and side seams. Attach a loop of CC to back seam for hanger.

DOLL: SANTA AND ELF (make 2 pieces): Beg at tip of hat with MC, cast on 2 sts. Work in stockinette st for 4 rows.

Row 5: K, inc 1 st. Work 3 rows even. Repeat last 4 rows once—4 sts.

Row 13: K, inc 1 st. P 1 row.

Row 15: K, inc 1 st—6 sts. Work 3 rows even. Repeat these 6 rows once—8 sts.

Face: Join pink. K 1 row, p 1 row, k 1 row.

Next Row: P, dec 1 st. Work 4 rows even.

Next Row: K, dec 1 st. P 1 row, then dec 1 st on next row—5 sts. Cut pink; join MC. * **Body:** P across, cast on 10 sts at end of row. K next row, cast on 10 sts at end of row—25 sts.

Arms: Work in stockinette st for 5 rows. Bind off 8 sts at beg of next 2 rows—9 sts. Work 5 rows even.

Next Row: P, dec 1 st at center of row—8 sts.

Legs: K 2, inc 1 st in each of next 2 sts, sl last 4 sts to a holder. Work even in stockinette st on 6 sts for 13 rows. Bind off. Sl 4 sts to needle. Join MC. Inc 1 st in each of first 2 sts, k 2. Work as for first leg. *

Belt: With CC, cast on 22 sts. K 3 rows. Bind off in k.

Hat Brim: With CC, cast on 17 sts and work as for belt.

Pompon: With CC, cast on 6 sts. K 7 rows. Bind off. Make 2 for elf.

SNOWMAN AND GINGERBREAD BOY (make 2 pieces): With MC, cast on 4 sts. Work in stockinette st for 2 rows.

Row 3: Inc 1 st each side. P 1 row. Repeat last 2 rows once.

Row 7: Inc 1 st each side—10 sts. Work 3 rows even.

Row 11: Dec 1 st each side. P 1 row. Repeat last 2 rows once.

Row 15: Dec 1 st at center of row—5 sts. Beg at first * on Body, work as for Santa and Elf from * to *.

FINISHING: Steam-press pieces. Overcast body pieces tog, stuffing as you go.

Note: Embroidery Stitch Details are on page 186.

GINGERBREAD BOY: Colors: Medium brown (MC), white (CC), black, and bright pink. Following General Directions, make stocking and doll. Embroider 3 groups of white lazy daisy sts with pink French knot centers on each side of stocking as shown. Outline one side of entire body with white chain sts; embroider 2 groups of white lazy daisy sts on body. Make small white straight sts for eyes with black French knot pupils; 3 white straight sts form bangs, a single strand of pink forms mouth.

SANTA: Colors: Red (MC), white (CC), pink, blue, and black. Following General Directions, make stocking and body. Sew pompon to tip of hat, brim at bottom of hat, belt around body. Embroider white straight sts for hair and beard. Make eyes as for Gingerbread Boy using blue and black; make red straight st mouth.

ELF: Colors: Green (MC), white (CC), pink, yellow, red, and black. Following General Directions, make stocking and body. Sew one CC pompon to tip of stocking, then tack pompon to stocking as shown. Sew on trims as for Santa, embroidering white lazy daisy sts on front of body. Embroider yellow beard and hair, green and black eyes, red mouth.

SNOWMAN: Colors: White (MC), black (CC), lime, and red. Following General Directions, make stocking and body.

Scarf: With lime, cast on 4 sts. Work in garter st for 11″ or desired length. Bind off. Tack around neck.

Hat: Top: With CC, cast on 20 sts. K 13 rows. Bind off. Sew ends tog; sew top seam (bound-off edge).

Brim: With CC, cast on 22 sts. K 1 row.

Next Row: K, inc 1 st in each st. K 1 row. Bind off. Sew ends tog; sew cast-on edge to top. Sew hat to head.

Buttons: With CC, cast on 4 sts. K 3 rows. Bind off. Sew into a ball; sew to body.

Eyes: With CC, cast on 3 sts. K 2 rows. Bind off. Sew into a ball; sew to face.

Crocheted Santa

Made in rounds of single crochet, this jolly Santa is 25" tall when hatless. (Shown on page 149.)

MATERIALS: Knitting worsted, about 6 ozs. red, 2 ozs. each of black and white, 1 oz. pink. Crochet hook size G. Small pieces of red, blue and black felt. Stuffing. Yarn needle. Glue. Red marker.

GAUGE: 7 sc = 2"; 4 rnds = 1".

Note: See Crochet Abbreviations and Stitches, page 184.

SANTA: HEAD: Beg at top of head, with pink, ch 2.

Rnd 1: 6 sc in 2nd ch from hook. Do not join rnds; mark end of each rnd.

Rnd 2: 2 sc in each sc around—12 sc.

Rnd 3: * Sc in next sc, 2 sc in next sc, repeat from * around—18 sc.

Rnd 4: 2 sc in each sc around—36 sc.

Rnds 5-8: Sc in each sc around.

Rnd 9: * Sc in 5 sc, 2 sc in next sc, repeat from * around—42 sc.

Rnds 10-20: Sc in each sc around.

Rnd 21: * Pull up a lp in each of 2 sc, yo hook and through 3 lps on hook (1 dec), sc in 5 sc, repeat from * around—36 sc.

Rnd 22: * Sc in 4 sc, dec over next 2 sc, repeat from * around—30 sc.

Chin: Rnd 23: Sc in each sc around.

Rnd 24: Sc in 10 sc, (dec over next 2 sc) 5 times, sc in 10 sc—25 sc.

Neck: Rnds 25-28: Sc evenly around.

BODY: Change to red. **Rnd 29:** Sc in 5 sc, 2 sc in next sc, ch 6 for shoulder, sc in 2nd ch from hook and in next 4 ch, sc in 6 sc, 2 sc in next sc, sc in 6 sc, 2 sc in next sc, ch 6, sc in 2nd ch from hook and in next 4 ch, sc in last 5 sc.

Rnd 30: Sc around, working on both sides of shoulder chains, inc 2 sc at end of each shoulder—52 sc. Work even on 52 sc for 37 rnds. End off.

Seat: With red, ch 20. **Row 1:** Sc in 2nd ch from hook and in next 18 ch—19 sc. Ch 1, turn each row.

Rows 2-8: Sc in each sc. End off. Stuff head and body firmly, sew seat in place to last rnd of body.

ARM (make 2): With black, ch 2.

Rnd 1: 6 sc in 2nd ch from hook.

Rnd 2: 2 sc in each sc around—12 sc.

Rnd 3: * Sc in 2 sc, 2 sc in next sc, repeat from * around—16 sc.

Rnds 4-13: Work even on 16 sc.

Rnd 14: Join red, dec 1 sc, sc in 14 sc.

Rnds 15-42: Work even on 15 sc. End off. Stuff arm leaving last few rnds unstuffed; gather top, sew to shoulder.

Thumb: With black, ch 2, 5 sc in 2nd ch from hook. Work 5 rnds even. End off. Stuff lightly; sew in place.

Nose: With pink, ch 2, 5 sc in 2nd ch from hook. Work 1 rnd of 5 sc. End off. Sew in place.

LEG (make 2): With black, ch 20, join with sl st to form ring. **Rnd 1:** Ch 1, sc in each ch around.

Rnds 2-11: Work even on 20 sc.

Rnd 12: Change to red, dec 2 sc evenly, work in sc—18 sc.

Rnds 13-42: Work even in sc. End off. Sew last rnd tog flat. Sew to lower front edge of body.

FOOT (make 2): With black, ch 2.

Rnd 1: 6 sc in 2nd ch from hook.

Rnd 2: 2 sc in each sc around—12 sc.

Rnd 3: * Sc in next sc, 2 sc in next sc, repeat from * around—18 sc.

Rnds 4-15: Work even on 18 sc. End off. Stuff; sew flat across back. Stuff leg; sew foot to bottom of leg, sewing instep of foot to front of leg to bring foot up in front.

LEG CUFF (make 2): With white, ch 20. Sl st in first ch to form ring. Work 3 rnds of 20 sc. End off. Sew in place.

ARM CUFF (make 2): With white, ch 16. Work as for leg cuff.

BODY CUFF: With white, ch 52. Work 4 rnds as for leg cuff.

BUTTON (make 3): With white, ch 2.

Rnd 1: 6 sc in 2nd ch from hook.

Rnd 2: 2 sc in each sc.

Rnd 3: * Sc in next sc, 2 sc in next sc, repeat from * around. End off. Sew buttons in place.

BELT: With black, work 2 rnds as for body cuff.

COLLAR: With white, ch 45.

Row 1: Sc in 2nd ch from hook and in each ch across. End off. Do not turn.

Row 2: Join yarn in first st of last row, sc in each sc across. End off. Do not turn. Repeat row 2 twice. Fold ends under, hem to wrong side. Sew collar around neck.

FINISHING: For beard, thread white yarn double in needle, work 3 rows of knotted loops about 1½" long around sides of face and chin. For moustache, glue 2 long loops of white yarn to each side of face under nose. For hair, sew long loops of white yarn to top of head along the "part," slightly to one side of head. Glue some of the hair to sides and back of head. For eyes, cut blue crescents and black pupils from felt; glue in place. Glue on narrow strip of red felt 1" long in curve for mouth. Add color to cheeks with red marker.

CAP: With red, beg at tip, ch 2.

Rnd 1: 3 sc in 2nd ch from hook.

Rnd 2: Sc in each sc around.

Rnd 3: 2 sc in next sc, sc in 2 sc.

Rnd 4: Sc in each sc around.

Rnd 5: 2 sc in next sc, sc in 3 sc.

Rnds 6 and 7: Sc in each sc around.

Rnds 8-34: Inc 1 sc on rnd 8 and every 3rd rnd, work 2 rnds even—13 sc.

Rnds 35-72: Inc 1 sc on rnd 35 and every other rnd, work 1 rnd even—32 sc.

Rnds 73-77: Inc 2 sc evenly each rnd—42 sc.

Rnds 78-84: Work 7 rnds even. Change to white. Turn work.

Rnd 85: Working around on wrong side of cap, inc 3 sc evenly around—45 sc. Work even for 4 rnds. End off. Turn up cuff; sew in place.

Pompon: With white, ch 10.

Row 1: Sc in 2nd ch from hook and in each remaining ch. Ch 1, turn each row.

Rows 2-9: Work even on 9 sc. End off. Gather edges and stuff piece, pulling into ball shape. Sew to tip of cap.

Striped Knitted Clown Doll

A pomponned clown to prop under the tree is knitted in stockinette stitch for 34" of brilliant color.

MATERIALS: Knitting worsted, 1 oz. white (W); about 5 ozs. various colors and shades. Knitting needles No. 6. Scraps of felt: green, black, red. Two small black shank buttons. Small piece lightweight cardboard. Cotton batting for stuffing. Glue.

GAUGE: 5 sts = 1"; 13 rows = 2".

Note: To give rainbow effect use shades of the same color in series. Stripe pattern consists of bands worked in stockinette st (k 1 row, p 1 row) in following number of rows: 6, 4, 4, 2, 2. When changing colors, leave 8" ends for sewing seams. See Knitting Abbreviations and Stitches page 184.

CLOWN: BODY (make 2): Beg at bottom, with first color, cast on 36 sts. Work in stockinette st for 6 rows, end p row.

Eyelet Row: With same color, * yo, k 2 tog, repeat from * across. Work 5 more rows in stockinette st (first color stripe), then change color and work in sequence (see Note). Work until there are 49 rows from eyelet row, end p row.

Shape Shoulders: Bind off 11 sts at beg of next 2 rows—14 sts. Change to W. Work 4 rows even for neck, end p row.

Shape Head: Inc 2 sts each side of next row. P 1 row. Repeat last 2 rows once—22 sts.

Next Row: Inc 1 st each side. P 1 row. Repeat last 2 rows once, then repeat inc row—28 sts. Work even for 7 rows.

Next Row: Dec 1 st each side. P 1 row. Repeat last 2 rows 3 times—20 sts.

Next Row: (K 2 tog, k 3) 4 times—16 sts. P 1 row. Bind off.

Top of Head: With W, cast on 12 sts. Work in stockinette st for 7 rows. Bind off.

Bottom of Body: With same color as first color on body, cast on 30 sts. Work in stockinette st for 12 rows. Bind off.

LEG (make 2): Beg at top, cast on 24 sts. Work in stripe pat for 42 rows.

Cuff: (K 2 tog) across—12 sts. P 1 row.

Next Row: Inc 1 st in each st across—24 sts. Work 5 rows even.

Next Row: * Yo, k 2 tog, repeat from * across. Work 3 rows even. Bind off.

FOOT (make 2): With same color as first color on body, cast on 11 sts. Work in stockinette st for 6 rows.

Rows 7 and 8: Bind off 3 sts at beg of each row—5 sts. Work 4 rows even.

Row 13: Inc 1 st each side—7 sts. Work 9 rows even.

Row 23: Repeat row 13—9 sts. Work 3 rows even.

Row 27: Dec 1 st each side. P 1 row.

Row 29: Repeat row 27. Bind off.

SOLE (make 2): With same color as foot, cast on 5 sts. Work in stockinette st for 8 rows. Beg with row 13, work as for foot.

ARM (make 2): Beg at top, cast on 20 sts. Work in stripe pat for 38 rows.

Row 39: (K 2 tog) across—10 sts. P 1 row.

Row 41: Inc 1 st in each st—20 sts. Work 3 rows even.

Row 45: Work eyelet row. Work 3 rows even. Bind off.

HAND (make 2): With W, cast on 10 sts. Work in stockinette st for 4 rows.

Row 5: (Inc 1 st, k 4) twice—12 sts. Work 3 rows even.

Row 9: (Inc 1 st, k 5) twice. Work 7 rows even.

Row 17: (K 2 tog, k 5) twice. P 1 row.

Row 19: (K 2 tog, k 4) twice. P 1 row.

Row 21: (K 2 tog, k 3) twice. P 1 row.

Row 23: K 2 tog across. Cut yarn leaving an end. Draw through sts, pull up; sew seam.

Thumb (make 2): With W, cast on 5 sts. Work in stockinette st for 9 rows. Cut yarn. Draw through sts, pull up; sew seam, stuffing as you go.

COLLAR: (Work 4 rows each of three shades of one color.) Cast on 26 sts. Work in stockinette st for 4 rows.

Row 5: (K 1, inc 1 st in next st) 13 times—39 sts. Work 3 rows even.

Row 9: (K 2, inc 1 st in next st) 13 times—52 sts. Work 3 rows even.

Row 13: With same color, work eyelet row, then work 3 rows even.

Row 17: With 2nd color, (k 2, k 2 tog) 13 times—39 sts. Work 3 rows even.

Row 21: With first color, (k 1, k 2 tog) 13 times—26 sts. Work 3 rows even. Bind off.

HAT: Working in same color sequence as body, cast on 48 sts. Work as for body through eyelet row, then work 7 rows even.

Row 15: (K 2 tog, k 6) 6 times. Work 3 rows even.

Row 19: (K 2 tog, k 5) 6 times. Work 5 rows even.

Row 25: (K 2 tog, k 4) 6 times. Work 5 rows even.

Row 31: (K 2 tog, k 3) 6 times—24 sts. Work 11 rows even.

Row 43: (K 2 tog, k 2) 6 times—18 sts. Work 15 rows even (working new color stripes when body pat is completed).

Row 59: (K 2 tog, k 4) 3 times—15 sts. Work 13 rows even.

Row 73: (K 2 tog, k 3) 3 times—12 sts. Work 3 rows even.

Row 77: (K 2 tog, k 2) 3 times—9 sts. Work 5 rows even.

Row 83: (K 2 tog, k 1) 3 times—6 sts. Work 3 rows even.

Row 87: K 2 tog across. Cut yarn. Draw through sts, pull up, fasten securely.

Nose: With a shade of red, cast on 9 sts. Work in stockinette st for 4 rows.

Row 5: (K 2 tog, k 1) 3 times—6 sts. P 1 row.

Row 7: K 2 tog across. Cut yarn. Draw through sts, pull up and fasten. Sew seam, stuff nose, then gather other side.

FINISHING: Steam-press pieces. With right sides facing, sew body and head pieces tog. Sew top of head in place. Turn hem on eyelet row to wrong side; sew in place, then sew bottom of body in place leaving one long edge open for front of body. Turn to right side and stuff. From wrong side, sew leg seam. Turn cuff on eyelet row to wrong side; sew in place. Turn to right side and stuff. Sew to front of body, then close bottom of front body seam. For foot, sew first 6 rows tog to form ankle (seam is back of ankle). Draw sole on cardboard and cut out. Glue p side of sole to cardboard. Stuff ankle; sew sole to foot, stuffing as you go. Sew ankle top inside leg, where cuff is hemmed. Sew arm seam; sew cuff as for leg. Stuff, leaving top ½" unstuffed. Sew top edge. Stuff hand. Sew thumb to hand; sew hand inside arm as for leg. Sew arms to top of body.

Fold collar in half on eyelet row; sew tog, then place around neck and sew back seam. Sew nose to center of face, 2" up from neck. Sew hat seam; sew brim in place. Stuff, then sew in place to top of head. Make two bunches of yarn for hair. Sew to sides of head; sew or glue a few strands at top of face for bangs. Cut two ⅞" red felt circles for cheeks, ¼" wide red felt strip for mouth. Glue in place as shown. For eyes, cut ¾" black felt circles; sew a shank button to each, then glue or sew in place. Cut an oval from green felt, 1½" wide by 1¾" long. Cut in half; fringe long edge. Glue above eyes for eyelids.

Make five full multicolored pompons. Sew one to tip of hat, two to body, and one to each foot.

Striped Knitted Stocking

A colorful array of gay stripes are knitted in stockinette to make this festive Christmas stocking, 18" from toe to top.

MATERIALS: Knitting worsted, 5 ozs. in shades of different colors. Knitting needles No. 6. Two stitch holders. Yarn needle.

GAUGE: 5 sts = 1"; 13 rows = 2".

Note: When changing colors, leave 8" ends for sewing seam. See Knitting Abbreviations and Stitches, page 184.

STOCKING: Beg at top, cast on 68 sts. Working in stockinette st (k 1 row, p 1 row), work 8 rows of first color.

Next Row (eyelet row): * Yo, k 2 tog, repeat from * across. Work 3 more rows. Change to next shade. Work 6 rows of next color, 4 of next color, 2 rows each of next 2 colors. Working in different colors and shades, work stripes in following number of rows: 6, 4, 4, 2, 2. Work striped pat for a total of 95 rows from eyelet row, end p row.

Divide for Heel: Sl first 17 sts and last 17 sts on 2 stitch holders.

Instep: Join next color, dec 1 st each side of first row—32 sts. Keeping to color rows, work even for 61 more rows, end p row.

Shape Toe: Row 1 (right side): Keeping to stripe pat, k 1, sl 1, k 1, psso, k across to last 3 sts, k 2 tog, k 1.

Row 2: Purl. Repeat last 2 rows until 10 sts remain.

Heel: Sl heel sts on one needle with back edges at center. Place 10 instep sts on a stitch holder.

Row 1 (wrong side): Join same color as first color of instep. Sl 1, p 2 tog, p across to last 2 sts, p 2 tog.

Row 2: * Sl 1, k 1, p across, repeat from * across.

Row 3: Sl 1, p across. Repeat last 2 rows until there are 27 rows, end p row.

Turn Heel: Work as for Green Embroidered Stocking, page 151.

Sole: Using same color as start of heel and instep and working in stripes to match instep, work as for Green Embroidered Stocking, page 151.

Shape Toe: Work as for instep toe shaping. Weave toe sts tog.

FINISHING: Steam-press stocking. Sew back and side seams. Turn hem on eyelet row to wrong side; hem in place. Crochet a chain or make a braid 5" long for hanger. Sew ends to inside top back of stocking.

Knitted Santa and Elf

Use the same basic instructions to knit and stuff these two delightfully floppy toys. Legs and arms are skinny tubes that twist and bend. Felt and yarn trim sets off features for Santa and his elf.

SIZE: About 27″ tall.

MATERIALS: Knitting worsted. For Santa, 4 ozs. red (R), 1½ ozs. each pink (P), white (W), 1 oz. black (B). For elf, 3 ozs. green (G), 2 ozs. white (W), 1½ ozs. each red (R) and pink (P). Set of dp needles No. 5. Scraps of felt (see individual directions). Cellophane tape. All-purpose glue. For elf, two pipe cleaners, three jingle bells.

GAUGE: 5 sts = 1″.

Note: See Knitting Abbreviations and Stitches, page 184.

Inc Note: K in front and back of st.

SANTA: HEAD: Beg at top of head, with P, cast on 9 sts and divide evenly on 3 dp needles. Join; k 1 rnd.

Rnd 2: Inc 1 st (see Inc Note) in each st around—18 sts. K 2 rnds even.

Rnd 5: (K l, inc l st in next st) 9 times—27 sts. K 2 rnds even.

Rnd 8: (K 2, inc l st in next st) 9 times—36 sts. K 2 rnds even.

Rnd 11: (K l, inc 1 st in next st) 18 times—54 sts. K 30 rnds even.

Next Rnd: (K 1, k 2 tog) 18 times—36 sts. K 1 rnd even.

Next Rnd: K 2 tog around—18 sts. K 8 rnds even. Bind off.

NOSE: With P, cast on 12 sts and divide evenly on 3 dp needles. Join; k 3 rnds.

Rnd 4: (K 2 tog, k 2) 3 times—9 sts. K 1 rnd.

Rnd 6: (K 2 tog, k 1) 3 times—6 sts. K 1 rnd. Run yard through sts, pull up, fasten.

BODY: With 2 dp needles (or 2 straight needles), and R, cast on 84 sts. Work back and forth in stockinette st (k 1 row, p 1 row) for 54 rows. Cut R; join W. Work 7 rows more. Bind off.

BOTTOM BOXING STRIP: With 2 dp needles and R, cast on 30 sts. Work in stockinette st for 9 rows. Bind off.

ARMS (make 2): Beg at top edge, with R, cast on 18 sts and divide evenly on 3 dp needles. Join; k 57 rnds. Cut R; join W. K 7 rnds more. Bind off. Sew top edge straight across.

MITTENS (make 2): Beg at top edge, with B, cast on 15 sts and divide evenly on 3 dp needles. K 7 rnds.

Rnd 8: (K 4, inc l st in next st) 3 times—18 sts. K 2 rnds even.

Rnd 11: (K 5, inc l st in next st) 3 times—21 sts. K 14 rnds even.

Rnd 26: K 2 tog, k around—20 sts.

Rnd 27: (K 2 tog, k 8) twice.

Rnd 28: (K 2 tog, k 7) twice.

Rnd 29: (K 2 tog, k 6) twice—14 sts. K 2 tog around. Run yarn through sts; pull up, fasten.

Thumbs (make 2): With dp needles and B, cast on 5 sts.

Row 1: K across. Do not turn; push sts to other end of needle. With yarn taut at back of work, repeat row 1 for 1½″. K 2 tog, k l, k 2 tog. Run yarn through sts; pull up, fasten.

LEGS (make 2): Beg at top edge, with R, cast on 21 sts and divide evenly on 3 dp needles. Join; k 58 rnds. Cut R; join W. K 7 rnds more. Bind off loosely.

BOOTS (make 2): Beg at top edge, with B, cast on 18 sts and divide evenly on 3 dp needles. Join; k 25 rnds. Mark end of rnd (back of boot).

Shape Foot: K 5, sl next 8 sts on a safety pin. With 2 dp needles, work back and forth in stockinette st on 10 sts for 8 rows. Divide 18 sts evenly on 3 dp needles. K 12 rnds.

Next Rnd: (K 2 tog, k l) around—12 sts. K 1 rnd. Repeat last 2 rnds once—8 sts. K 2 tog around—4 sts. Run yarn through sts, pull up, fasten.

HAT: Beg at lower edge, with W, cast on 54 sts and divide evenly on 3 dp needles. Join; k 7 rnds. Cut W; join R; k 10 rnds.

Rnd 18: (K 16, k 2 tog) 3 times—51 sts. K 4 rnds even.

Rnd 23: (K 15, k 2 tog) 3 times—48 sts. K 4 rnds even. Continue in this manner, dec 3 sts every 5th rnd having 1 st less between decs, until 3 sts remain. Run yarn through sts, pull up, fasten.

HAIR: Loop W back and forth on sticky side of cellophane tape making loops about 12" long (6" on each side of tape). Machine stitch down center of tape. Carefully remove tape.

BEARD (make 3): Loop W back and forth on 6"-7" piece of tape making loops 1½" long, having top loops on tape. Machine stitch ⅛" down from top. Remove tape. Make moustache in same way on 1" piece.

FINISHING: Steam-press flat pieces. Weave side edges of body piece for front of body. Turn up W trim at bottom; sew in place. Pin boxing strip in place at bottom of body; sew. Stuff body. Sew top of head; stuff firmly, including neck. Insert neck about ¼" into center of body. Sew neck to body; weave shoulder seams. Stuff arms up to W cuff; turn up cuff. Stuff mitten; sew on thumb. Sew mitten to arm under cuff. Sew arms to top of body (they should swing freely). Sew and stuff legs as for arms. Stuff boots; sew up gusset. Insert leg; sew in place. Sew legs to body at front, ½" each side of center seams. Cut ¾" wide strip of black felt long enough to fit around body. Glue on 2½" from W trim.

For features, from felt, cut blue oval outer eyes, 1" x 1⅜". Cut off top quarter as shown. Cut two black ¾" circles for pupils. Cut thin red strip for mouth. Glue on features. Stuff nose; sew in place at center of face. Sew hair, moustache and beard in place. See illustration, page 157. For eyebrows, thread needle with 16" piece of W. Beg at other end, run needle in and out of yarn every ½". Pull needle and yarn through, pull up and sew to face over eyes.

On hat, turn up W brim; sew in place. For pompon, wind W 70 times around a 2" piece of cardboard. Slip loops off, tie at center, cut loops on both ends; trim. Sew to hat.

ELF: HEAD: Work as for Santa.

BODY: With G, work as for Santa for 54 rows. Bind off.

BOTTOM BOXING STRIP: With G, work as for Santa.

NOSE: With P, cast on 9 sts and divide evenly on 3 dp needles. Join; k 3 rnds.

Rnd 4: (K 2 tog) twice, K 5—7 sts. K 5 rnds even.

Rnd 10: (K 2 tog) twice, k 3—5 sts. K 5 rnds even. Run yarn through sts, pull up, fasten (tip).

RIGHT EAR: Beg at inner edge, with P and 2 dp needles, cast on 6 sts. K 1 row, p 1 row.

Row 3: K, inc 1 st each side. P 1 row.

Row 5: K, inc 1 st in first st, k across. P 1 row. Repeat last 2 rows once—10 sts.

Row 9: Inc 1 st in each of first 2 sts, k across —12 sts. P 1 row.

Row 11: Dec l st each side. Bind off in p.

LEFT EAR: Work same as for right ear, reversing shaping (inc at end of rows 5, 7 and 9).

ARMS: With G only, work same as Santa for 64 rnds. Bind off; finish as for Santa.

MITTENS: Working as for Santa, with W, cast on and work first 7 rnds. Drop W; join G. Work rnds 8-10. Drop G.

Rnd 11: With W, (k 5, inc 1 st in next st) 3 times—21 sts. Work 3 rnds even. Drop W, join R. K 2 rnds. Cut R; with W, k 5 rnds.

Next Rnd: K 2 tog, k around—20 sts. Cut W. With G, finish as for Santa from rnd 27.

Thumb: With W, work as for Santa.

LEGS (make 2): Beg at top edge, with W, cast on 18 sts and divide evenly on 3 dp needles.* (K 7 rnds W, 3 rnds G, 4 rnds W, 2 rnds R) 5 times, end k 7 rnds W, 3 rnds G. * Mark end of rnd (back of foot). With G only, work as follows:

Shape Foot: K 5, sl next 8 sts on a safety pin. With 2 dp needles, work back and forth in stockinette st on 10 sts for 8 rows. Divide 18 sts evenly on 3 dp needles; k 12 rnds even.

Next Rnd: (K 2 tog, k 4) 3 times—15 sts. K 1 rnd even.

Next Rnd: (K 2 tog, k 3) 3 times—12 sts. K 1 rnd even. Continue in this manner, dec 3 sts every other rnd having 1 st less between decs, until 6 sts remain. K 11 rnds.

Next Rnd: (K 2 tog) 3 times. Run yarn through sts, pull up, fasten.

DICKEY: Beg at top edge, with 2 dp needles and W, cast on 24 sts. Working in stockinette st, work 2 rows even. Work in stripe pat as follows: 2 rows R, 4 rows W, 3 rows G, 4 rows W, 2 rows R, 4 rows W; **at the same time,** dec 1 st each side every k row—4 sts. Run yarn through sts, pull up, fasten.

HAT: Beg at lower edge, with G, cast on 54 sts and divide evenly on 3 dp needles. Join; work in ribbing of k 1, p 1 for 7 rnds. Beg at *, work stripe pat same as for legs from * to *; **at the same time,** dec 3 sts evenly spaced every 5th row (as on Santa's hat), until 3 sts remain. Run yarn through sts, pull up, fasten.

BEARD AND HAIR: With R, make 3 strips as for Santa's beard. Make hair same as beard, having strip 9″ long.

FINISHING: Steam-press flat pieces. Weave side edges of body piece for front of body for 5″ beg at bottom edge (bound-off edge). Insert dickey. Sew 7 sts on each side of dickey to 7 sts on back of body, leaving center 10 sts free on both. Sew dickey to front. Pin boxing strip in place at bottom of body; sew. Stuff body. Sew top of head; stuff firmly, including neck. Insert neck about ¼″ into center opening. Sew neck in place. Weave remainder of shoulder seams. Turn up last 7 rows of arms for cuffs. Stuff arms. Stuff mitten; sew on thumb; sew mitten to arm under cuff. Sew arms to body. Stuff feet, inserting a double piece of pipe cleaner at tips. Bend into shape. Sew up gussets. Stuff leg; sew to body as for Santa. Stuff nose, inserting a small double piece of pipe cleaner. Bend into shape. Sew nose to center of face. Sew ears to head in line with nose, knit side to front.

For features, cut green outer eyes, black pupils, red mouth as for Santa, leaving outer eyes complete ovals. Glue in place. Sew on beard. Sew hair strip at back and sides. Sew a jingle bell to top of hat, one to each foot.

Clockwise from top: Beanbag Knitted Elf, page 165; Snowman, Santa and Gingerbread Boy Stocking Trio, page 160; Granny Stocking, page 160.

Granny Stocking

Granny squares are quick to crochet for a stocking that holds lots of goodies. (Shown on page 159.)

SIZE: 20″ long.
MATERIALS: Knitting worsted, 4 ozs. green, 2 ozs. red, 1 oz. white. Crochet hook size I or J.
GAUGE: Each motif is 4″ square.
Note: See Crochet Abbreviations and Stitches, page 184.
FRONT: MOTIF (make 7): With green, ch 4. Sl st in first ch to form ring.
Rnd 1: Ch 3 (counts as 1 dc), 2 dc in ring, ch 1, (3 dc in ring, ch 1) 3 times. Join to top of ch 3 with sl st. End off.
Rnd 2: Join white in any ch-1 sp, ch 3, 2 dc in sp, ch 1, 3 dc in same sp, (3 dc, ch 1, 3 dc in next sp) 3 times. Join to top of ch 3. End off.
Rnd 3: Join red in any ch-1 sp, ch 3, 2 dc in sp, ch 1, 3 dc in same sp, (3 dc in next sp between groups of 3 dc, 3 dc, ch 1, 3 dc in next ch-1 sp) 3 times, 3 dc in next sp between groups of 3 dc. Join to top of ch 3. End off.

Sew 5 motifs tog in a row, sewing through back lps of dc's. Sew last 2 motifs in a row and to side of last motif to form foot.
BORDER: Join green in ch-1 sp at top left corner, ch 3, 2 dc in sp, ch 1, 3 dc in same sp; working down back edge * (3 dc in next sp) twice, 3 dc in seam between motifs, repeat from * 3 times, (3 dc in next sp) twice, work corner as before in heel, work as for border on back across bottom of foot, 3 dc in ch-1 sp at corner, (3 dc in next sp) twice, 3 dc in ch-1 sp at top corner of toe, work as for border on back across foot motifs to inner corner, work 1 dc in inner corner, work as for border on back up front, work corner at top, work across top; join to top of ch. 3. End off.
Next Row: Join green in sp after 3 dc in corner at top of toe, sc in same sp, (3 dc in next sp) 4 times, dc in dc at inner corner, (3 dc in next sp) 5 times, (3 tr in next sp) 6 times, 3 tr, ch 1, 3 dc in top corner, (3 dc in next sp) 3 times, 3 dc, ch 1, 3 tr in next corner, (3 tr in next sp) 6 times, (3 dc in next sp) 6 times, sc in next sp. End off.
BACK: Work as for front, reversing position of foot motifs and working border to correspond to front.
FINISHING: With red, ch 8 for hanger; working through both thicknesses, with front piece toward you, sc front and back of stocking tog down back, around foot and up front, working 1 sc in each st; end at top of front edge. End off. Sew end of hanger in place.

Crocheted Stocking Trio

Three identical stockings are worked in single crochet, then appliquéd with their own delightful crocheted motif: a snowman, a Santa or gingerbread boy. Each stocking is 17″ long. (Shown on page 159.)

SIZE: About 17″ long.
MATERIALS: Knitting worsted weight yarn: 2 oz. white, 2 ozs. red, small amounts of black and green for Snowman Stocking; 2 ozs. white, 2 ozs. green, small amounts of red, black and pink for Santa Stocking; 4 ozs. white, 1 oz. brown, small amount of black for Gingerbread Boy Stocking. Crochet hook size I. Scrap of red felt. Glue.
GAUGE: 4 sc = 1″; 5 rows = 1″.
Note: See Crochet Abbreviations and Stitches, page 184.

STOCKING (make 2 pieces): Beg at bottom, with white, ch 36.
Row 1: Sc in 2nd ch from hook and in each ch across—35 sc. Ch 1, turn each row.
Row 2: 2 sc in first sc, sc in each sc across to last st, 2 sc in last sc—37 sc.
Rows 3 and 4: Repeat row 2—41 sc.
Row 5: 2 sc in first sc (toe), sc in each sc across—42 sc.
Row 6: Sc in each sc to last sc, 2 sc in last sc—43 sc.
Row 7: Repeat row 5—44 sc.

Rows 8-14: Work even.

Rows 15-23: Dec 1 st at toe end every row (to dec, pull up a lp in each of 2 sc, yo and through 3 lps on hook)—35 sc.

Row 24: Sc in each of 23 sc. Ch 1, turn.

Row 25: Work even on 23 sc. For Snowman Stocking, change to red; for Santa Stocking, change to green. Work even for 53 rows. End off.

SNOWMAN: Head: With white, ch 2.

Rnd 1: 6 sc in 2nd ch from hook.

Rnd 2: 2 sc in each sc—12 sc.

Rnd 3: * Sc in next sc, 2 sc in next sc, repeat from * around—18 sc.

Rnd 4: Sc in each sc around. End off.

Body: With white, ch 5.

Rnd 1: Sc in 2nd ch from hook, sc in each of next 2 ch, 3 sc in last ch. Working along opposite side of ch, sc in each of next 2 ch, 2 sc in next ch.

Rnd 2: 2 sc in first sc, sc in each of next 3 sc, 3 sc in next sc, sc in each of next 4 sc, 2 sc in last sc.

Rnd 3: 2 sc in first sc, sc in each of 5 sc, 2 sc in each of next 2 sc, sc in each of 5 sc, 2 sc in last sc.

Rnd 4: (3 sc in next sc, sc in each of 8 sc) twice—22 sc.

Rnd 5: (2 sc in each of 3 sc, sc in each of 8 sc) twice. Work sc in each of next 5 sc for neck edge; ch 1, turn; work sc in 4 sc. End.

ARMS: Work as for Body through rnd 1. End off.

Sew pieces to front stocking piece, wrong side out, padding lightly with yarn or cotton.

SCARF: With green, ch 8.

Row 1: Sc in 2nd ch from hook and in each remaining ch. Ch 4, turn.

Row 2: Sc in 2nd ch from hook and in next 2 ch, sc in 7 sc. End off. Sew narrow part to neck. Fringe end.

HAT: Brim: With black, ch 11. Work 1 row of 10 sc. End off.

Top: With black, ch 7. Work 4 rows of 6 sc. End off. Sew above head, padding with yarn scraps; sew brim in place.

EYES: With black, ch 2. Sc in 2nd ch from hook. Sew into round shape, run the 2 loose ends through appliqué and tie securely to wrong side of stocking.

Make nose same as eyes.

Make 2 buttons like eyes but work 2 sc in 2nd ch from hook. Glue on red felt mouth.

FINISHING: Sew front and back of stocking tog. Join white at top back, work 3 rnds of sc around top. For hanger, ch 25. Work 1 row sc in ch. Sew ends inside at back seam.

SANTA: BODY: With white, ch 11.

Row 1: Sc in 2nd ch from hook and in each ch across—10 sc. Change to red.

Row 2: Sc in first 2 sc, dec 1 sc (to dec, pull up a lp in each of 2 sc, yo and through 3 lps on hook), sc in each sc across—9 sc. Ch 1, turn each row.

Row 3: Repeat row 2—8 sc.

Rows 4 and 5: Work even.

Row 6: Dec 1 sc each side—6 sc. Work 5 rows even. End off.

HEAD AND HAT: With pink, ch 5. Sc in 2nd ch from hook and in each remaining ch. Work 5 more rows of 4 sc. Change to white, work 2 rows even. Change to red, work 1 row even. Dec 1 sc on next row; work 3 rows even. Dec 1 sc on next row; work 5 rows even. Dec to 1 sc. Work 1 row. End off.

Pompon: With white, ch 2. Work 4 sc in 2nd ch from hook. Sew into a ball, sew to tip of hat.

LEGS: With black, ch 5, sc in 2nd ch from hook and in each remaining ch. Ch 1, turn. Sc in 2 sc; ch 1, turn each row. Work 1 row even; change to white. Work 2 rows even; change to red. Work 3 rows even. End off. For 2nd leg, work as for first leg through first row. Turn. Sl st in each of 2 sc, sc in each of last 2 sc. Ch 1, turn. Sc in 2 sc. Ch 1, turn. Finish as for first leg.

ARMS: With black, ch 3. Work 2 rows on 2 sc. Change to white, work 2 rows even. Change to red, work 7 rows even.

FINISHING: Sew pieces to front piece of stocking, padding head, body, arms and legs lightly. Have tops of legs under body. Leave cap and mittens free. Sew white straight sts for hair and moustache, loops for beard. Glue on felt mouth. Embroider black eyes, or glue on felt pieces. Finish stocking as for Snowman Stocking.

GINGERBREAD BOY: HEAD: With brown, ch 2.

Rnd 1: 6 sc in 2nd ch from hook.

Rnd 2: 2 sc in each sc around.

Rnd 3: Sc in each sc—12 sc.

Rnd 4: 2 sc in each sc around.

Rnd 5: Sc in each sc—24 sc. End off.

BODY: With brown, ch 7.

Rnd 1: Sc in 2nd ch from hook and in next 4 ch, 3 sc in last ch. Working on opposite side of starting ch, sc in 4 ch, 2 sc in same ch with first sc. Work around in sc for 4 more rnds, inc 3 sc evenly spaced at each end each rnd—38 sc. End off.

LEGS AND ARMS: With brown, ch 5. Work around as for body, inc 3 sc each rnd for 2 rnds. End off.

FEET: Work as for leg for 1 rnd. End off.

FINISHING: Sew pieces of Gingerbread Boy, wrong side out, to stocking, padding lightly. Work white chain st around figures. Make eyes, nose, buttons same as for Snow-man. Glue on red felt strip for mouth. Sew front and back of stocking tog. Join brown at top back, work 5 rnds of sc around top, white chain st around center of cuff.

Santa Hand Puppet

This 12" high Santa is made in single crochet and given a flowing yarn beard to steal the show as a delightful hand puppet. (Shown on page 163.)

SIZE: 12" high.
MATERIALS: Knitting worsted weight yarn, 1½ ozs. red, 1 oz. white, ½ oz. pink. Crochet hook size J. Cotton batting. Felt scraps.
GAUGE: 4 sc = 1".
Note: See Crochet Abbreviations and Stitches, page 184.
PUPPET: Beg at lower edge, with red, ch 35. Join with a sl st in first ch to form ring.
Rnd 1: Ch 1. Sc in each ch around. Mark end of rnd. Work even on 35 sc for 3".
First Dec Rnd: Work in sc, dec 2 sc in rnd (to dec 1 sc, pull up a lp in each of 2 sc, yo and through 3 lps on hook)—33 sc. Work 2 rnds even.
2nd Dec Rnd: Work in sc, dec 3 sc evenly spaced around—30 sc. Work 2 rnds even.
3rd Dec Rnd: Work in sc, dec 4 sc evenly spaced around—26 sc. Work 1 rnd even.
Arms: * Ch 8. Sc in 2nd ch from hook and in each of next 6 ch, sc in each of next 13 sc (front of body). Repeat from * once. Mark end of rnd after 13 sc for back of body.
   * Sc in each of 7 ch of arm, sc in each of 7 sc of arm, sc in 13 sc on body, repeat from * once—54 sc. Work even on 54 sc for 5 more rnds. End off.
   Sew tops of arms tog, leaving center 7 sc on back and front free for neck edge.
Head: Rnd 1: Join pink at side, sc in each sc around, working 1 extra sc at each side to avoid holes—16 sc.
Rnd 2: Sc in each sc around.
Rnds 3-6: Inc 1 sc at each side each rnd—24 sc.
Rnds 7 and 8: Sc in each sc around.
Rnd 9: Inc 1 sc each side—26 sc.
Rnds 10-13: Sc in each sc around. Cut pink; join red.
Hat: Rnd 1: with red, sc in each sc around.
Rnds 2 and 3: Dec 1 sc each side each rnd—22 sc.
Rnd 4: Dec 5 sc evenly spaced around—17 sc.

Rnds 5-7: Sc in each sc around.
Rnds 8 and 9: Dec 1 sc each side each rnd—13 sc.
Rnds 10 and 11: Sc in each sc around.
Rnd 12: Dec 1 sc each side—11 sc.
Rnd 13: Sc in each sc around.
Rnd 14: Dec 1 sc each side—9 sc.
Rnds 15-17: Sc in each sc around.
Rnd 18: Dec 1 sc each side—7 sc.
Rnds 19-23: Sc in each sc around.
Rnds 24-29: Repeat rnds 18-23—5 sc.
Rnd 30: Dec 1 sc each side—3 sc. End off.
Pompon. With white, ch 10. Sc in 2nd ch from hook and in each remaining ch—9 sc. Ch 1, turn. Work 8 more rows of 9 sc. End off. Run yarn around edges of square and pull up, stuffing with cotton. Sew to tip of hat.
Hands: With pink, ch 4. Sc in 2nd ch from hook and in each of next 2 ch. Ch 1, turn. Work 5 more rows of 3 sc. End off. Fold in half, sew side edges, sew to ends of arms.
Finger Hole for Head: With pink, ch 8.
Row 1: Sc in 2nd ch from hook and in each remaining ch. Ch 1, turn.
Rows 2 and 3: Sc in each sc across—7 sc. Ch 1, turn.
Row 4: Sc in each of 6 sc. Ch 1, turn.
Row 5: Sc in each of 5 sc. Ch 1, turn.
Rows 6-14: Sc in each sc. Ch 1, turn each row. End off. Turn puppet inside out. Place finger piece on back of head, row 4 at neck edge, 10 rows of 5 sc extending up. Sew to head around sides and top of these 10 rows only, leaving flap free at bottom. Turn puppet to right side. Stuff head and 9 rnds of hat. Turn body inside out and sew flap over stuffing to front neck edge.
Hat Trim: With white, ch 25. Sc in 2nd ch from hook and in each remaining ch. Ch. 1, turn. Work 1 more row of 24 sc. End off. Sew around hat edge.
Cuffs: With white, ch 10. Sc in 2nd ch from

hook and in each remaining ch. Ch 1, turn. Work 1 more row of 9 sc. End off. Sew around edge of arm.

Suit Trim: With white, ch 30. Work as for hat trim. Sew around body. Make another piece the same with ch 14. Sew up front of body.

Hair and Beard: Cut white yarn into 5″ lengths. Fold a strand in half. Insert hook through st of face, catch folded end of strand, pull loop through st, pull 2 ends through loop.

Tighten knot. Knot strands in this way around back and sides of head under hat trim, for hair. Knot 2 strands at front of head. Cut shorter. Knot strands at sides and bottom of head, for beard. Knot 2 strands at center front of face, for moustache. Bring 2 ends out at each side, curl upward and glue in place.

Features: From felt, cut red crescent mouth, round blue eyes, black pupils. Glue or tack in place.

Top a stocking, trim a tree with Santas, Santas, Santas—some to knit, some to crochet, and others to sew. Santa Hand Puppet, page 162; Furry Santa, page 168; Knitted Santa Gift Cover, page 166; Tiny Santa, page 169; Knitted Beanbag Santa, page 165; Terry Santa, page 167; Crocheted Santa, page 164.

Crocheted Santa

This Santa in single crochet is stuffed to a full 12″ height.
(Shown on page 163.)

SIZE: 12″ high.
MATERIALS: Knitting worsted weight 1½ ozs. red, ½ oz. each of pink, white, and black. Crochet hook size E. Four 12″ chenille sticks. Cotton batting. Scraps of felt. Glue.
GAUGE: 5 sc = 1″; 6 rows = 1″.
Note: See Crochet Abbreviations and Stitches, page 184.
SANTA: BODY: Beg at top edge of back, with red, ch 11.
Row 1: Sc in 2nd ch from hook and in each remaining ch—10 sc. Ch 1, turn each row.
Rows 2-40: Sc in each sc across. End off. Last row is top edge of front.
SIDE, LEG AND FOOT (make 2): Beg at top edge of side, with red, ch 4.
Row 1: Sc in 2nd ch from hook and in each remaining ch—3 sc. Ch 1, turn each row.
Row 2-17: Sc in each sc across. At end of row 17, ch 4, turn (beg at leg).
Row 18: Sc in 2nd ch from hook, sc in each of next 2 ch, sc in each of 3 sc, ch 4, turn.
Row 19: Sc in 2nd ch from hook, sc in each of next 2 ch, sc in each of 6 sc—9 sc. Ch 1, turn.
Rows 20-27: Sc in each sc across. Cut red. Join black.
Row 28-33: Sc in each sc across.
Row 34: Dec 1 sc at beg and end of row. To dec, pull up a lp in each of 2 sts, yo and through 3 lps on hook.
Rows 35-38: Sc in each sc across—7 sc.
Row 39: Repeat row 34—5 sc.
Rows 40-42: Sc in each sc across. End off.
SHOULDER, ARM AND HAND (make 2): Beg at neck edge, with red, ch 4.
Row 1: Sc in 2nd ch from hook and in each remaining ch—3 sc. Ch 1, turn each row.
Rows 2-4: Sc in each sc across.
Row 5: Sc in each sc, ch 3, turn (beg of arm).
Row 6: Sc in 2nd ch from hook and in next ch, sc in 3 sc, ch 3, turn.
Row 7: Sc in 2nd ch from hook and in next ch, sc in 5 sc—7 sc.
Rows 8-23: Sc in each sc across.
Row 24: Dec 1 sc at beg and end of row—5 sc. Cut red. Join black.
Rows 25-28: Sc in each sc across.
Row 29: Dec 1 sc in row—4 sc.
Row 30: Sc in each sc. End off.

HEAD: Beg at top of head, with pink, ch 2.
Rnd 1: 6 sc in 2nd ch from hook.
Rnd 2: * Sc in next sc, 2 sc in next sc, repeat from * around—9 sc.
Rnd 3: 2 sc in each sc around—18 sc.
Rnd 4: * 2 sc in each of next 2 sc, sc in next sc, repeat from * around—30 sc.
Rnds 5-12: Sc in each sc around.
Rnd 13: Sc around, dec 3 sc in rnd.
Rnd 14: Sc in each sc around—27 sc.
Rnd 15: * Sc in next sc, dec 1 sc in next 2 sc, repeat from * around—18 sc.
Rnds 16-19: Sc in each sc around. End off.
CAP: With red, ch 33.
Row 1: Sc in 2nd ch from hook and in each ch across. Ch 1, turn each row.
Rows 2 and 3: Sc in each sc across—32 sc.
Row 4: Dec 4 sc evenly spaced across.
Row 5: Sc in each sc across—28 sc.
Row 6: Repeat row 4—24 sc.
Rows 7-9: Sc in each sc across.
Row 10: Dec 6 sc evenly spaced across.
Rows 11-13: Sc in each sc across—18 sc.
Row 14: Dec 3 sc evenly spaced across.
Rows 15-18: Sc in each sc across—15 sc.
Row 19: Repeat row 14—12 sc.
Rows 20-22: Sc in each sc across.
Row 23: Repeat row 14—9 sc.
Rows 24-28: Sc in each sc across.
Row 29: Repeat row 14—6 sc.
Rows 30-34: Sc in each sc across.
Row 35: Repeat row 14—3 sc.
Rows 36 and 37: Sc in each sc. End off.
Pompon: With white, ch 6.
Row 1: Sc in 2nd ch from hook and in each remaining ch—5 sc. Work even for 5 more rows. End off. Gather edges of square, stuff with cotton and pull into a ball. Sew to tip of cap.
Cap Cuff: With white, ch 33. Work 3 rows of 32 sc. Sew around bottom edge of cap.
ASSEMBLE BODY: Fold body in half. Sew side between front and back edges of body with leg at fold. There will be a slight opening. Sew shoulder to front and back of body at top leaving an opening for neck. Repeat on other side. Twist 2 chenille sticks tog for arms. Insert through holes under shoulders. Stuff around stick with cotton and sew up arm seams. Twist 2 sticks tog for legs. Insert

through holes at bottom of sides. Stuff around stick with cotton and sew up leg seams. Stuff body. Sew tops of legs and arms to body at holes. Stuff head; sew to neck opening.

FINISHING: Arm Cuffs: With white, ch 9. Work 3 rows of 8 sc. Sew to sleeves.

Leg Cuffs: With white, ch 10. Work as for arm cuffs on 9 sc. Sew to legs.

Suit Cuff: With white, ch 29. Work 4 rows of 28 sc. Sew around body above legs.

Front Trim: With white, ch 13. Work 4 rows of 12 sc. Sew in place.

Thumbs: With black, ch 4. Sc in 2nd ch from hook and in each of 2 ch. End off. Sew in place.

Hair and Beard: Thread white double in needle. For hair, take long straight sts from top of head to back of suit and shoulders and some shorter sts on forehead. For beard, take straight sts from sides and bottom of face to front of suit. For moustache, run 4 strands through st at front of face. Curl up ends each side and glue to cheeks.

Features: From felt, cut blue eyes, black pupils, red mouth. Glue in place.

Knitted Beanbag Elf and Santa

These jolly fellows can perch high in the tree or cavort on the ground as amusing little beanbags. (Elf shown on page 159; Santa shown on page 163.)

SIZE: About 10″ tall.

MATERIALS: Knitting worsted (see individual directions). Double-pointed needles No. 5. Large dried beans, about ½ to ¾ cup for each beanbag. Cotton for stuffing. Yarn needle.

GAUGE: 11 sts = 2″.

Note: See Knitting Abbreviations and Stitches, page 184.

GENERAL DIRECTIONS: BODY, FACE AND HAT: Cast on 36 sts; divide evenly on 3 dp needles. Join; k 8 rnds.

Rnd 9: K, dec 1 st at beg of each needle. K 4 rnds even. Repeat last 5 rnds twice—27 sts.

Rnd 24: Repeat rnd 9—24 sts.

Rnds 25-36: Knit around.

Rnd 37: Dec 1 st at beg of each needle. K 3 rnds even—21 sts.

Rnd 41: Repeat rnd 37—18 sts. K 4 rnds.

Rnd 46: Repeat rnd 37—15 sts. K 3 rnds. Repeat last 4 rnds 3 times—6 sts.

Next Rnd: K 2 tog 3 times. Cut yarn, draw through sts, pull up and fasten.

ARMS: Cast on 9 sts; divide on 3 needles. Join; k 20 rnds.

Next Rnd: Dec 1 st at beg of each needle. Cut yarn, draw through sts, pull up and fasten.

BOTTOM: With MC and 2 dp needles, cast on 15 sts. Work back and forth in stockinette st (k 1 row, p 1 row) for 8 rows. Bind off.

FINISHING: Sew bottom to body on 3 sides, leaving one long edge open. Stuff face and hat with cotton. Fill body with beans. Sew opening closed. Stuff legs with cotton. Sew to front of body at seam. Stuff arms with cotton; sew to sides of body.

SANTA: 1 oz. red (MC), small amounts pink, black, white, blue.

BODY: With white, cast on 36 sts; divide evenly on 3 needles. (K 1 rnd, p 1 rnd) twice; change to MC. Beg with rnd 5, follow General Directions through rnd 24. Work rnds 25-34 with pink; change to white, (k 1 rnd, p 1 rnd) twice. Beg with rnd 39, complete hat with MC.

ARMS: Following General Directions, work first 13 rnds with MC; change to white; k 1 rnd, p 1 rnd. Change to pink. Beg with rnd 16, complete hand.

LEGS: With MC, cast on 12 sts; divide evenly on 3 needles. Join; k 12 rnds.

Rnd 13: Change to white. K, dec 1 st at beg of each needle. P 1 rnd.

Rnd 15: Change to black. K 6 rnds even.

Heel: Rnd 22: (K 4, turn; p 4, turn) twice. Working on all sts, k 6 rnds.

Next Rnd: Dec 1 st at beg of each needle. Cut yarn, draw through sts, pull up and fasten.

HAIR AND BEARD: Thread long piece of white yarn in needle. Beg at back of head, under brim, * wind yarn 3 times around two fingers tightly. Take st in head going through loops on finger; knot yarn around loops. Take st in head bringing needle up ⅜″ away. Repeat from * around back of head and face, as shown.

Embroider blue eyes, black pupils, red nose

and mouth. Draw two strands of white yarn, 4" long, below nose for moustache. Curl ends, glue in place on face.

Pompon: Wind white yarn around index finger 50 times. Tie one end; cut other end. Trim; sew to top of hat.

ELF: 1 oz. Green (MC); small amounts pink, red, white, brown, black.

Striped Pattern: 3 rnds white, 2 rnds red, 2 rnds white, 1 rnd green. Repeat these 8 rnds for striped pat.

BODY: Following General Directions, work with MC through rnd 24; work rnds 25-34 with pink. K 1 rnd MC; complete hat in striped pat, following General Directions.

ARMS: Following General Directions, work first 16 rnds in striped pat; complete arm with pink.

LEGS: With white, cast on 12 sts; divide evenly on 3 needles. Join; work in striped pat for 19 rnds. Change to red. K 2 rnds.

Heel: Rnd 22: (K 6, turn; p 6, turn) twice. Working on all sts, k 7 rnds.

Dec Rnd: Dec 1 st at beg of each needle. Work 1 rnd even. Repeat last 2 rnds once. Repeat dec rnd. Work 5 rnds even—3 sts. Cut yarn, run through sts, pull up. Sew tip over to front of foot.

RIGHT EAR: With pink and two needles, cast on 5 sts. K 1 row, p 1 row.

Row 3: Inc 1 st in first st, k across. P 1 row. Repeat row 3. Bind off.

LEFT EAR: Work as for right ear, inc at end of rows.

Sew cast-on edge of ear to side of face.

BEARD: With brown yarn, work as for Santa's beard around face. Sew two loops to front for bangs. Embroider features as for Santa, using green for eyes. Make red pompon as for Santa. Sew to hat.

Knitted Santa Gift Cover

With a beard of fluffy angora, here's Santa all ready to deliver his gifts in person. (Shown on page 163.)

SIZE: 7" tall plus hat.

MATERIALS: Knitting worsted, 1 oz. red (R), ½ oz. pink (P), ¼ oz. black (B). White angora (W), 1 10-gram ball. Double-pointed (dp) needles No. 6. Size F crochet hook. Scraps of felt: blue, white; sewing thread to match. Cotton for stuffing. 4" hollow plastic egg to be filled with candy or small gift, or solid styrofoam egg.

GAUGE: 5 sts = 1"; 7 rows = 1" (stockinette st).

Note: See Knitting Abbreviations and Stitches, page 184.

SANTA: BODY AND HEAD: With B, cast on 40 sts; divide on 3 needles. Join; work around in ribbing of k 1, p 1 for 1". Change to R. Work in stockinette st (k each rnd) for 20 rnds.

Rnd 21: K 4, k 2 tog, (k 8, k 2 tog) 3 times, k 4—36 sts. K 1 rnd.

Rnd 23: K 3, k 2 tog, (k 7, k 2 tog) 3 times, k 4—32 sts. K 1 rnd.

Shape Neck: Rnd 25: (K 2 tog) around—16 sts. Change to P.

Rnds 26 and 27: K around.

Shape Head: Rnd 28: Inc 1 st in each st—32 sts. K 8 rnds even.

Rnd 37: K 7 P, drop P; join R and work bobble in next st for nose (to work bobble: k 1, p 1, k 1, p 1, k 1 in next st, turn; p 5, turn; k 5, turn; p 2 tog, p 1, p 2 tog, turn; k 3, turn; p 3 tog). Cut R; finish rnd with P. K 7 rnds even.

Rnd 45: K 3, k 2 tog, (k 6, k 2 tog) 3 times, k 3—28 sts. K 1 rnd.

Rnd 47: K 2, k 2 tog, (k 5, k 2 tog) 3 times, k 3—24 sts. Cut yarn leaving a long end; weave top of head tog.

ARMS (make 2): With R, cast on 12 sts. With two needles only, work back and forth in stockinette st (k 1 row, p 1 row) for 8 rows. Change to W; work 2 rows. Change to P; work 3 rows, end k row.

Row 14: P 2 tog, p 8, p 2 tog. Bind off. Sew side and end seam.

HAT: With W, cast on and divide 34 sts on 3 needles. Join; work in ribbing of k 1, p 1 for 3 rnds. Change to R; k around for 20 rnds. Cut yarn, draw through sts, pull up and fasten.

Pompon: Wind W around a 1" piece of cardboard 50 times. Tie one end; cut other end. Trim; sew to tip of hat.

HAIR AND BEARD: Cut 2½" strands of

W. Fold in half and, with crochet hook, attach to face having 3 rows for beard and 2 rows for hair. Sew hat to head above hair. **Features:** From felt, cut ½″ blue circles for pupils, ¾″ white circles for eyes. Sew in place. Embroider red mouth.
FINISHING: Stuff head and arms with cotton. Sew arms to body. Insert egg in body.

Terry Santa

Here's a lean and lanky Santa stitched in terry cloth from the top of his hat to the tip of his boots. (Shown on page 163.)

EQUIPMENT: Paper for pattern. Pencil. Ruler. Scissors. Straight pins. Needle.
MATERIALS: Terry cloth fabric, 45″ wide: ⅝ yd. red; small amounts of pink and white. Red and white sewing threads. Scraps of black, red, and pale blue felt. All-purpose glue.
DIRECTIONS: Enlarge patterns (at right) by copying on paper ruled in 1″ squares; complete half-patterns indicated by dash lines.

To make body, cut piece of red terry cloth 18″ x 26″; fold in half crosswise, bringing 18″ sides together. Fold in half again crosswise so that piece measures 6½″ x 18″. Roll up sideways to form 6½″-long tube. Turn loose edge under; sew to roll. For legs, cut two pieces of red cloth each 5½″ x 7½″. Turn a narrow hem on each longer side; sew in place. Roll each with hemmed edges at top and bottom of roll. Turn loose edge under; sew to roll. Pinch one end of leg roll as flat as possible; sew this end of each leg to one edge of body roll (front). Cut red cloth circle the diameter of body roll, adding ⅛″ all around for seam allowance. Turn in seam allowance; sew circle to body bottom. Using pattern, cut two shoes of red terry cloth. Reverse pattern; cut two more shoes. With right sides facing, sew two matching pieces together with ⅛″ seam, leaving small opening. Turn to right side; stuff with scraps of terry cloth; turn edges of opening in and slipstitch closed. Make second shoe in same manner. Having toes pointing inward, sew one to each leg end, with X on shoe pattern at back of leg. For arms, cut two pieces of red cloth each 5½″ x 6½″. Hem the 6½″ sides same as for leg. Finish as for leg. Sew one to top of body roll at each side. Using pattern, cut two gloves. Reverse pattern: cut two more gloves. Sew up and stuff as for shoes. Sew one to each arm end with thumbs to front.

For neck, cut piece of pink cloth 9″ x 9″. Fold in thirds and roll up sideways. Turn loose edge under; sew to roll. Sew one end of

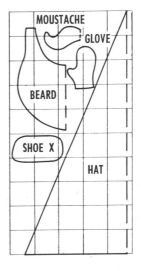

roll to body top. For head, cut pink cloth 8¼″ x 15″. Fold in thirds lengthwise, making strip 2¾″ x 15″. Wrap around neck with top edges even and seam in back; turn in and sew loose edge to roll. Sew bottom of head around neck.

For jacket trim, cut strip of white cloth 1½″ x 24″. Fold in half lengthwise; sew long ends together. Refold so long seam is at center (wrong side). With wrong side to body, sew one end to neck, and pin down center front of body, around bottom back, and up body front again to neck. Turn raw ends under; sew edges to body. For sleeve and pants trims, cut for each, a piece of white cloth 1″ x 3″; wrap around in place. Turn all raw edges under; sew in place. Using pattern, cut hat out of red cloth. With right sides facing, fold in half lengthwise. Sew up side edges, making ¼″ seam; leave bottom open. Turn to right side. Pull hat about 1″ onto head; sew in place. For trim, cut 1″ x 8″ strip of white cloth. Sew around hat as for other trims. For pompon, cut 3″-diameter circle of white cloth. Make gathering stitch around the edge; place some fabric scraps in center to stuff and pull gathering thread tightly to form ball; knot thread. Sew to tip of hat.

For beard and moustache, cut two each of white cloth. With right sides facing, place two of each together. Sew edges together, making ⅛″ seams; leave small openings for turning; turn to right side. Turn edges of opening in and sew closed. Sew beard and moustache in place.

For outer eyes, cut two ½″ circles of light blue felt; for inner eyes, cut smaller circles of black felt. For nose, cut ¼″ circle of red felt; for mouth, cut curve of red felt about ¾″ long. Glue all to Santa head.

Furry Santa

Colorful felt and furry fabric add an especially inviting texture to this happy Santa. (Shown on page 163.)

EQUIPMENT: Paper for pattern. Pencil. Ruler. Scissors. Straight pins. Sewing needle. Tape measure.
MATERIALS: Fur fabric, 60″ wide: ½ yd.

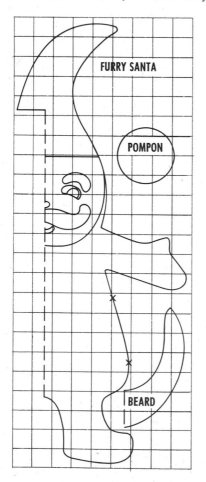

red; ¼ yd. white. Felt: White, 8″ x 10″; pink, 5″ x 6″; scraps of light blue, red, black. Red and white sewing thread. Dacron fiberfill for stuffing. All-purpose glue.
DIRECTIONS: Enlarge pattern at left by copying on paper ruled in 1″ squares; complete half-patterns indicated by dash lines.

Fold red fabric in half with right sides facing; pin complete Santa pattern to fabric; mark around pattern with pencil on wrong side. Cut two Santas out of fabric, adding ¼″ all around for seam allowance. With right sides facing, sew the two Santas together, making ¼″ seam and leaving open between X's. Clip seam allowance at curves. Turn to right side. Stuff fully. Turn edges of opening in; slip-stitch closed. Cut two pompons of white fabric, adding ¼″ seam allowance all around each. With right sides facing, sew edges together making ¼″ seam; leave small opening. Clip into seam allowance all around. Turn to right side. Stuff. Turn edges of opening in; slip-stitch closed. Sew pompon to tip of hat.

Cut face of pink felt; glue to Santa. Cut inner eyes of black felt, outer eyes of blue felt, nose and mouth of red felt; glue to face. Cut eyebrows of white fur fabric; glue to face. Cut beard and moustache each out of white fur fabric and white felt, adding ¼″ all around for seam allowances. With right sides facing, sew matching beards together and matching moustaches together, leaving small openings for turning. Clip into seam allowances; turn to right side. Turn edges of opening in and slip-stitch closed. Slip-stitch beard and moustache in place.

For trims, cut 1¼″-wide strips of white fabric to fit down front and around Santa "hem"; glue in place. Cut 1″-wide strip of white fabric to fit around "hat"; glue.

Tiny Santa

A child's white sock forms the body for this tiny little Santa,
dressed in a velveteen suit and carrying his jolly pack.
(Shown on page 163.)

EQUIPMENT: Paper for patterns. Pencil. Ruler. Scissors. Sewing and large-eyed needles. Straight pins.

MATERIALS: Child's white sock, size 4½-5. Small piece of cord. Red cotton velveteen, ¼ yd. White fur fabric (with knit backing) for trims, ⅛ yd. Dacron fiberfill for stuffing. Red, white, and black sewing thread. Small piece of black plastic. Small buckle (watchband size). Small pompon from white ball fringe. Red and black felt-tipped pens for features. Small amount of Dacron fiberfill for hair, beard, and moustache. All-purpose glue. Red yarn 12″ long.

DIRECTIONS: Enlarge patterns by copying on paper ruled in 1″ squares; complete half-patterns indicated by long dash lines. Short dash lines indicate folds. When cutting fabric pieces, add ¼″ for seam allowances, except on boot and top edge of bag. Pin pieces together before sewing.

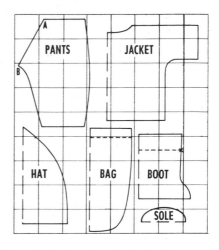

To make body, refold and flatten sock so that heel reinforcement is in center back. With sock in this position, cut from top of sock through center front and back of ribbing and sock to top of heel. Cut off 2″ from ribbing crosswise (these pieces will be used for arms). Stuff toe and foot of sock fully up to back of heel; this will form head and body. Separate the remaining cut sections to form legs. Turn under raw edges along each inner side of legs and at top edge of heel (crotch); whip edges together, leaving ends open. Stuff legs fully. For head, tie cord around sock about 2½″ from toe end. For arms, fold each 2″ ribbed piece in half lengthwise; stitch one end closed. Turn to other side. Turn lengthwise raw edges under and stitch. Stuff each arm fully; whip ends closed. Sew an arm to each side of body ½″ down from neck cord.

For nose, cut a 1″-diameter circle of red fabric; make a gathering stitch around edge; place small amount of stuffing in center; pull gathering thread tightly; knot. Sew nose to head on opposite side from heel. With black pen, mark eyebrows; with red pen, mark mouth.

Using pattern, cut two jackets; with right sides facing, sew shoulder seams. Cut down center of one piece to make jacket front opening. Cut a 1″-wide strip of white fur fabric to fit around each sleeve end; pin right side of fur fabric to wrong side of velvet around each sleeve end with edges flush. Stitch together ¼″ from sleeve end. Turn fur cuffs over to right side. With right sides facing, sew underarms and side seams. For jacket trim, cut 1¼″-wide strip long enough to go around neck, front opening, and bottom edges of jacket plus ½″ overlap. With right side of strip facing wrong side of velveteen, pin strip to jacket edge, starting at front top corner, going around neck, down front opening, across bottom and up other side of front opening to starting corner. Turn overlap edge under. Stitch all around ¼″ from edge. Turn fur strip to right side. Pin free edge to right side of jacket; miter corners neatly. Topstitch fur all around jacket ⅛″ from inner edge.

For pants, cut four pieces out of red velveteen. With right sides facing, sew two together from B to A for front. Repeat with other two pieces for back. With right sides facing, pin front and back pants pieces together along sides and inner legs; sew seams. Hem waist edge.

To make padded stomach, cut two 3″-diameter circles of scrap fabric; stitch together close to edge; leave small opening for stuffing.

Stuff fully and whipstitch opening closed. Put pants on doll. Insert stomach pad into pants. Gather pants leg ends to fit tightly around legs.

For each leg, cut boot and sole of black felt. Fold boot piece in half crosswise. Whip from bottom of toe up to X. Whip sole around bottom edge of boot. Stuff boot fully nearly to top. Pull boots over ends of legs; turn top edge down to form cuff. Slip-stitch boots to legs.

For belt, cut strip of black plastic ⅜" wide, 10" long. Fit one end on buckle; stitch to secure. Cut other end to a point. Put jacket on Santa and place belt around waist. Make hole at point where belt fits tightly in buckle. Tack cuffs near ends of arms.

Cut two hats of red velveteen. With right sides facing, sew sides together. Cut 1"-wide strip of white fur fabric long enough to fit around bottom edge of hat. Pin right side of strip to wrong side of velveteen; stitch together all around hat with ¼" seam. Turn hat to right side; turn fur over to right side. Topstitch inner edges of fur to hat. Sew pompon to hat tip.

For hair, glue a strip of fiberfill around head. To form moustache and beard, glue on fiberfill cut to proper shape. Tack hat on head.

Cut two bag pieces of velveteen; with right sides facing, sew together around sides and bottom. Fold top edge to wrong side; hem. Turn bag to right side. With large-eyed needle, run red yarn in and out of top edge to make drawstring. Stuff bag and tie string.

Needlepoint Argyle Stocking

A fresh new look in argyles is worked on needlepoint canvas in an easy upright bargello stitch.

EQUIPMENT: Paper for patterns. Pencil. Ruler. Scissors. Tapestry needle. Sewing needle. Waterproof felt-tipped marking pen. Masking tape. **For Blocking:** Soft wooden surface. Brown paper. Rustproof tacks.

MATERIALS: Mono needlepoint canvas, 16-mesh-to-the-inch, 16" x 24". Tapestry yarn, 8.8-yard skeins: 9 dark green, 8 each light green and white, 4 red, 1 yellow. White wool dress fabric, 13" x 21". Matching sewing thread. Interfacing, 13" x 21". Green lining fabric, 26" wide, ⅝ yard.

DIRECTIONS (Note: Test felt-tipped pen to be sure it is waterproof.) Enlarge stocking pattern by copying on paper ruled in 1" squares. Cut out pattern. Place pattern on canvas, allowing 2" margin of canvas all around. Mark around outline of stocking. Darken all argyle lines, and heel, toe, and cuff on pattern with marking pen. Place pattern under canvas, matching outline of pattern to outline on canvas. Pattern lines will show through canvas. Carefully mark lines of argyle on canvas; mark toe, heel, and cuff line. Bind raw edges of canvas with masking tape to keep from raveling.

Cut yarn strands 18" long and work with one strand in needle throughout.

Heel, toe, and cuff areas are worked in rows of horizontal stitches over four threads of canvas, with a row of backstitch between (see Detail 1). With dark green yarn, begin working cuff area at upper left, making first row down to lower edge (Fig. 1). Continue working rows from top to bottom in this manner to cover area. Between each row, make a row of backstitches from top to bottom (Fig. 2) in same spaces as ends of horizontal stitches.

Work heel and toe areas in same manner, with straight rows from top of area to bottom.

Argyle area is worked in rows of vertical stitches over four threads of canvas (Detail 2). For argyle design, follow shading and key for colors of each diamond. Single line stripes are worked in dark green (dash line) and yellow (dotted line). Work vertical stitches across from right to left in each area (Fig. 3). Single lines are worked in same vertical stitch, each row down moving one mesh to right or left to form diagonal stripe.

Blocking: When needlepoint is finished, block. Cover wooden surface with brown paper. Mark canvas outline on paper. Place needlepoint right side down over guide. Fasten canvas with tacks about ½" apart along edge of canvas, stretching canvas to match guide. Wet thoroughly with cold water; let dry. Remove from board.

To Finish: Using stocking pattern and adding ½" seam allowance all around, cut one stocking from wool fabric and interfacing and two stockings from lining fabric. Cut off excess canvas ½" beyond needlepoint. Baste interfacing to wrong side of wool fabric stocking. Place needlepoint and fabric stocking together with right sides facing. Stitch together along edge of needlepoint, making ½" seam and leaving top open. Turn to right side. With right sides facing, stitch the two lining pieces together. Insert lining into needlepoint stocking. Turn in ½" at top of stocking on canvas, fabric, and lining. Slip-stitch lining to outer boot all around top.

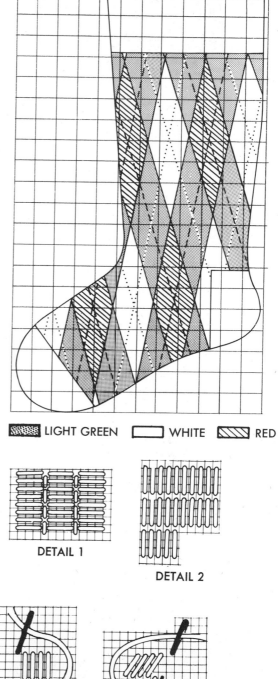

LIGHT GREEN ☐ WHITE ▨ RED

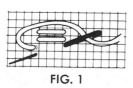

DETAIL 1

DETAIL 2

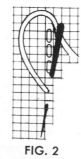

FIG. 1

FIG. 2

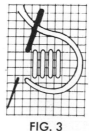

FIG. 3

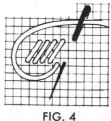

FIG. 4

Needlepoint Tree Stocking

*Red and green trees are quickly worked on needlepoint canvas
in a horizontal version of the bargello stitch.*

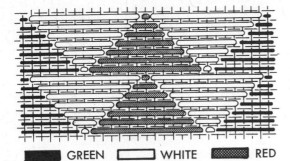

GREEN ☐ WHITE ▨ RED

EQUIPMENT: Paper for patterns. Pencil. Ruler. Scissors. Tapestry needle. Sewing needle. Waterproof felt-tipped pen. Masking tape. **For Blocking:** Soft wooden surface. Brown paper. Rustproof tacks.

MATERIALS: Needlepoint canvas, 10-mesh-to-the-inch, 16″ x 24″. Red wool dress fabric, 13″ x 21″. Red lining fabric, 26″ wide, ⅝ yd. Persian yarn (3 ply): red, 52 yards; white, 40 yards; green, 19 yards. Matching sewing thread. Interfacing, 13″ x 21″.

DIRECTIONS: (**Note:** Test felt-tipped pen to be sure it is waterproof.) Use basic pattern for Needlepoint Argyle Stockings (page 171) and enlarge by copying on paper ruled in 1″ squares. Cut out pattern. Place pattern on canvas, allowing 2″ margin all around. Trace stocking outline on canvas with felt-tipped pen. Place pattern beneath canvas, matching

outlines. Mark cuff line across top, heel and toe outlines with pen.

Bind raw edges of canvas with masking tape to keep from raveling.

To work needlepoint, use all three plys of yarn in needle throughout. Cut strands to 18″ lengths. Cuff, heel, and toe areas are worked in rows of Slanting Gobelin Stitch (see Fig. 4, page 171). Starting at upper left corner of cuff area, work row across using red yarn. Fill in at each end of row with shorter stitches to square ends. Work next row below in same manner, with top ends of stitches meeting in same mesh as bottom of first row. Continue working rows across to cover cuff area. Work heel and toe areas in same stitch, making rows across within outlined areas.

For tree design on remainder of stocking, follow the chart and Color Key for colors. Pattern is worked in horizontal stitches: First stitch over one thread of canvas (top of tree); next stitch over three threads; next stitch over five threads, etc., down to last row of tree, which is over 13 threads (see chart). Starting at top center of area with red yarn, work a row of trees down to bottom. Following chart, repeat with white (trees upside down) and green. Fill entire area of stocking, alternating red, white, and green.

Block and finish following directions for Needlepoint Argyle Stocking, page 171.

"Fur-Topped" Boot

*Put a fancy, furry look on an original Christmas stocking—a
bright green boot decorated with a star-splashed repeat
design in machine embroidery.*

EQUIPMENT: Paper for patterns. Pencil. Ruler. Scissors. Pins. Dressmaker's tracing (carbon) paper. Zigzag sewing machine.

MATERIALS: Green felt, ⅜ yd., 36″ wide. White fur fabric, 2″ wide, 21″ long. Interfacing, 13″ x 17″. Narrow gold braid, 10″ long.

Absorbent cotton. Sewing thread to match felt. For machine embroidery, gold metallic thread and red sewing thread. Twelve gold sequins.

DIRECTIONS: Enlarge boot pattern and embroidery design by copying on paper ruled in 1" squares. Pin pattern to doubled felt and cut two boots, adding ⅜" seam allowance all around. Cut one boot from interfacing, adding ⅜" seam allowance.

Pin interfacing piece to wrong side of one boot piece for front; stitch all around ⅜" in from all edges. Trim interfacing close to stitching. Trace and transfer design for machine embroidery onto boot front.

Following pattern, use narrow satin stitch and gold thread for wavy stripes; use red thread and a long and short scalloped pattern stitch for stars. Tack on gold sequins to center of red stars.

With right sides facing, pin front and back pieces of boot together. Stitch around sides and bottom, making ⅜" seams. Clip into seam allowance at curves close to stitching. Turn to right side.

At top of boot, turn 1¼" to inside; stitch in place. Pin a piece of white fur fabric 2" x 16" around top of boot. Hand sew fur to boot, making sure stitching does not show.

From remaining fur, cut two 2" squares. Trim corners of squares, shaping each into a circle. With heavy white thread, make wide running stitches along edge of each circle,

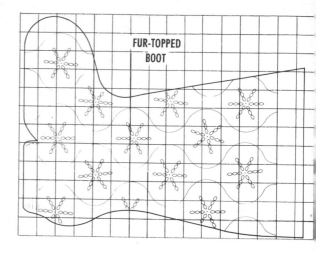

FUR-TOPPED BOOT

leaving a length of thread to pull. Roll small pieces of absorbent cotton into two balls, stuff for center of each circle. Pull thread to gather circle into a ball. Attach one end of 10"-long gold braid in center opening of each ball. Tie center of braid into bow; tack bow to back edge of boot.

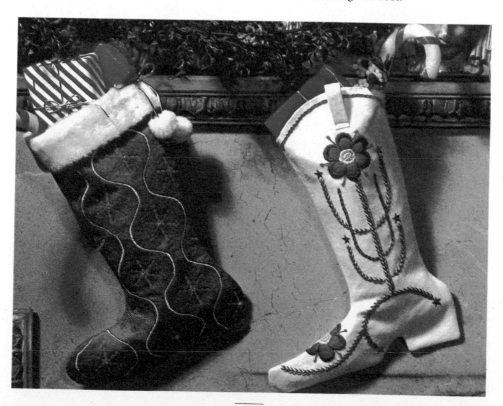

Cowboy Boot

Santa goes western! Here's a high-stepping white felt cowboy boot to embroider with colorful strands of pearl cotton.

EQUIPMENT: Paper for pattern. Pencil. Ruler. Scissors. Tracing paper. Embroidery needle. Straight pins.
MATERIALS: White felt, 36" wide, ⅜ yd. Polyester lining, 12" x 16". Pearl cotton #3, 1 skein each: red-orange, green, gold, blue.

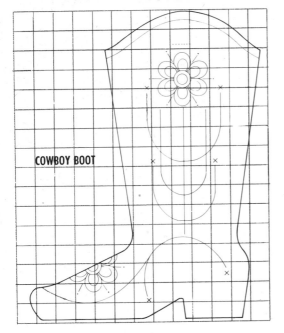

COWBOY BOOT

Sewing thread to match felt. Red star sequins, 6. Glue stick.
DIRECTIONS: Enlarge pattern for boot and embroidery by copying on paper ruled in 1" squares. Pin pattern to doubled felt; cut two boots. From lining fabric, cut a piece for front of boot.

Stitch lining to wrong side of one (front) piece of felt ¼" in from edges. Trim lining close to stitching. Trace pattern for embroidery onto boot front.

Following color illustration on page 173 and referring to Stitch Details on page 186, embroider flower petals and outer circle of flower center in satin stitch; work French knots for area in each flower center. For radiating lines between petals, work straight stitch, ending each with French knot. For remaining lines, work connecting fly stitches, except for second branch from top and line around top of boot; for these lines, use chain stitch.

With right sides facing, pin front and back pieces of boot together. Stitch around sides and bottom making ¼" seams. Clip into seam allowances at curves. Turn to right side. Glue on star sequins at X's on pattern.

For hanging loop, cut a white felt strip 5" x 1½". Turn in each long side edge ¼"; glue. Fold strip in half crosswise. Stitch to outside of front piece just above top flower as indicated by dashes.

Embroidered Felt Boot

Bold Christmas motifs decorate a large felt stocking; all pieces are assembled and appliquéd with the blanket stitch.

Size: 15" tall.
EQUIPMENT: Paper for pattern. Pencil. Ruler. Scissors. Straight pins.
MATERIALS: Felt: White, 16" x 26"; royal blue, 10" x 12"; scraps of bright colors. Six-strand embroidery floss to match all colors.
DIRECTIONS: Enlarge pattern on paper ruled in 1" squares. Complete half-pattern for cuff. Make a separate pattern for each appli-

qué piece. From white felt, cut two boots; from royal blue, cut two boot cuffs. Cut one of each appliqué piece out of felt.

Pin all pieces in place on one white boot, following pattern. With matching floss, work blanket stitch around each piece (see Stitch Details on page 186) to attach. With edges flush, pin two boots together. With white floss, work blanket stitch around edge of boot

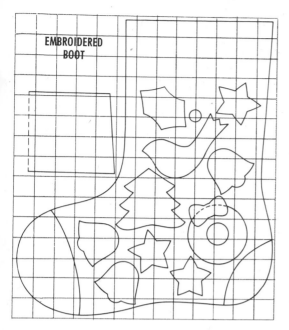

EMBROIDERED BOOT

through both thicknesses, leaving top open. Stitch top of each cuff piece to top of boot with running stitch. Turn cuff down over boot. With white floss, stitch sides together with blanket stitch; work blanket stitch around edge of cuff.

For hanger, cut two 10″ x ⅝″ strips of felt. Tack together at one end to back inside of boot. Tie other ends together with overhand knot.

A Pair of Stocking Children

Felt cutouts and bits of trim are glued to felt stocking to make a whimsical yarn-haired girl and a smiling soldier boy.

EQUIPMENT: Paper for patterns. Pencil. Ruler. Scissors. Straight pins. Needle.

MATERIALS: Felt: Two pieces approximately 12″ x 18″ for each basic stocking: apple green for Girl, red for Soldier; large and small pieces of magenta, apple and olive green, medium and pale orange, black, white, navy blue, aqua. Sewing thread: apple green, red, navy blue. Yarn: bright orange and pink knitting worsted. Black string. Trims, such as gold braid ¾ yard, white lace ¾ yard, two medium-size orange pompons from ball fringe. All-purpose glue.

GENERAL DIRECTIONS: Enlarge patterns by copying on paper ruled in 1″ squares. Make separate pattern for each piece, Short dash lines indicate where pieces are overlapped. For each stocking, use basic stocking shape given with Soldier pattern; cut out up to short dash line. Cut two basic stocking pieces and other pieces of felt for each; assemble as indicated in individual directions. Partial stocking shape is given on Girl's pattern to show position. All sewing is done ³⁄₁₆″ from edges, topstitching by machine. Leave top open between crosslines on Girl. Glue on trims as indicated below.

Girl: Cut stocking front and back of apple green felt, extending top to curve shown on Girl's pattern. Cut head and arms of white felt; legs, center and outside stripes of dress of magenta; cheeks, berry, and remaining dress stripes of medium orange; eyes of black; leaf of olive green. Sew stocking front and back together.

To make bangs, wrap orange yarn around

175

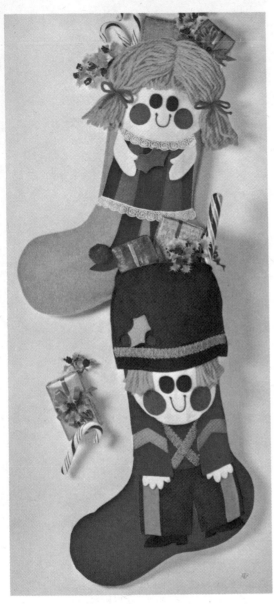

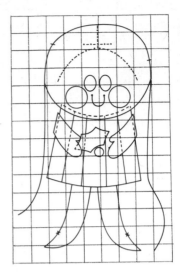

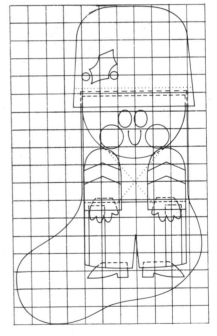

four fingers 15 times; slip off and sew near top of head at horizontal dot-dash line on pattern. For pigtails, wrap yarn around 17″ piece of cardboard 17 times. Place yarn loops across top of head; spread loops 1¾″ down from top; sew across loops from top, down center of head, making part. Glue top of head with hair on stocking front; cut hair loops. Using pink yarn, tie hair at sides (see dot-dash line for drape); glue in place. Trim hair as desired.

Glue on dress stripes with top ends under head; glue on remainder of head. Glue on legs with dress edges overlapping. For mouth, knot ends of 3″ piece of black string; glue features on head. Glue strip of lace across top, bottom of dress. Glue orange pompon on each shoe at X's.

Soldier: Cut stocking front and back of red felt; pants and two hats of navy blue; face and hands of white; sleeve stripes of pale orange; sleeves and one berry of magenta;

cheeks and one berry of medium orange; leaf of apple green; pants' stripes of aqua; eyes and shoes of black.

Pin head to one hat. On each side of head, insert eight short loops of orange yarn between head and front hats, as shown in illustration. Sew across lower edge of hat, securing pieces. Pin face and hat front to stocking front. Sew across over previous stitching. Sew hat back to stocking back. Glue top edge of stocking front to front hat, and top edge of stocking back to back hat. Sew front and back stockings, with hats, together. Glue face down with ends of braid trim glued under. Crisscross braid and glue at dotted lines on pattern. Glue pants on, overlapping braid. Glue on shoes as indicated. Glue on pants' stripes and stripes on sleeves. Glue sleeves in place with hands. For mouth, knot ends of 3¼" piece of black string; glue in place. Glue braid across hat; glue leaf and two berries on hat as shown in illustration.

Two Felt Whimsy Stockings

Felt "Santa train" and two smiling teddy bears will charm the youngest members of the family, and deck the mantelpiece with color. Trims of felt, lace, fringe and pompons are glued in place once the stocking shapes are sewn together.

EQUIPMENT: Ruler. Pencil. Paper. Scissors.
MATERIALS: Felt: For Baby, white 11" x 18", scraps of pale pink, bright pink, deep pink, red, bright green, light blue, turquoise; for Train, bright green 12" x 18", turquoise 6" x 7", scraps of red, white, pale pink, deep pink, dark green, light blue. Trims such as narrow lace edging, baby rickrack, lace motifs, pompons from ball fringe, moss fringe. Sewing thread to match background felt. All-purpose glue. Thin white cardboard for the Baby Stocking.
GENERAL DIRECTIONS: Enlarge patterns for each stocking by copying on paper ruled in 1" squares. Make a separate pattern for each piece; short dash lines show overlapped pieces. Small dotted lines on patterns indicate braid or lace edging; single small dots are lace motifs; large dots are pompons from ball fringe.

Following individual directions, cut two complete stocking pieces. Stitch together with matching thread around sides and bottom. Cut all felt design pieces indicated by solid outlines, and glue in place on stocking front. Glue braids and lace edgings along dotted lines. Glue pompons at large dots.
Baby Stocking: From white felt, cut one complete stocking, including two teddy bear heads (for front); cut one stocking for back with just the bottom bear head (cut top edge off straight across). Cut a separate bear head using top of pattern and adding ½" across bottom of head, from white felt, and also from cardboard. Stitch front and back stockings together. Glue separate head to back of top head with cardboard between.

Cut one stocking cuff, hat and collar for bottom bear of bright green felt; cut hat for top bear of red. Cut features for both: pale pink inner ears, light blue eyes with turquoise pupils, bright pink cheeks, deep pink noses, red mouths. Cut heel and toe portion of stocking and letters BABY of deep pink felt. Glue all pieces in place following pattern. Glue red baby rickrack down sides and bot-

tom of stocking along dotted line. Glue lace edging along remaining dotted lines. Glue a large white pompon at very large dot at tip of top bear's hat; glue regular red pompons at other large dots.

Santa Train Stocking: From bright green felt, cut two complete stockings, including bottoms of wheels, but not smokestack. Stitch together around sides and bottom.

From turquoise felt, cut stocking cuff, two wheels, semicircle below smokestack, and top and bottom smokestack stripes. Cut wheel spokes and top cuff stripe of bright green. Cut train window, smokestack, and wide headlight stripes of dark green. Cut stripes on headlight, smokestack, stocking cuff, and Santa's mittens of deep pink. Cut Santa's face of pale pink felt; eyes of light blue with turquoise pupils; white beard, moustache, cuff and hat trim; red hat and jacket. Glue all felt pieces in place following pattern. Glue white baby rickrack along dotted line at top of cuff, under smokestack, and in front of headlight. Glue white lace edging around window. Glue turquoise moss fringe at bottom dotted line of cuff.

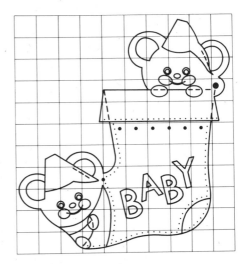

"Patchwork" Stockings Paired with Dolls

A jester hand puppet and little doll with braids keep careful watch over their matching "patchwork" stockings filled with toys for eager little friends on Christmas morning.

EQUIPMENT: Paper for pattern. Pencil. Ruler. Scissors. Straight pins. Embroidery and sewing needles.

MATERIALS: Patchwork fabric, 36" wide, ¾ yd. Lining, 36" wide, ¾ yd. Piece of cotton batting, 26" x 22". Matching and contrast-ing sewing thread. Contrasting color of embroidery floss. Bells (optional). One curtain ring for each.

DIRECTIONS: Enlarge stocking pattern by copying on paper ruled in 1" squares. From doubled patchwork fabric, lining, and batting,

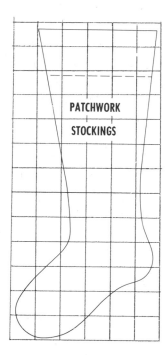

PATCHWORK STOCKINGS

cut two stockings each, adding ¼″ seam allowance all around. Mark dash line indicated on pattern on right side of lining pieces.

For front and back stocking pieces, pin lining to each piece of patchwork fabric, having right sides together. Pin batting on top of each lining piece. Stitch together all around, making ¼″ seam and leaving an opening to turn. Clip into seam allowance at curves close to stitching. Turn to right side, with batting between fabric and lining. Slip-stitch opening closed.

With contrasting color of embroidery floss and needle, stitch outline of patches on fabric with chain stitch (see Stitch Details on page 186), starting from bottom of stocking and working up to dash line. Or, with contrasting sewing thread, quilt along outline of patches, with small running stitches, starting from bottom up to dash line.

With right sides of patchwork facing, pin front and back stocking pieces together. Stitch around bottom and up sides to dash line, making ¼″ seam. Clip into seam allowance at curves close to stitching. Turn to right side. Stitch sides together above dash line, making ¼″ seam.

For cuff, turn top of stocking down to outside along dash line. Tack on ring for loop at top on heel side of stocking. If desired, tack on bells along front cuff edge.

LITTLE GIRL WITH BRAIDS

EQUIPMENT: Paper for patterns. Pencil. Ruler. Scissors. Pinking shears. Straight pins. Sewing needle. Embroidery needle.

MATERIALS: Green cotton fabric, 36″ wide, ½ yd. Patchwork fabric, 8″ x 10″. Cotton batting, 8″ x 10″. Matching sewing thread. Yellow knitting worsted, ½ oz. Scraps of felt: Pink, blue, black, red, and white. Small amount of black embroidery floss for quilting. Three small (⅜″ diam.) white buttons. All-purpose glue. Absorbent cotton for stuffing.

DIRECTIONS: Enlarge pattern by copying on paper ruled in 1″ squares. Complete half-pattern indicated by long dash line. Make separate patterns for complete body, head, dress, and collar.

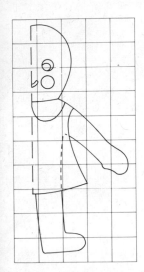

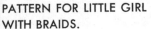

PATTERN FOR LITTLE GIRL WITH BRAIDS.

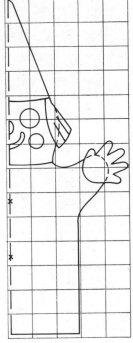

PATTERN FOR JESTER HAND PUPPET.

From doubled green fabric, cut two complete dolls and two dresses for lining, adding ¼″ seam allowance all around. From doubled patchwork, cut two dresses, adding ¼″ seam allowance all around. From batting, cut two dresses, adding ¼″ seam allowance.

With right sides facing, pin doll pieces together. With matching thread, stitch ¼″ in from edges all around, leaving an opening to turn. Clip into seam allowance at curves close to stitching. Turn to right side. Push out corners and curves smoothly. Through opening, stuff doll fully. Stitch closed.

For dress front, pin one patchwork dress and one lining together with right sides facing. Place one batting dress on wrong side of lining. Stitch pieces together around neckline, armholes, and bottom, making ¼″ seams. Repeat with remaining dress pieces for back. Turn dress front and back so that batting is between patchwork and lining. With patchwork sides facing, stitch dress front and back together, ¼″ in from edges along shoulders and sides. Turn to right side.

For quilting, use embroidery needle and black floss, and chain stitch (see Stitch Details on page 186) outline of patches on fabric. Or, with black sewing thread, quilt along outline of patches.

From pink felt, cut two head pieces. Glue to front and back of doll's head. For hair, cut yellow yarn into 45 pieces, each 18″ long. Place center of yarn pieces at center of head, starting at top front, to approximately two-thirds down back of head. With matching thread, stitch yarn at center of head. Divide yarn into two sections. Braid each section and tie ends with matching yarn. Stitch braids to sides of head. For bangs, cut four strands; wrap around little finger to make loops. Stitch to front of head.

From blue and black felt, cut circles for eyes. From red felt, cut cheek circles and smiling mouth. From white felt, cut two collar pieces. Glue on all felt pieces. Sew on three small white buttons down center of dress.

Using pinking shears, cut triangle for scarf from green fabric. Tie scarf onto doll.

JESTER HAND PUPPET

EQUIPMENT: Paper for pattern. Pencil. Ruler. Scissors. Sewing needle.
MATERIALS: Patchwork fabric, 36″ wide, ¼ yd. Lining, 36″ wide, ¼ yd. Cotton batting, 16″ x 14″. Matching and contrasting sewing thread. Scraps of yellow cotton fabric. Scraps of white, green, yellow, and red felt. Ruffled white trim, ¼ yd. Two bells. Two plastic movable eyes. All-purpose glue.
DIRECTIONS: Enlarge pattern by copying on paper ruled in 1″ squares. Complete half-pattern indicated by long dash line. Make separate patterns for hair, face, and hands.

From plaid fabric, lining fabric, and batting, cut two complete puppet shapes, including hat (without hands and hair). With right sides facing, pin one plaid and one lining piece together for both front and back. Baste one batting piece to lining side of each. Stitch together across straight bottom only. Fold each right side out and pin lining to plaid. Quilt front and back pieces by machine, stitching with contrasting thread between each block of plaid. From white felt, cut one face, adding ¼″ seam allowance along each side. Baste face to plaid side of one puppet piece for front. With plaid sides facing, stitch front and back puppet pieces together ¼″ from edges, leaving bottom open. Turn to right side.

Cut two hands from white felt. Cut mouth,

nose, and cheeks from red felt. Cut eyes from green felt. Cut two hair pieces from yellow felt; slash on lines of pattern to fringe. Glue features to felt face. Insert a little extra batting inside face for padding, with glue to hold in place; glue face on head. Glue plastic eyes to felt eyes. Glue hands to ends of arms. Slip-stitch ruffling around neck, catching in bottom edge of face.

For hat band, cut a strip of yellow fabric 2″ x 8″. Fold in half lengthwise. Stitch long edges together, making ¼″ seam. Turn right side out; turn in ends. Pin band around head over top edge of face, overlapping ends on back. Slip-stitch band in place. Glue one hair piece to each side of head at bottom edge of band. Sew a bell to front of puppet at each X on pattern.

Patchwork Angel

This plump patchwork angel, with a head of curly yarn hair, will charm any child on your list. Bright red wings in a pretty calico print are puffed with padding. Solid base lets her stand up to show off her 14″ height.

EQUIPMENT: Paper for patterns. Pencil. Ruler. Scissors. Sewing needle. Stiff paper.
MATERIALS: Small pieces of different red and green print cotton fabrics. Scraps of light pink cotton fabric. Yellow rug yarn. Sewing thread to match fabric and rug yarn. Polyester fiberfill for stuffing. Lightweight cardboard, 4″ x 11″. Small amount of six-strand embroidery floss, red and blue. Scraps of light pink felt. Thin white lace trim, 6½″ long. All-purpose glue.
DIRECTIONS: Enlarge patterns by copying on paper ruled in 1″ squares. Complete half and quarter-patterns indicated by dash lines. Make separate patterns for each dress piece, including one complete half for dress back. Before cutting, add ¼″ all around each piece for seam allowance. From print fabrics, cut the following: two half-dress pieces for back; five front dress pieces; four sleeve pieces; two wing pieces; one bottom piece. From light pink fabric, cut two head pieces and four hand pieces. From pink felt, cut two circles for cheeks. From cardboard, cut bottom piece for base of angel minus the seam allowance.

With right sides facing, stitch long edges of the five front pieces together, making ¼″ seams. With right sides facing, stitch back pieces together, making ¼″ seam, leaving seam open between crosslines indicated on pattern. Stitch neck edge of head pieces to top of front and back pieces. Embroider head front using three strands of floss in needle: With blue floss, embroider eyes in satin stitch; with red floss, embroider mouth in outline stitch (see page 186 for Stitch Details).

With right sides facing, pin front and back pieces together. Stitch around sides and head, making ¼″ seam; leave bottom open. Clip into seam allowance at curves, close to stitching. Pin bottom piece around lower edges. Stitch, making ¼″ seam. Clip into seam allowance at curves close to stitching. Turn angel to right side. Push out corners and curves smoothly.

Through opening at back seam, insert cardboard piece for base. Stuff doll fully with fiberfill. Slip-stitch opening closed.

With right sides facing, pin two pieces together for each sleeve. Stitch ¼″ in from edges, leaving end open for hands. Clip into seam allowance at curves. Turn to right side; turn in edges at open ends. Stuff sleeves.

Stitch hand pieces together in same manner, leaving open at wrist. Turn to right side.

Stuff. Insert ends of hands inside sleeves and slip-stitch in place. Tack sleeves to dress at X's indicated on pattern.

Stitch wings together, leaving an opening to turn. Turn to right side; stuff. Slip-stitch opening closed. Attach to back of dress at top center.

For hair, cut strips of stiff paper 1″ wide. Cut strands of rug yarn about 48″ long. Wrap yarn around paper strip in a single layer; stitch across center of loops. Remove paper strip. Tack looped yarn around sides and top of head over seamline. Make and tack on enough looped yarn strips to cover back and top of head.

For collar, tack white lace trim around neck of angel, stitching ends closed.

Glue on pink felt circles for cheeks. Sew tips of hands together.

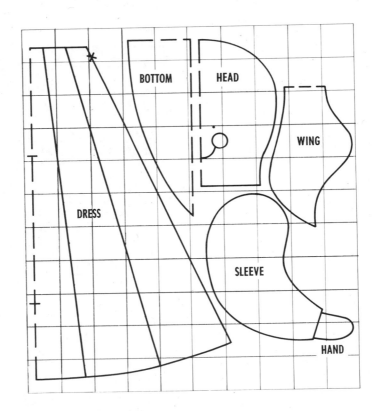

HOW-TO'S and STITCH DETAILS

How to Enlarge or Reduce Designs

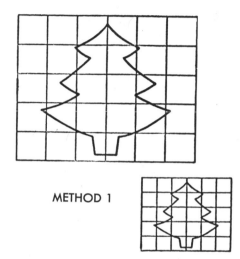

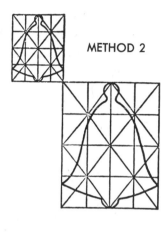

METHOD 2

METHOD 1

Note: Charts can be enlarged to actual size by photostat service.

There are various ways of enlarging or reducing designs so that all parts remain in proportion. The most commonly used are the "square" method, No. 1, and the diagonal method, No. 2.

Method 1: If design is not already marked off in squares, make a tracing of original design. Mark off tracing with squares ⅛" for small designs, and ¼", ½", or 1" for proportionately larger designs. On tracing paper, mark off the same number of squares, similarly placed, in the space to be occupied by the enlarged design. For instance, if you want to make the original design twice as high and twice as wide, make the squares twice as large. Copy outline of design from smaller squares to corresponding larger squares. Reverse procedure for reducing designs.

A "trick of the trade" is to place a fine wire screen over the original design for "squaring off." For a different shortcut, transfer original design to graph paper.

Method 2: Make a tracing of original design. Draw a rectangle to fit around it. Immediately next to and below this rectangle, draw a second rectangle of same proportions to fit desired size of design (drawing diagonals from corner to corner of each rectangle as illustrated). In each rectangle, the point where diagonals meet is the center. Draw one horizontal and one vertical line to divide each rectangle into four equal rectangles. In each of these, draw diagonals to find center, and divide into four equal rectangles. Copy outlines of original design in corresponding divisions of second rectangle.

An easy way to divide the rectangles into spaces described above is to fold a paper desired size of design into halves, quarters, and sixteenths.

How to Make a Star

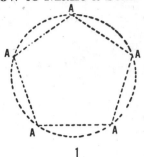

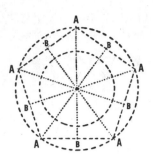

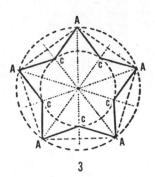

1　　　　**2**　　　　**3**

1. Draw a circle desired size of star. With compass or dividers, find five equidistant points A on circumference of circle. Draw connecting lines to form pentagon.

2. Using same center of circle, draw another circle inside larger circle as illustrated (distance of inner circle from outer circle controls depth of star points). Find centers of five sides of pentagon (points B). From these centers, draw lines through center of circle to opposite points A.

3. Draw lines from points A of pentagon to where dividing lines intersect inner circle (points C) to form star.

How to Make a Tassel

Wind yarn around cardboard cut to size of tassel desired, winding it 20 or more times around, depending on thickness of yarn and plumpness of tassel required. Tie strands tightly together around top as shown, leaving at least 3″ ends on ties; clip other end of strands. Wrap piece of yarn tightly around strands a few times, about ½″ or 1″ below top; then tie and knot. Trim the ends of the tassel to a uniform length.

How to Make a Pompon

Cut two cardboard disks desired size of pompon; cut out ¼″ hole in center of both. Thread needle with two strands of yarn. Place disks together; cover with yarn, working through holes. Slip scissors between disks; cut all strands at outside edge. Draw strand of yarn down between disks and wind several times very tightly around yarn; knot, leaving ends for attaching pompon. Remove cardboard disks and fluff out pompon.

Knitting and Crochet Abbreviations and Stitches

▶ **Knitting: Abbreviations, Stitches**

k—knit	MC—main color
st—stitch	CC—contrasting color
yo—yarn over	p—purl
inc—increase	sts—stitches
dec—decrease	sk—skip
tog—together	pats—patterns
dp—double-pointed	lp—loop
psso—pass slip stitch over	sl—slip
beg—beginning	rnd—round

▶ **Crochet: Abbreviations, Stitches**

beg—beginning	rnd—round
ch—chain	bl—block
st—stitch	sts—stitches
cl—cluster	p—picot
sl st—slip stitch	pat—pattern
yo—yarn over	sp—space
sc—single crochet	sk—skip
dc—double crochet	lp—loop
tr—treble crochet	inc—increase
dtr—double treble	dec—decrease
hdc—half double crochet	

Pick Up and Knit Stitches on Edge—From right side, insert needle into edge of work, put yarn around needle, finish as a k st. When picking up on bound-off or cast-on edge, pick up and k 1 st in each st (going through 2 lps at top of each bound-off st); pick up and k 1 st in each knot formed on edge of each row on front or side edges.

To Slip a Stitch—Insert needle in st as if to knit st (unless directions read "as if to p") and sl st from one needle to the other without knitting or purling it.

Psso (pass slip stitch over)—This is a decrease stitch. When directions read "sl 1, k 1, psso," insert left-hand needle from left to right under slipped stitch on right-hand needle, bring it over the knit stitch and off needle.

Garter St—K every row.

Stockinette St—K 1 row, p 1 row. When knitting round and round on circular or dp needles, k every row.

Sc (Single Crochet)—To make a single crochet, start with a loop on hook, insert hook in work, draw yarn through, yarn over hook and draw through both loops.

Dc (Double Crochet)—Start with a loop on hook, put yarn over hook, insert hook in work, draw yarn through, yarn over hook and draw yarn through two loops, yarn over again and draw through the two remaining loops on hook.

Hdc (Half Double Crochet)—Start with a loop on hook, put yarn over hook, insert hook in work, draw yarn through, yarn over hook and draw through all three loops on hook.

Tr (Treble Crochet)—This is made the same way as double crochet, with the yarn wrapped around the hook twice instead of once and then worked off—yarn over and through two loops, yarn over and through two loops, yarn over and through two loops.

Sl St (Slip Stitch)—Insert hook through st, catch yarn, and with one motion draw through both the st and the one lp on hook.

* (asterisk)—Repeat directions following * as many extra times as directed. For example "* 2 dc in next st, 1 dc in next st, repeat from * 4 times" means to work directions after first * until second * is reached, then go back to first * 4 times more, repeating directions. Directions are worked 5 times altogether.

( ) (parentheses)—When parentheses are used to show repetition, work directions in parentheses as many times as specified. Example: "(dc, ch 1) 3 times" means to do what is in ( ) 3 times in all.

Work Even—Work in same pattern stitch without increasing or decreasing.

To Sew in Sleeves—Place the sleeve seam at center underarm and center of sleeve cap at shoulder seam. Ease in any extra fullness evenly around. Backstitch seam.

Weaving or Kitchener Stitch: Break off yarn, leaving about 12″ end on work. Thread this into a tapestry needle and proceed as follows: Working from right to left, * pass threaded needle through first st on front needle as if to knit and slip st off needle; pass yarn through 2nd st on front needle as if to purl but leave st on needle; pass yarn through first st on back needle as if to purl and slip st off needle; pass yarn through 2nd st on back needle as if to knit but leave st on needle. Repeat from * until all sts are woven together. Fasten off yarn.

Duplicate Stitch: Duplicate stitch embroidery on knitted garments looks the same as knitted-in designs and is worked after garment is finished. Start to work (far left); then work vertically (center) or work diagonally (near left) as shown by white.

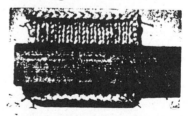

▶ **You Must Be Sure to Check Your Gauge**

Be sure you can knit or crochet to exact gauge specified in directions. To test your knit gauge, cast on 20 to 30 stitches, using needles specified. Work 3″ in pattern stitch. Smooth out swatch; pin down. Measure across 2″ as shown, then down 2″, counting number of stitches and rows; if you have **more** stitches and rows to inch than directions specify, use larger needles; if you have **fewer** stitches and rows to the inch, use smaller ·needles. Knit new swatches until gauge is correct. Test crochet same way.

EMBROIDERY STITCHES

STRAIGHT STITCH

BACKSTITCH

BLANKET STITCH

FRENCH KNOT

SATIN STITCH

RUNNING STITCH

WHIPPED RUNNING STITCH

FLY STITCH

OUTLINE STITCH

SPLIT STITCH

BUTTONHOLE STITCH

CHAIN STITCH

TURKEY WORK

COUCHING

STAR FILLING

LONG AND SHORT STITCH

CROSS-STITCH

LAZY DAISY STITCH

FEATHERSTITCH